D0671263

Republic of the Philippines
OFFICE OF THE CIVIL REGISTRAR GENERAL

CERTIFICATE OF DEATH

Registry No. **2013-CHA269**

Municipality **PASAY CITY**

2. SEX (Male/Female) **Female**

(First)	(Middle)	(Last)
ELIZABETH	LOGAN	GREENWOOD

3. DATE OF DEATH (Day, Month, Year) **7 July 2013**

4. DATE OF BIRTH (Day) (Month) (Year) **28 April 1983**

5. AGE AT THE TIME OF DEATH
- [1] IF 1 YEAR OR ABOVE
- [2] Completed years **30**

b. IF UNDER 1 YEAR
- [1] Months **July**
- [c] [0] Days **2**

7. CIVIL STATUS (Single, Married, Widower/Annulled/Divorced) **Married**

6. PLACE OF DEATH (Name of Hospital/Clinic/Institution/House No., St., Barangay, City/Municipality, Province)
SAN JUAN DE DIOS GEN. HOSPITAL-Pasay City

10. RESIDENCE (House No., St., Barangay, City/Municipality)
Unit 303 Central Park Condominium St.Pasay City

8. RELIGION/RELIGIOUS SECT **Catholic**

9. CITIZENSHIP **American**

13. MAIDEN NAME OF MOTHER (First, Middle, Last) **Diana Logan**

11. OCCUPATION **Businesswoman**

12. NAME OF FATHER (First, Middle, Last) **Philip Greenwood**

MEDICAL CERTIFICATE
(For ages 0 to 7 days, accomplish items 14-19a at the back)

Interval Between Onset

19b. CAUSES OF DEATH (If the deceased is aged 8 days and over)

I. Immediate cause : a. **Car Accident**

Antecedent cause : b.

Underlying cause : c.

II. Other significant conditions contributing to death:

19c. MATERNAL CONDITION (If the deceased is female aged 15-49 years old)
- a. pregnant, not in labour
- b. pregnant, in labour
- c. less than 42 days after delivery
- d. 42 days to 1 year after delivery

19d. DEATH BY EXTERNAL CAUSES
- a. Manner of death (Homicide, Suicide, Accident, Legal intervention, etc.)
- b. Place of Occurrence of External Cause (e.g. home, farm, factory, street, sea, etc.)

21b. If attended, f

21a. ATTENDANT
- 1 Private Physician
- 2 Public Health Officer
- **X** 3 Hospital Authority
- 4 None
- 5 Others (Specify)

From

22. CERTIFICATION OF DEATH
I hereby certify that the foregoing particulars are correct as near as same can be ascertained and I further certify that I have not attended the deceased and that death occurred at ___ am/pm on the date of death specified

REVIEWED BY:

Signature

Name in Print **DR. R. H. FAJARDO M.D.**

Title or Position **Physician**

Address **San Juan de Dios Gen.Hospital-Pasay City**

Date **July 17, 2013**

Signature Over Printed Name

Date **07-19**

24a. BURIAL/CREMATION PERMIT
Number **04351876**
Date Issued **07-19-2013**

24b. TRANSFER PE
Number
Date Issued

23. CORPSE DISPOSAL (Burial, Cremation, if others, specify) **burial**

25. NAME AND ADDRESS OF CEMETERY OR CREMATORY
Manila Memorial Park-Sucat,Paranaque

27. PREPARED BY

Signature

26. CERTIFICATION OF INFORMANT
I hereby certify that all information supplied are true and correct to my own knowledge and belief.

Name in Print **ROBERTO L.**

Title or Position **Record**

Date **July 19, 20**

Signature

Name in Print **WILLIAM LOGAN ROBERT**

Relationship to the Deceased **Cousin**

Address **same as above**

Date **July 17, 2013**

29. REGISTERED BY THE CIVIL RE

Signature

Name in Print **DA**

PLAYING DEAD

A JOURNEY THROUGH
THE WORLD OF DEATH FRAUD

ELIZABETH GREENWOOD

SIMON & SCHUSTER

NEW YORK   LONDON   TORONTO   SYDNEY   NEW DELHI

Simon & Schuster
1230 Avenue of the Americas
New York, NY 10020

Research for this book was conducted between 2010 and 2016. Certain names and identifying characteristics have been changed and certain events have been reordered for narrative clarity.

First Simon & Schuster hardcover edition August 2016

SIMON & SCHUSTER and colophon are registered trademarks of Simon & Schuster, Inc.

For information about special discounts for bulk purchases, please contact Simon & Schuster Special Sales at 1-866-506-1949 or business@simonandschuster.com.

The Simon & Schuster Speakers Bureau can bring authors to your live event. For more information or to book an event, contact the Simon & Schuster Speakers Bureau at 1-866-248-3049 or visit our website at www.simonspeakers.com.

Interior design by Lewelin Polanco

Manufactured in the United States of America

10 9 8 7 6 5 4 3 2 1

Library of Congress Cataloging-in-Publication Data

Names: Greenwood, Elizabeth, 1983– author.
Title: Playing dead : a journey through the world of death fraud / Elizabeth Greenwood.
Description: New York : Simon & Schuster, [2016]
Identifiers: LCCN 2015038731
Subjects: LCSH: Missing persons—Case studies. | Fraud—Case studies. | Absence and presumption of death.
Classification: LCC HV6762.A3 G74 2016 | DDC 364.16/3—dc23 LC record available at http://lccn.loc.gov/2015038731

ISBN 978-1-4767-3933-5
ISBN 978-1-4767-3936-6 (ebook)

For my mom.
For everything.

Everyone forgets that Icarus also flew.

—JACK GILBERT, "FAILING AND FLYING"

CONTENTS

INTRODUCTION   xi

1: *How to Disappear*   1

2: *How to Be Found*   41

3: *The Canoe Man*   85

4: *The Believers*   139

5: *Collateral Damage*   177

6: *Faking My Death with Mr. Clean and Mr. Bean*   201

EPILOGUE   235

ACKNOWLEDGMENTS   245

The fixer's phone lit up with a text message:

"Your friend is dead."

I'd been waiting with him and his associate in the frigid Manila hotel lobby all morning for this news. Though the fixer and I were not friends in any conventional sense of the word, we had gotten to know each other through small talk over a half-dozen $5 Cokes. We discussed kids, the weather, how best to fake your death in the Philippines, and, as an added bonus, how to slay an assailant with a ballpoint pen. Aside from getting into the particulars about purchasing cadavers on the black market and murder techniques with ordinary household objects, most of our chitchat could have taken place in the buffet line of a wedding reception. We were killing time, waiting for the forger to produce my death certificate.

And now it was ready. We sprang up from our seats, and

I charged the Cokes to my room. This—obtaining documents that would pronounce me dead without actually ending my life—was what I'd been waiting to do for years.

Now that the moment had finally arrived, I felt a little uneasy. We walked through the megamall, connecting to the underground parking garage to find the car in which we would wend through metro Manila in the evening rush hour to meet the forger's conduit, who, in his hot hands, possessed a dossier that, in effect, could kill me. I compensated by laughing too hard at the guys' jokes about their wives.

How did I end up sweating in the backseat of a Mercedes in the Philippines, driving to obtain evidence of my own death? I'm pretty happy with my life, for the most part. I loathe adrenaline and unnecessary risk. I don't even like to go downhill fast on my bike. And while I present as effervescent to the degree of ditziness, that warmth can quickly curdle into an animal rage, festered and heightened by ten years of living in New York by my own wits, especially toward strange men who want to take my money.

I sought out these fixers because I wanted to know if it was possible to fake your own death. And, if this handoff went as planned, I'd be dead within the hour.

======

FAKING YOUR DEATH—BOTH AS a concept and as an act people attempt with surprising frequency—first occurred to me two years earlier, when I was having dinner with my friend Matt. We had met teaching public school in the Bronx. That evening, as we sat in a cheap Vietnamese restaurant, I was feeling sorry for myself. I'd recently abandoned teaching to go back to school full-time, which meant foolishly taking out several dozen thousand dollars in student loans to heap upon the $60,000 debt from my undergraduate education, bringing the sum total to a bloated figure in the six digits. At the beginning of the semester, I felt alive and nourished and like I was on vacation after a career of corralling second graders. Then, a few weeks in, I realized what I had done. I'd screwed myself financially, big-time (for the second time!), and had nobody to blame but the creep in the mirror.

In the dim crepuscular light of early winter, I was bemoaning my self-imposed financial plight to Matt, who was exhausted and smelled slightly like the syrup from the school cafeteria. He looked less than amused.

I revealed my latest vision of the future over greasy spring rolls:

"So the plan is to become, like, a towering luminary and highly sought-after public intellectual, and, I mean, my TED Talk alone will obviously pay back my private loans, but in the very off chance that the film offers don't come knocking straightaway, I've come up with plan B: Belize."

"What does that even mean?" Matt asked, his eyelids sagging after a day of coaxing eight-year-olds into mastering fractions.

"You know, just slip through the cracks. Find a sun-bleached country with a rickety government and no extradition policy and kick back on the beach, avoiding the feds for the rest of my life."

Would Sallie Mae and the US Department of Education really deploy a repo team to a tiny Central American country in search of a certain debt-laden Rubenesque bottle blonde? What's a little $100,000 deficit to them? (Well, actually closer to a half million after the lifetime of accrued interest.) This conversation took place in the wake of the 2008 financial collapse, when it had become evident that the middle-class ideal of playing by the rules in search of the American dream was for chumps. Flouting it like the goons on Wall Street was the only way to profit and evade consequences. Defaulting on debts was very much in the zeitgeist—plus I could score a vacation in the meantime. I was pretty pleased with my plan, though the fantasy was more of a pressure valve than a blueprint. The puritan in me, while realizing how the system is rigged, still paid her taxes and got regular teeth cleanings. But the idea of throwing on a wig and some shades and starting over was appealing, even though I was still relatively young at the time. I joked about it, but my student loan debt, though not unique in any way, made me feel definitively and inextricably fucked. Two options presented themselves: a Dickensian debtors' prison or a life on the lam.

"Or you could fake your own death," Matt said casually, shoving another spring roll into his mouth.

"Or I could fake my own death," I parroted back, the thought undulating through my skull like squid ink.

Why hadn't that occurred to me? Faking my own death. An untimely end would make a far superior story for the bill collectors than simply vanishing one day. Sloughing off the past, shucking the carcass of my impoverished self, to be reborn, unblemished as a sunrise. My "death" would not be a conclusion but a renaissance—a shot at an alternative ending. The dross of life would not inflict itself upon me: I could arrange and edit to suit my specifications. Faking death could be a refusal, a way to reject the dreary facts, a way to bridge the chasm between who you are and who you want to be. From bit player in your life, you become the auteur. From being pressed up against a wall, you carve a tunnel.

That night, when I got home to my apartment, before I took off my coat, I marched straight to my laptop and Googled "fake your own death." I don't know what I was expecting to find in those search results, but I encountered a diverse and vibrant ecosystem: amateur forums where anonymous avatars traded tips on how to score fake IDs and stash money undetected; stories of low-budget con men who ripped off life insurance companies; urban legends of Elvis and Michael Jackson staging death hoaxes and walking among us. There were experts dispensing advice with a steep price tag about how you can maintain your privacy in the digital age and how-tos for erasing yourself in the physical world. Nothing was what it seemed, anything was possible, and you needed only not to repeat the mistakes of those who'd gotten caught in order to stay good and gone. Was that it? Were the people who got busted just too messy, their exits too hastily planned?

While my initial search was rooted in a despairing thought experiment, my stumbling upon this world seemed perfectly timed. My debt informed decisions large and small: Should I use my tax refund to backpack in Nicaragua or pay back my faceless oppressor? Should I slog through another decade at a job that was turning my brain into porridge to ensure that I could meet the minimum monthly payments? If declaring bankruptcy at the tender age of twenty-seven were an option, I would have done it in a heartbeat. But student loans cannot be absolved with the stroke of a judge's pen, or else Millennials would be skipping around town with ruined credit and buoyant hearts.

Beyond the money I owed dictating the shape of my day and my future, my world was looking fixed. Pleasant enough, but calcifying. I was living in a rent-controlled apartment in

Chelsea with Elijah, a reformed heartbreaker musician who'd given me the runaround for years. I was in a relationship I'd fought for, in a New York real estate wet dream. I'd wake up before him and read in the embrace of an overstuffed red armchair I bought at a Housing Works thrift store with my first freelance check, positioned in a corner to absorb the sun glinting off the Hudson River. Eventually he'd stumble out of bed after a late-night gig, and we'd cradle mugs of coffee and drape over each other as horns sounded seven stories below us on Ninth Avenue. We'd recently adopted Bonnie, a Jack Russell–Chihuahua who sparked commentary from friends and relatives on the good practice she provided for the caprices of a human child. The mail seemed to bring a new batch of wedding invitations every month, and each week was a rinse-repeat cycle of the same café table, the same bills to pay, the same commute. It was a comfortable rhythm of what I wanted. Or thought I wanted. Or was supposed to have wanted. A familiar refrain echoed in my head: Is that all there is?

I took out the first batch of loans seeking escape. In high school in my New England rust belt town, I logged nearly as many hours in the parking lot smoking cigarettes as I spent in class. After graduation, I waitressed, telemarketed, delivered food, and worked at a residential facility for troubled teens not much younger than me. I didn't apply to college right away and knew that I'd be paying for most of it on my own, as my mom was raising my sister and me on an assistant professor's salary. My dad, who lived in a different state, was in no position to contribute. But I knew I wanted to get as far away as possible from binge drinking, the cult of the Red Sox, and North Face fleeces. So I took out $60,000 in loans to go spend four years studying American history at the University of San Francisco.

I'd never been west of Colorado until moving into the dorms. I went to college in between tech bubbles and paid $600 a month for a room in a Victorian off Alamo Square. I drove a red Vespa motor scooter through the troughs of hills and up the slope of the Presidio. I made out with surfers. I taught English at a day labor collective. I tasted freedom.

While I'd gone into debt in order to fund my escape from the parochial cradle of central Massachusetts, I'd actually screwed myself into stasis. Owing a massive amount that never diminished despite $400 monthly payments made new movement a mere fantasy. So my mind wandered. Could I annihilate the self that owed the money? Or would I have to annihilate my entire being?

What would be lost? Should I have carried on the sensible slog of teaching elementary school in favor of a nebulous goal? Should I just have cemented myself onto the same bar stool in Worcester? How does it happen that what once seemed like the deepest fulfillment of desire could turn out to betray my future freedom?

What those search results revealed to me that first night wasn't only a vast ecosystem but also an alternative. I was concerned that the choices I'd been making were hemming me in and limiting my options. But here were people who designed their lives around proxy identities, subterfuge, shirking responsibilities. Here was freedom. I had to know everything, to satisfy my nagging intellectual curiosity—and because my life felt stopped up, and I wanted to punch a hole in it.

Each link I clicked opened up a new facet of faking death, and every new aspect elicited a fresh set of questions. Is it possible to fake your death at all? Proving a negative is impossible, because the people who pull it off are simply presumed dead.

So what lessons could one extract from those who had been caught? What is the best way to stage your fatal accident? How do you occupy your days in your second life? And can you even disappear in the twenty-first century, when every move is monitored, if not by the US National Security Agency then by closed-circuit TVs and drones, phones transmitting our coordinates, and obnoxious friends tagging us on Facebook?

While the idea of manipulating one's own mortality was dark, I also delighted in its inherent black comedy. As ideas go, faking your death is one of those things—like homeschooling or a bad haircut—that is, to me at least, timeless comedic gold. The stories I encountered were almost the stuff of B movies: a Wall Street huckster who was to report to jail but then faked his suicide and lived in an RV; a man who was in deep real estate debt paddling away in a kayak off the northern coast of England and presumed to have drowned, only to have a photo of him in a Panamanian real estate office emerge five years later; a money manager who staged a plane crash but then made the mistake of inadvertently leading the feds to the campsite where he was holed up. It seems that while en route, he'd discarded a road atlas with several pages torn out of it. The lawmen who found it simply purchased the same atlas at a nearby gas station and followed the missing pages.

These unlucky endings were punch lines, if propelled by unfunny setups. If one sides with the many philosophers who believe that death is the ultimate absurdity of human existence, then faking death might represent a slapstick sketch of human ingenuity and folly.

But beyond the intriguing practical logistics and poignant hilarity of the last resort, I became keenly interested in what it takes emotionally and spiritually to kill off the person you once were. What happens to the people you leave behind? If you kill yourself in order to live anew, what dies with you? Is it ever worth it? And who *are* the people who traffic in "pseudocide" (industry jargon, I learned, for faking one's death)? It became very clear to me that I had stumbled into a bizarre underworld made up of people with forbidden knowledge and those seeking it. And while my intention to fake my death might not have been as earnest as that of the commenters in the forums I was frequenting, I had definitely become a seeker as well.

As I sat in a winter coat, hunched over a computer, these questions piqued a curiosity in me that would end up leading me across the globe years later.

———

AS I GAZED OUT the window of the Mercedes in the monsoon season, humidity smudging the edges of Manila, on the way to pick up my death certificate, I felt myself about to cross over from seeker to expert. I had wanted to see how close I could come to faking my death, short of actually doing it. Was it possible? I was about to find out.

But before the forger and the death certificate, before Manila, I'd have a lot to learn.

PLAYING DEAD

1

HOW TO DISAPPEAR

When Sam Israel III woke up on a hot Monday in June 2008, he had already decided it was a good day to die. He'd lost everything. He had lost his job as founder and CEO of the Bayou Hedge Fund Group, his reputation as a guy who could double your money, and his family in an ugly divorce. And more than $450 million of his investors' dollars.

That day, Sam was supposed to be reporting to Devens Prison in Massachusetts. At his sentencing hearing a few months earlier, he'd been handed twenty-two years for financial malfeasance and fraud—one of the harshest punishments a white-collar criminal had ever received. His Ponzi scheme was one of the largest to date, until Bernie Madoff's crimes surfaced eight months later. Sam thought he'd do three to five, but the judge surprised him with seventeen more than he had expected.

Something about Sam Israel rubbed people the wrong way. He always seemed to be smirking. He refused to mimic the narrative of regret and atonement so many scammers adopt, at least after they get busted. Even the feds in court that day were stunned by the severity of Judge Colleen McMahon's decision. As he was being led out of the courtroom, an FBI agent leaned in and whispered to Sam, "I have two words for you: Costa Rica."

Going on the run hadn't crossed Sam's mind, but the agent's words stuck with him. And since an officer of the court had presented him with the idea, though jokingly, he thought he'd been given the green light. By now, Sam understood that things were often not what they seemed. In his mind, his crime had not been typical Wall Street greed or a pyramid scheme. As he understood it, he'd been tapped by the Octopus, an international conglomerate that dictated all financial markets. He had entered a world where he believed that a shadow market secretly controlled the Federal Reserve and that he had survived attempts on his life. While others thought he'd been a pawn in a long con, Sam now saw the world's power structures as deeply connected and profoundly duplicitous. Messages could be anywhere, and an FBI agent was not the most outlandish emissary.

After his sentencing in April 2008, a limousine dropped off Sam with his mother and his girlfriend in the driveway of the house he'd been renting since his divorce. They were all in shock. Twenty-two years. He was forty-nine; he might as well have been handed a life sentence. Bright yellow pollen from budding trees blanketed the GMC Envoy truck that he rarely drove—it was simply one among his fleet of a half dozen cars. His mother asked Sam what he was going to do. In the neon scrim of pollen dust, he traced the message "suicide is painless" onto the hood.

She told him the joke (which also happens to be the theme song from *M*A*S*H*), if it was one, was not in any way funny.

Costa Rica. Of course! The country was a metaphor for escape. It meant save yourself; don't go down without a fight. And he would heed the advice. But he wouldn't defect south of the border. Inspired by the Robin Williams comedy *RV* that Sam happened to catch on late-night TV one night around the time of his sentencing, he realized that he'd already seen the world, but not much of his own country. Why not hide in plain sight, in a mobile home? In just a few short weeks between his sentencing and surrender date, he cobbled together an exit plan. Disguised in a hat and sunglasses, he bought a laptop at Best Buy in the Palisades Mall. He found an RV for sale on Craigslist, just like the one Williams commandeered in the film, and purchased it from an elderly Long Island couple for $55,000 cash. He told them he was a professional poker player.

Sam tapped the former CIA and Mossad connections he had established through the Octopus. They helped him score IDs and a Social Security number in the name of David Klapp, an Iowa man who had died in 2001. He got a parking permit for all five boroughs of New York, a gun permit, a library card, and signed up as a night school student at a local community college. In three days, he had a new identity and the authenticating documents to prove it.

He told a friend he had business to take care of at West Point, and needed a ride. He wanted to check out the Bear Mountain Bridge as a place to stage his suicide but knew he needed to avoid photos of his own car being taken at the tollbooth. Sam didn't spot any cameras on the bridge itself, and he noticed that the southern lane was cordoned off, with construction nets hanging beneath. If he could swing it, he could step out over the ledge and fall into the net. He'd look like just another disgraced Wall Streeter who would as soon take his own life before paying his debt to society and his investors. No one would miss the man who had lost millions, whose constant smirk reporters' cameras had plastered on the nightly news.

On that Monday in June, Sam parked the RV at a truck stop off Route 684 in Brewster. He paid Hassan, the twentysomething nephew of one of his Mossad associates, a wad of hundreds to help him stage his death. Hassan would tail the convicted man's truck and wait for him on the other side.

Sam had several cars he could've driven that day, but he took the Envoy because the family rarely used it. It got such little mileage that he'd forgotten the prescient suicide note he'd written on the hood weeks prior. He parked the truck at a vista point overlooking the Hudson River and then got into Hassan's Nissan. They drove back over the bridge at fifteen miles per hour to make sure that repairmen weren't working on the construction site that day. Sam thought back to the FBI agent's Costa Rica suggestion. He'd been given the green light, right? There would be sacrifices. He wouldn't have contact with his family, and he'd have to go underground for a few years. The thought of not seeing his kids—a boy in junior high and a girl in high school—was distressing. Even in the throes of his divorce and legal troubles, they'd never spent more than a week apart. But anything was better than rotting in prison.

When Hassan dropped him back off at the Envoy, Sam started to obsess over the things he'd be leaving behind for the cops to find. His own wallet, IDs, and credit cards were on the passenger seat. He considered writing a real suicide note but decided against it. That'd be too cute. Let them figure the fucking thing out, he thought. He opened up the back tailgate and smoked a cigarette. He walked over to Hassan's car. They were both jumpy with nerves.

"I have to be out of my mind," Sam told Hassan.

"Look, man," Hassan said, "either way, you are dead. So at least now you'll choose your own end. This is crazy, but you may live and be free. You know you're crazy," he added. "So just do the fucking thing!"

In that loaded moment, Sam received Hassan's wisdom— that he was fucking crazy and to just do the fucking thing—as from a divine oracle. He would do it. But he'd given Hassan's uncle a contingency plan. Late the night before, they'd been drinking Scotch, and Sam said that if things went south—if he missed the narrow construction net and plummeted to the Hudson River below—Hassan should give $200,000 to Sam's girlfriend and the rest to his son. Sell the RV, but wipe it of any evidence and fingerprints first.

He paused, as if waiting for some act of God to intervene, something that would prevent him from slamming the truck door shut and doubling back across the bridge. But nothing happened. So Sam climbed in, alone, and turned on the engine. He reflected on his life as he drove. What had brought him to this point? How the fuck did it come to this, man? He'd believed he was a good person, but in the last few years, he'd gotten away from himself. He'd lied to his investors when he didn't have to. He'd gotten divorced, and he had never considered himself the type to end a marriage. He'd joined an underworld where se- crets ran deep. Nothing was what it seemed.

But as he circled the rotary back across the bridge, he smiled. No matter what, he was free already. It didn't matter how much work lay ahead of him, or if he lived another fifty years or fifteen minutes. The decision had been made. Today was a good day to die.

He drove up and paid the toll.

=====

"HIS WHOLE 'SUICIDE IS painless' thing?" Frank Ahearn says. "What, did he think the feds were going to show up and say, 'Hmmmm, he wrote a suicide note on his truck, he must have jumped off the bridge! All right, fellas, let's go home!'" Frank shakes his head wearily. "He conforms to a category of a thief with no walk-away plan."

I'm talking to Frank Ahearn to get an expert opinion on faking death in general and on Sam Israel in particular. We are sitting in his garment district office in New York City: a converted factory ensconced between a modeling agency and a drag queen costumer. Frank is the coauthor of *How to Disappear: Erase Your Digital Footprint, Leave False Trails, and Vanish Without a Trace*, a manual for those who want to do just that, and he took a special interest in Sam's case, one of the higher-profile instances of pseudocide in recent years. Sam is one of Frank's favorite "morons and idiots." He fits a certain death fraud trend that's all too familiar. "None of these white-collar criminals plan their exit. They just keep going until it all falls down. If he'd thought about his exit plan as smartly as he'd thought about his crime, he'd be in a lovely locale right now, enjoying his money."

Frank knows all about planning the exit. Billing himself as a "privacy consultant," Ahearn is the self-proclaimed "world's top expert" on helping people dissolve their identities, physically and digitally. In other words, he helps people disappear—which, he instructed me, is a very different act than helping someone to fake his or her death. Frank is in his fifties and resembles a Hells Angel. The word *Freedom* is tattooed across his broad shoulders. His speech is prone to Bronx inflection, and he uses profanity in a way that borders on Zen poetry. ("Some days, life is a shitty piece of shit.") He doesn't buy politicians' platitudes: "I think the government blows, in plain English. They're a bunch of lying mothafahkas." And he believes in the right to protect and conceal one's privacy. Though he does not recommend pseudocide, and claims that he never helped any of his clients fake a death, he wrote a chapter in his book on the phenomenon.

I sought out Frank because of his peculiar expertise. A question had been plaguing me, one I hadn't yet been able to answer with any satisfaction: Is it possible to fake your death in the twenty-first century, and, if so, what does it really take? Here was someone who had made a business out of obscuring people, so the most dramatic kind of disappearance—pseudocide— must have crossed his desk. For someone who helps people disappear for a living, Frank works very much out in the open. He has lent his expertise to the *New York Times* and National Public Radio on famous missing persons cases such as the Boston gangster Whitey Bulger, who evaded capture for sixteen years, and fabled hijacker D. B. Cooper, who in 1971 parachuted out of a Boeing 727 with $200,000 in ransom money and has never been seen since. If Sam were a case study in how not to fake your own death, I hoped that Frank would be my Rosetta stone for how to pull it off.

But obtaining an audience with the world-famous privacy consultant proved more difficult than finding him in the first place. I'd tried to meet with Frank for over six months before he finally relented. He would cancel at the last minute every time. He bailed on me while I was waiting for him at a Starbucks on a rainy March afternoon, and when I was downstairs from his office in a skuzzy roller-rink-smelling lobby that shares an address with Fabric Czar USA. He simply texted me "Sry Cant Today."

As with a bad boyfriend, the more Ahearn pushed me away, the more determined I became to win him over. If he was going to play hard to get, I would meet him with equal and opposing resolve. Each time I set out to meet Frank, my well-intentioned friends warned me to be careful. Why the heck would I need to be careful? This guy charges more for his services to disappear people than I make in a year, so I felt pretty confident he wouldn't do me in for free.

One steamy summer afternoon, I head out for yet another meeting, steeled for disappointment and prepared to reverse course back home when he cancels. But moments before our appointed time, my phone has yet to buzz and deliver bad news. Even the elevator ride up to meet him feels victorious. I have finally managed to move beyond the lobby. An unmarked white door swings open, and Frank, six foot four, with his hair scraped into a thin ponytail, extends a meaty hand, splotchy blue tattoos coiling up his forearms. "How ya doin', hon?" he says before leading me through a honeycomb of offices separated by flimsy particleboard. After all his evasions, this is like getting an audience with the Pope.

He is warm and engaging, a far cry from the slippery front he'd used to stonewall me. I ask him why he'd blown me off for so long, and he admits that he thought I was merely posing as a writer and was actually going to serve him papers. He takes precautions with nosy inquirers: "If you look me up, you'll find an address in the Bronx for me, which is actually my brother, and if you ring the doorbell, he'll stick a gun in your face." And given the fuzzy area of the law his work occupies, he possesses a healthy skepticism about anyone who contacts him. "You're a cop, a criminal, or crazy until proven otherwise," he says. And he doesn't help criminals.

Frank is a god of high bullshit. Not the kind of bullshit that is necessarily lying, but the kind of storytelling that seduces anyone, anywhere. His infinite yarns—from growing up on the city's mean streets to scoring criminal records from a pay phone—establish an immediate intimacy, as he inserts your name into the million hypothetical scenarios he constructs to illustrate his dark work. Frank tells his story like an origin myth, replete with American up-by-your-bootstraps redemption, self-made entrepreneurship, and the right to individual privacy. And a little bit of bullshit.

To my dismay, it turned out that Frank frowns upon death fraud. But only out of pragmatism: he says it simply doesn't work. "If your purpose is to defraud an insurance company, there are guys who are paid to check you out," he explains. "Grave robbing—finding a kid who died at a young age—doesn't work today. Twenty years ago, you could walk into the Social Security office and say, 'I've never worked, but I just got a job, and I need a card,' and they would give it to you if you had a fake birth certificate. Death records are now connected to Social Security records, but it didn't used to be like that."

As Eileen Horan, Frank's former employee, ex-fiancée, and coauthor of How to Disappear, would explain later, "There's always one factor you can't count on when you fake your death. You're doubling your chances of getting caught." Ahearn echoed her sentiments: "Think about any crime. Usually police don't catch them in the act, they catch them for the broken headlight on their car."

Which is exactly what happened to Bennie Wint, who had been presumed dead since staging his drowning off the coast of

Daytona Beach, Florida, in 1989. He'd been involved in a narcot-
ics ring, and, swept up in paranoia, he believed the cops were
onto him. He was vacationing at the beach with his fiancée,
Patricia Hollingsworth. After swimming about a mile down the
shore beyond the breakers and vanishing from view with $6,500
stuffed into his swim trunks, he emerged from the water, dried
off, and bought a T-shirt at a nearby store. While Hollingsworth
reported him missing to the beach patrol, he hitched a ride
with a trucker to Ozark, Alabama, and ran a business selling
NASCAR merchandise for twenty years, going by the name William James Sweet. During his tenure as Sweet, he shacked up
with a common-law wife and had a son, whom he named after
himself. But he never filed for an ID under his new alias.

So twenty years later, when he was pulled over in North Carolina, where he'd been living with his new family, for not having
a $1.50 lightbulb over the license plate of his car, he couldn't
produce a driver's license and was booked in jail as John Doe. But
Bennie Wint left behind a grieving fiancée and a four-year-old
daughter from a previous marriage. Wint took the precaution of
avoiding identity fraud but got caught on the most mundane in-
fraction instead. He was charged with driving without a license
and giving a false name to the police. After coming clean, he told
reporters, "The person I was died, in my opinion. I will never be
that person again. I will always be Bill Sweet."

Wint's case illustrates the problem of determining any re-
liable statistics for how many people successfully fake their
deaths and disappear: we learn only about the failures. On average, ninety thousand people are missing in the United States
at any time. But how many of those people disappear inten-
tionally? In my highly unscientific data collection via Google
alerts, I noticed a would-be death fraudster making headlines

every few weeks. Since the Coalition Against Insurance Fraud, a national alliance of consumer groups, public interest organizations, government agencies, and insurers, began keeping records in 1990, 564 cases of life insurance fraud were reported. That averages out to roughly 23 cases per year that get flagged. Not exactly endemic, but two dozen industrious people faking their deaths and getting caught still speaks to a lot of folks with equal parts chutzpah, greed, and shoddy planning skills.

But what of death fakers who don't attempt to collect on a policy, or remember to replace their license plate lightbulb? For every Israel and Wint, perhaps there is an undead doppelganger kicking back in Margaritaville, or maybe even walking among us.

I couldn't help but wonder if the people who'd gotten caught faking their deaths simply hadn't been proactive enough. Are they really "morons and idiots"? Or is it possible that they just aren't doing it right? Or are their foiled attempts perhaps inevitable in our digital age?

=====

IN HIS AUTHOR PHOTO on *How to Disappear*, Frank Ahearn is lit from the side like a late-career Marlon Brando. Despite the book's large print and his liberal deployment of the word *fuck* as noun, adjective, and verb, he has written an exhaustive guide to disappearing in the twenty-first century, and it sells more than 150 copies per week. It hit the *New York Times* Nonfiction Best Sellers list in 2014, four years after it was published. Disappearing is clearly on the minds of many. In his book, Frank discourages readers from faking their deaths, claiming that it's "highly illegal." But, in fact, there is no law on the books called "faking your death." Sam Israel got two years heaped onto his prison sentence for obstruction of justice. If you don't file a police report or death certificate, making it *look* like you are deceased violates no law except perhaps that of good taste. Promoting the idea that you have met an untimely end when in fact you are lazing beachside, paying for your daiquiris with a suitcase full of cash, is perfectly legal.

"In those narrow confines, it wouldn't create any legal issue," says Judge Daniel Procaccini, a Rhode Island Superior Court judge who dealt with the legendary case of Adam Emery. Adam and his wife, Elena, appeared to have plunged from the Claiborne Pell Bridge in Newport in 1993. The young couple abandoned their Toyota Camry on the bridge, also leaving behind packaging for eighty pounds of strap-on weights. This occurred just three hours after he was convicted of stabbing a twenty-year-old man to death but somehow was allowed out on bail. In September 1994, pieces of Elena's skull were positively identified. Adam's remains have never been found. After eleven years with no sign of him, Judge Procaccini pronounced Emery dead so that his family could collect life insurance money.

If you even try to rent a bike or apply for a library card with another identity, and especially if you try to cash in a life insurance policy, then you are committing fraud. But to make believe that you are dead poses no crime. "It's surprising more people don't do it," the judge says.

But some do. Petra Pazsitka, a German woman, seems to have pulled off a fully legal faked death for over three decades. Paztiska was a twenty-four-year-old computer science student in 1984 when she was last seen boarding a bus in Braunschweig. One year earlier, a fourteen-year-old girl had been murdered in the vicinity. Her parents reached out to a crime stoppers television show to solve the cold case, and in 1985 a carpenter's apprentice, a nineteen-year-old known as Gunter K., was arrested and confessed to murdering the fourteen-year-old, and later to murdering Pazsitka as well. Petra was declared dead. At fifty-five years old, she was resurrected when she alerted police to a burglary taking place at her Dusseldorf home. When police asked her for identification, she introduced herself as "Mrs. Schneider," but couldn't produce any official documents. She had spent the past thirty-one years bouncing between different German cities, without any government ID or bank accounts, and paying for everything in cash. She told police she "wanted nothing to do with her family" and no contact with the public. She refused to give any motive for her disappearance. Since she committed no life insurance or identity fraud, she was not charged with any criminal offense. She did, however, have to register herself with German authorities as alive.

I find this refreshing. As morally questionable as faking death might be, at least you can pull it off while still being a good citizen. As Frank explains, "Picking up your suitcase and going to the bus stop is not a crime. Is it against the law to walk out on your wife or husband? I don't think so." Not that being on the right side of the law much interested Frank Ahearn. He didn't start out in the disappearing business. He actually got his start finding people in the course of a fifteen-year stint as a skip tracer. A skip tracer, in Frank's words, is a "liar for hire." Skip tracers locate people and uncover their most intimate information. The difference between a private investigator and a skip tracer is that a PI must be licensed. Kurt Duesterdick, a PI himself and a friend of Frank's, explains: "The state police perform a crazy background check to license PIs. Let's just say there are a lot of skip tracers who couldn't get licenses." Skip tracers can extract hard-to-get information for police, PIs, lawyers, and anyone else with enough cash, because they don't get bogged down in pesky details such as warrants or privacy laws. Frank has tracked down deadbeat dads and missing witnesses, and accessed the checking accounts of financiers suspected of embezzling money. He has worked with tabloids targeting celebrities. One of his main clients was a British tabloid that hired Frank to locate famous people. In 1998 it sent him the as-yet-unknown name Monica Lewinsky.

"I had no idea who she was," he says. He called her home, saying he was from UPS and had a water-damaged package for Ms. Lewinsky that was about to be sent back. The housekeeper who answered the phone told him just to leave it on the door-step. Frank unwittingly broke the scandal of the White House intern simply by verifying her identity and whereabouts. "My client told me to watch the news that night," he says, "and when I did, I discovered who she was." As a practical joke, he would page his friends with celebrities' phone numbers, having them call Britney Spears and Nick Nolte.

In his time as a skip tracer, Frank—whose formal education concluded in the ninth grade—obtained criminal, phone, and banking records and scored intelligence from the FBI and Scotland Yard. "All a skip tracer needs is charm and a telephone," he says. He could access any piece of privileged information by posing as someone else and providing false pretenses (such as posing as a UPS deliveryman), a routine he dubbed "pretext-ing." If a client wanted the phone records of a cheating spouse, for example, Ahearn would simply pick up the phone and call the company, pretending to be the cheating spouse himself. "I'd say, 'How ya doin'? This is so-and-so, and I just want to make sure I'm on the best calling plan, and by the way, could you read me my call history for the month?'" He likens his tech-nique to the scorched-earth policy deployed by creepy guys everywhere. "It's like dating: every no leads to a yes," he explains. "If I get some twenty-year-old guy on the phone, I start shooting the shit, like 'Hey, I'm going to the Caribbean over the weekend with the guys; nothing but booze, beer, and babes!' Or I get the middle-aged woman, and I'll talk about how my daughter is getting married on Sunday." For someone who considers himself a misanthrope, he sure knows how to connect with people, at least when there's something to gain. "Skip tracing is really about taking the person on the other end of the phone away from their day," he says.

At the height of his skip tracing business, in the 1990s, Ahearn lived in an affluent New Jersey suburb with his wife and employed a staff of fifteen who helped him locate people and information. Single moms, he claims, were the best workers, because he allowed a flexible schedule and found them to be quite motivated to earn commissions on top of their base salary. One could easily take home up to $1,500 per week for telling a few lies on the phone. "We had a lot of fun. Everyone was dysfunctional," he recalls. His former employees remember Ahearn as a generous boss who treated them to lunch regularly and surprised them with cakes on their birthdays. The staff nabbed records and documents from the Canadian newspaper publisher Conrad Black, who was worth millions and subsequently imprisoned for fraud. Ahearn still relishes the fact that his team contributed to Black's demise, because, as he likes to brag, "the highest level of education in that office was a GED." With the help of his team, Frank says he located more than forty thousand people.

Skip tracing provided instant gratification, a rush of adrenaline, and more money than Frank could ever have imagined. Assuming a new identity for each pretexting phone call allowed him to slip away from himself, to disappear for a moment.

Perhaps Frank's aversion to death fraud is because his ethos is built like a chest of drawers, with comfortable compartments in which to stow different levels of deception. Lying never bothered him. "If your name came across my desk, you had probably done something wrong," he rationalizes. The part of his mendacity that did bother him, however, was his natural facility. "The thing that played in my mind was 'Why am I so good at this deception thing?' Like, why did I grab that bag when I was born? Why didn't I grab the bag for being good at painting?"

His inauguration ten years ago as a "privacy consultant," or disappearance concierge, occurred not so much by choice as by accident. After 9/11, Frank's business crumbled, along with his life. With the economy in the tank and new privacy laws that made it illegal to pretext banks, skip tracing became more difficult. The Internal Revenue Service caught up with him for unpaid taxes, his wife divorced him, and he "had the misfortune of quitting drinking." After he and his wife separated, he slept on a couch in his office and kept all his clothes in the trunk of his car, waking in the early morning to shower in the office bathroom, wiping the water drops off the shower curtain, and slipping out so no one would catch on. "I'd bounce around for a few hours and roll into the office at nine thirty with a cup of coffee. No one knew anything," Frank says. He paid his employees a small severance with the money from the sale of his house after the divorce. The day his skip tracing office closed, he packed up whatever he could stuff into his car, unable to pay the deposit on a moving van. "I looked back at this vacant office, just a sea of empty desks, and said, 'There's my empire.'"

Newly sober—without the help of Alcoholics Anonymous, he is quick to point out—he attempted to skip trace for regular people instead of PIs and police. Frank placed an ad on the website EscapeArtist, a community bulletin board for expats, but soon got an email from the administrator saying that *locating* people kind of went against its mission, so why didn't he write a short article about disappearing instead? And from his "crappy, unedited" piece about the mistakes people make and the slipups that get them caught, he started receiving emails and calls from all over the world requesting his consulting services to help people make their getaway. So Frank inverted his business model and used his insider knowledge to aid those desperate for a respite from their lives. Because he knew how to find people, he also knew how to help them hide.

But why disappear rather than fake your death? Frank maintains strongly that the two are very different things. To him, simply disappearing—walking out on your life without leaving a trace, rather than staging an elaborate accident suggesting your death—is the way to go because of its austere elegance. But it still didn't make sense to me. If you're not leaving behind anything outstanding in your wake—like a jail sentence or impoverished investors—wouldn't people just assume you died if it looked like you died? If you're not planning on coming back, the illusion of death might actually be gentler. Then at least your loved ones can mourn your memory rather than try restlessly to solve the mystery of your disappearance. It seemed to me that people would be more suspicious if you simply vanished without a trace. Wouldn't *someone* come sniffing around as to your whereabouts? And wouldn't you have to assume another identity anyway?

Although there is no law on the books explicitly against death fraud, Frank holds firm that even tiny auxiliary crimes can get a person in trouble, like the authenticating details that bolster the credibility of a death scene: "You blow up your house, you chop your fingers off, you leave your fingers behind—that's a crime. If somewhere down the line you find out they paid your wife a hundred thousand dollars in insurance, that's a crime." It occurred to me that he was talking about people with quite a bit of baggage, the baggage one accumulates over a lifetime of chasing the American dream: a wife, a house, a family, a little trouble with the law trying to get more. But me? I was an unencumbered, footloose and fancy-free, unmarried, childless young adult. I had only garden-variety six-figure student loan debt. It's true that the debt was incurred in service of chasing that elusive American dream, but that did not make me special. So how dire, how irreversible, do your problems need to be to "kill" the person— you—responsible for them, rather than just walking away?

———

WHEN A PERSON DECIDES to disappear, the stakes are high. Prior to meeting Frank, I'd thought that my debt qualified as pressing, but compared with someone like Sam Israel, who was looking down the barrel of two decades in prison and a half-billion-dollar IOU, my little problem was just a drop in the death-faking bucket. Ahearn sorts his clients' motives into two categories: money and violence. Occasionally you could file it in the category of "love," like when the husband wants to run away with a woman (or man) who is not his wife, but this motivation is an outlier.

Ahearn estimates that from 2001 to 2012, he helped around fifty people disappear, charging up to $30,000 per case for his services. More than half of his clients were men, whom he charged full freight to help underwrite his female clients. Men came to him with money problems; they had come into money or had lost it all and his female clients had violence problems: stalkers or abusive husbands. If the woman contacting Frank felt like her life was in imminent danger, he wouldn't charge her anything.

"Most of the men were in search of the palm-tree lifestyle," Frank explains, referring to middle-aged men who lit out for places like Belize or Panama (countries where you can open an anonymous corporation with little oversight and hassle), free from the IRS or the "ex-wife sucking him dry." He never helped people with offshore banking but instead set up his clients as "virtual entities." He'd then funnel money to fund their livelihoods—from phone bills to rent—under a limited liability company (LLC), which, depending on the state, can be set up with varying degrees of anonymity. Along with a variety of other undetectable methods, such as prepaid cell phones and credit cards, Ahearn could make his clients invisible *without* their assuming false identities: "The minute you open up a bank account with a fake identity, you're violating so many laws," he says. "And how do you know whose identity you're buying? What if the person is a pedophile?" Good point.

But even to get to the point of "undetectable"—and Ahearn maintains that these days "everything" is traceable, even cash and burner phones (disposable cell phones unlinked to a credit card or social security number)—one must go to great lengths. Methods that at one time seemed viable, like the anonymizing software application Tor, have all proved fallible to a baby hacker. Whatever new technology comes along promising citizens privacy will inevitably become obsolete in a matter of moments. And Big Brother's surveillance is very real. Your image can be captured on Google Street View, by drones, by security cameras everywhere. Erasing a digital footprint is now impossible, Frank maintains, but you can take measures to disconnect yourself from the trail.

This involves a method of outsourcing the dirty work that Frank dubs "stretching the footprint." He illustrates his point

with a surprisingly wholesome example, given his rakish personal presentation: "Say you ask the bully's girlfriend to dance,
and now he's coming to kick your ass. You duck from him, but
then a week later you're delivering pizza because that's your
job. You show up at the house, and you realize, 'Oh shit! It's his
house.' If you ring the doorbell, he's going to open the door and
punch you in the face. How do I accomplish my goal of delivering the pizza and getting paid without him realizing it's me?
You go to the schoolyard, you get a kid, and say, 'Hey, listen,
deliver this pizza; keep the tip money.' I give the pizza money
to my boss, I keep my teeth, and we're all happy."

   The idea is to create buffers with other people in other
places to insulate you from detection. How can I remove myself from the picture and have somebody else leave my digital
footprint for me? Frank describes how he stretches his connection when making contact with a client who really, really
does not want to be linked to the privacy consultant: "If I need
to email somebody in Romania, I will never email them from
frankahearn.com. I have a circle of third-party people in all different parts of the world who work as assistants for companies
like oDesk [a freelancer service] who will have a prepaid cell
phone to call this person in Korea, and I will dictate an email.
They will email it to a location email address. I will have someone in Norway access it, copy it, and then they shut down that
email. Then they email it to where I want it to go in Romania.
Is it perfect? No. But the average person can't get that. Can law
enforcement get it? Sure, but it's going to take a little time, and
by then you're gone. You're going to create the digital footprint
no matter what, so make your footprints few and far between."

   But even getting the prepaid phone requires some extra planning. People get so wrapped up in the digital footprint, Frank

says, that they forget about being out in the real world, where a security camera captures a picture of them buying the phone at CVS. "I have certain clients who will contact me, and they'll just email me a word. And I'll know what that word means and where to call. So I will shoot to Times Square and find myself a homeless guy. I'll say, 'Go buy me a prepaid phone,' and I'll pay him a hundred dollars. His face is on the camera buying it. I make sure I'm not walking deep into Times Square where my face is being picked up on camera, nor am I being picked up at the location where he's giving me the phone. Now that phone is anonymous; nobody knows Frank Ahearn used that phone."

It seems like an awful lot of trouble. But that is the price of doing business. If you want to disappear, and do it right, the planning is not for the faint of heart, or the careless. "It's a pain in the ass," Frank admits. Which is part of the reason why people who want to disappear hire him to do the grunt work. It's a fraught and lonely world out there on your own.

So how does a woman with little disposable income and even less time ditch a madman hot on her trail? "The less money you have, the easier it is to disappear. Give me a waitress with shitty credit who doesn't own a house, all I have to do is skip trace her information and see what she needs to do. Piece of cake," Frank says. With fewer assets, there's less to detect. Of course, I can project myself into that model, with my own lack of funds, shitty credit, and history of verbal leases. No real estate, no inheritance, nothing to hide. I could walk out of Frank's office and into the thick humidity of the August afternoon and dissolve easier than I thought. Confronting the flimsiness of my life, at least on paper, I recognized a certain lightness of being. I felt as if I could blow away.

Frank's process disappears people in three easy steps. The

first step is "misinformation," which means destroying any information available, from closing bank and phone accounts to removing your name from online databases. Then he creates "disinformation," or false leads to throw off pursuers. So if the waitress is repairing to Kansas in February, Ahearn starts diverting traceable leads to Chicago in January. She will place calls to realtors, utility companies, and restaurants that might be hiring. "If I'm a stalker and I hire a skip tracer, the first thing I'm going for is your phone records. Anyone who is looking for you is going to look at that January information." If she has enough money, she can travel to Chicago for the day and meet with realtors to see apartments. If a skip tracer brings up her credit report, he will see an inquiry from a Chicago realtor.

Once Frank has sufficiently engineered enough false leads and set her up in the next place, he calls the woman to say it's go time. Fleeing under these conditions means leaving behind almost everything. "If you live with the guy, you just pack that one fahkin' bag, and you go. You don't risk hiring a moving company." To escape her pursuer, the woman might hire a PI to do surveillance and make sure he's out of the way. And, of course, the woman should take an indirect route to Kansas by buying a bus ticket to Chicago with a credit card and paying for her Kansas ticket with cash.

Now begins the off-the-grid life. When the woman makes the move to Kansas, she will pay her rent and bills from an LLC. But how to earn a living? "You can't be a regular employee or a licensed professional, like an accountant or a nurse," Frank says. "But you can work off the books—as a waitress, or graphic designer, or house cleaner—and claim the cash you make. I would never tell anyone not to claim their cash," he adds with a smile. "That would be un-American." A Massachusetts lawyer retained Frank's services to help her escape an ex-boyfriend who was stalking her. Since she could no longer practice law ("She'd have to join the bar in that state, and all the guy would need to do is make fifty phone calls. There are fifty states, right?"), she became a legal consultant in New Hampshire to avoid registering her address in the very public state bar association database and filed her taxes as an independent contractor.

I was shocked to learn that a woman who felt her life was in danger from a deranged stalker would merely cross a single state line to hide. Couldn't they plausibly run into each other at the gas station? But many of Frank's disappearees have relocated to towns just hours away. Most stayed close because they couldn't afford a big move, but, as Frank says, "Sometimes disappearing two hours away is better than going cross-country because you're hiding in plain sight." To keep in touch with loved ones left behind, Frank devised codes in the form of Craigslist postings and classified ads. "If Mom wants to find you, all she needs to do is look up '1974 Cadillac Seville with whitewall tires' and switch the last two digits of the phone number in the ad to call your prepaid cell phone." Some of his clients corresponded by using a single email account, with each user having the password, and not sending their messages but saving them as drafts so that no electronic trail could be recovered. Other clients did the same with unpublished blogs. "I'm good," he chuckles.

One of Frank's favorite clients was a man named Louie, a gruff older gentleman who had amassed a small fortune from hot dog carts and food trucks. "He cursed and smoked cigars and had a lawyer son who was a prick and wanted his money," Frank recalls. Louie's wife had died recently, and he regressed into bachelorhood, buying sports cars and dating women decades younger. The son thought Louie was acting irresponsibly, so he filed a petition for power of attorney. "He wanted his son off his back, and he knew the best way to do that was to disappear. Move to the Caribbean. Enjoy his fortune and a cold Corona next to the bright blue sea," Frank writes in *How to Disappear*. Louie read an article about Frank and had his lawyer contact him.

"The lawyer said, 'He doesn't need your help getting from point A to point B; he just wants to make sure no one finds him when he gets to point B. And he wants to create "fahk you" things for the son to find when he goes after him.'" So Frank went to town creating disinformation for the son's private investigator to find. Frank hired an expensive escort ("I didn't want a two-bit hoo-ar") to live in a luxury apartment in Louie's name. The PI staked out the doorman building, and, after days of not spotting Louie, he approached the escort, who handed him an envelope with a phone number. Louie's son dialed the phone number but was looped to his own home answering machine, as Frank had set up a call-forwarding service by pretexting a phone company.

———

FAKING DEATH IS HARDLY a new phenomenon. Rather, it seems as if people in the past gave it a whirl with far fewer technologies at their disposal and for less urgent motives than the money or violence Frank cites. Up until relatively recently, faking one's death was as easy as placing an obituary in the local newspaper. In 1913, French police investigated the "queer case" of a wealthy Côte d'Azur contractor who'd built many of the gleaming Mediterranean-style mansions dotting the Riviera. The contractor's son, a wealthy Parisian playboy, had run up steep debts in his father's name. The contractor's obituary ran in the local paper, and a funeral procession departed from his gigantic villa, Star of the Sea, and marched to the village cemetery—where his empty coffin was buried. His mansion fell into disrepair. The manicured lawns grew ragged weeds and jungle vines. The banks in Paris closed the case on the debt. But a few months later, a friend spotted the contractor crossing the street in Cannes. Other reported sightings came in from Nice and Antibes. When authorities announced that they planned to dig up the coffin, one villager came forward and revealed that the funeral invitations had been penned in the dead man's handwriting.

While the financial motive remains common, the stakes weren't always so high. One young Englishman, William Mellor, registered his own death in 1885 because he was wanted for stealing a horse. The contraband horse was located in Manchester, where Mellor had sold it for £18. Mellor's pseudocide was just the anticlimactic coda to a life of petty crime. According to the London *Pall Mall Gazette*, which documented Horsegate, the nine-year-old Mellor collected alms for a youth group of missionaries. He took his meager donations to get drunk at a pub and then burned his alms box. Two decades later, Mellor fraudulently obtained a government loan to stock a farm that did not exist. When an inquiry officer paid him a visit to check up on Her Majesty's investment, Mellor toured him around a thriving farm down the road, which belonged to neighbors he knew to be out of town. Mellor was not heard from again until ten years later, when he reported himself dead. But police were suspicious of the fortuitous timing of his death. Officers speculated that he "succeeded in escaping to America with the proceeds of the horse robbery." The newspaper editorialized, "not a few hope he has made his escape good." Faking death has always been the province of low-rent con men.

While Frank maintains that romance is a distant third motivation to fake one's death, in 1879 one fanciful young woman fulfilled every jilted lover's fantasy. Twenty-one-year-old Ida M. Eddy placed her own obituary in two Boston-area newspapers, saying she had died of heart disease, replete with lurid details of belabored breathing and coughing up blood. But her plan had a sinister twist: on the morning of publication, she furiously called the newspapers herself, upbraiding the editors for running her death notice without fact checking. She was very much alive, and accused Jennie Bessom (whom the *Boston Advertiser* described as a "respectable young woman") of writing her obituary. Ida had organized the subterfuge because "a young man had transferred his affections from Miss Ida Eddy to Miss Jennie Bessom, and that the former had since endeavored to win him back by composing malicious forged letters written to herself, purporting to have come from the latter." It was a sublime revenge scenario: Ida would illustrate to her ex-boyfriend the agony of what life would be like without her while simultaneously maligning the new girl's character, painting her as an amoral home wrecker. When police investigated the story, they found "the animus of the whole affair 'appears' to have been a desire to destroy Miss Bessom's reputation." Ida eventually admitted her dastardly hoax and was ultimately fined $100. It is unknown whether she was able to reignite the young man's affections.

Not all pseudocides intended to teach a heartbreaker a lesson end so whimsically. Some romantic ploys have ended up in lives cut tragically short. In a 1935 article entitled "Wife Dies in Ketchup Case," the *New York Times* reported that after a domestic dispute, a Yonkers policeman "smeared his face with ketchup and then fired his pistol into the floor of their home after his wife had threatened to leave the house after a quarrel." When she saw her husband covered in what she thought was blood, she grabbed the pistol and fatally shot herself.

STORIES OF FAKED DEATH are proto narratives. The founding myth of the Talmud features Rabbi Yohanan ben Zakkai faking his death so that he can escape Jerusalem during the Jewish rebellion against the Romans in the first century AD: "Pretend you are sick, and let everyone come to visit you. Bring something rotten and place it with you, and they will say you died." It's a theme that resurfaces frequently in literature. In Nathaniel Hawthorne's 1835 story "Wakefield," for example, a man leaves his London home "under the pretense of going on a journey" but instead takes an apartment around the corner where he can watch his own life progress without him, from a ghost's perspective. Huck Finn smears pig's blood around a cabin and plants clumps of hair on an ax, orchestrating a hoax to "fix it now so nobody won't think of following me," and sets off on the adventure of a lifetime, unencumbered by the adults who would want to "sivilize" him. Juliet downs a tincture to make her "stiff and stark and cold, appear like death," to leave her family's warring tribal politics and live happily ever after with Romeo. But much like the ketchup fiasco, this plan, too, went awry. Men in crime novels by John Grisham and Tom Clancy disappear or fake their own deaths regularly, like their cultural predecessors in pulpy noir paperbacks. To become invisible is to cast yourself as both the villain and the hero of your story.

And now more than ever, audiences hunger for stories of deliberate disappearance. Everywhere I looked, there they were: Monica Ali's 2011 novel *Untold Story* suggests that Princess Di faked her own death. Gillian Flynn's 2012 bestseller *Gone Girl* is plotted around a staged murder. One of the computer-generated suggestions in my Netflix queue was a self-produced documentary entitled *Alive! Is Michael Jackson Really Dead?* (one of the most popular instant-streaming choices at the time). In September 2011 the Discovery Channel debuted a new series called *I Faked My Own Death,* which chronicled some of the "morons and idiots" referred to by Frank. *Gossip Girl*'s steely robber baron Bart Bass returns from the dead in the penultimate season, a classic soap opera trope. Don Draper on *Mad Men* ditched Dick Whitman in the Korean War and assumed a dead man's identity. And everyone's favorite antihero, Walter White on the TV show *Breaking Bad,* hired a consultant like Frank to deliver him to a new life off the grid.

Pseudocide boasts an eternal fascination—think Elvis and Tupac—but why the seeming ubiquity? Perhaps I was just experiencing the phenomenon of naming the thing and then seeing it everywhere, but new death fraud cases kept popping up with uncanny frequency. Even Paul Walker, the blandly handsome action hero of *The Fast and the Furious* movie franchise, was rumored to have staged the car accident that claimed his life in 2013. It was as if people needed the fantasy as a place to project their longing for a different ending, or even a resurrection.

Today, disappearing seems virtually impossible. This, I think, is what accounts for our renewed fascination with it. We are burdened with our search histories and purchase histories and data stats that constitute our profile, to then be lumped and farmed out and sold to the highest bidder. Disappearing means disconnecting—unimaginable yet totally captivating. Precisely because it has become less feasible, that deep urge to be anonymous, or even to be someone else, exists ever more powerfully within us. The desire to disappear doesn't go away just because times change and technology strangles us. That we cannot fulfill the urge as easily is perhaps the greatest tragedy.

The economy has been in the toilet for the better part of a decade, and Americans find themselves saddled with more personal debt than ever before in human history. Like my own plight, many feel they might never recover from their financial turmoil, or have been set so far back that they have little investment in playing by the rules that have screwed them. Prospects we once trusted—home ownership, a comfortable retirement, hard work leading to a decent life—crumble every day. The typical college student graduates burdened with $35,000 in debt, the average household owes $15,706 to credit card companies, and if you are lucky enough to qualify for a mortgage, you'll owe in the ballpark of $156,474. Disappearing seems like a reasonable daydream to indulge.

The fantasy might also represent a pendulum swing away from the hypervisibility of our age. We project pieces of ourselves in humble braggy status updates and clever hash tags, and refuse even the blood and viscera of speaking on the phone. Instead of expressing emotion, we have emojis. One has not experienced the present moment until it has been photographed, posted, and liked. Our lives are processed through cables and screens, and filtered through Mayfair, X-Pro II, and Valencia. We are only as sensitive as the ironic graffiti we notice and post, as sexy as the selfies we flaunt. The fevered curating and monitoring weigh us down while simultaneously abstracting us from relationships IRL.

A 2010 University of South Carolina study suggests that loneliness increases with time spent on the internet, reinforcing a 1998 study, published in the journal *American Psychologist,* which finds that digital dependence leads to depression, loneliness, and neglect of existing relationships. Psychologist Sherry Turkle, famed professor at the Massachusetts Institute

of Technology, wrote in the *New York Times*, "We think constant connection will make us feel less lonely. The opposite is
true. If we are unable to be alone, we are far more likely to be
lonely." Perhaps faking death and disappearing appeals to the
part of us that still craves authenticity and unfettered solitude,
the truest antidote to loneliness.

Having others reflect and validate our existences back at us
is exactly what the narcissism of social media has conditioned
us to expect. Consider the temptation to check in on yourself,
once you have disappeared, by logging on to Facebook through
a bogus account to monitor your in-memoriam profile. It's the
twenty-first-century equivalent of Tom Sawyer showing up at
his own funeral.

The temptation was too much for Patrick McDermott,
Australian singer Olivia Newton-John's longtime boyfriend.
He faked his death on a fishing trip in 2005 shortly after the
couple had broken up. He'd chartered a boat and allegedly fell
overboard at night, drowning in the waters off the coast of Los
Angeles. His motive appeared to be monetary. He had filed for
bankruptcy while still with Newton-John, and, according to
various news sources, might have wanted the proceeds from
a $100,000 insurance policy to go to his son. A group of pri-
vate investigators hired by *Dateline* located McDermott when
they noticed a centralized cluster of IP addresses originating
near Puerto Vallarta, Mexico, all clicking onto a site dedicated
to tracing his whereabouts. Keeping tabs on oneself through
the disembodied filter of the computer screen highlights how
egomaniacal one must be to fake one's death in the first place.
But perhaps McDermott thought he was harnessing technology
to his own advantage: a real-time report of where his pursuers
were searching for him. His case shows how easy it is to get

yourself caught, even off the grid. "Disappearing makes you infinite," Frank says. "If you disappear, people will always talk about you." Somehow the mystery of the disappeared makes more present the person who has gone.

Surprisingly, Frank maintains that technology has actually made disappearing much easier today than in the analog days of yore. He too has noticed an increased fancy for the world of disappearance, and he too agrees it's because things are shitty. But he also thinks it's because the fantasy is less of a hassle to enact: "Twenty years ago, if you wanted to disappear to Belize, you would have to go to a bookstore and buy a book about Belize. Then you'd have to call the tourist bureau down there, but first you'd have to call directory assistance to get a long-distance line—fourteen dollars later—and then, 'Hi, I'm looking to move to Belize,' and they'll send you a brochure. Then you'd have to call airlines to see who flies to Belize. It would be a weeks-long project. Today all you need to do is sit in front of your computer for twenty minutes. You can rent an apartment, buy plane tickets, and you're gone." But what about the fact that you could be traced just as easily? "The internet is a double-edged sword," Frank admits. In his view, "it all comes down to who's better at it: the person looking or the person disappearing?"

That's why Frank has set his sights on a new frontier, retooling and revamping his business yet again, to help clients bury negative information available about them online. While disappearing clients typically seek his services for reasons of money or violence, his digital-deception clients' needs vary. Frank cites a common scenario: "The problem with information is that it's starting to affect the average Joe. Say that before you were born, your father had a DUI and killed a kid in Iowa. And now, all of a sudden this small newspaper from Iowa is putting up all their issues online, and all of a sudden there's this information about your father. That's a problem, because some guy has changed his life and now has to pay the price. I find it fahked up because at the end of the day, the only reason that newspaper is putting that online is so they can make more money on ads." He deals with people like the hypothetical DUI dad who seeks to distance himself from the sins of his past (he clarifies again, "I'm not talking about a pedophile or someone like that!") or people who might want to hide only certain parts of their identities, such as a world-traveling photojournalist who also happens to be a millionaire, or a prosecutor who has sent murderers to jail and doesn't want the convicts to know the particulars of her family life and residence.

The notion of making the move from physical to digital disappearance occurred to Frank when he was a guest on a local New York cable TV show in 2010. He was on for his expertise in the art of disappearance. The other guest was Michael Fertik, CEO of Reputation.com, who Skyped in from a conference in Washington, DC. Fertik's company offers a variety of services, including "helping people establish a positive online visibility" and "combat[ting] negative content." The two guests could not have been more different. Frank, in his uniform of sunglasses and black T-shirt, spoke of his trademark recipe of manipulating information to disappear, while Fertik rhapsodized about reinvention as an American ideal and the internet as the locus of a "collective permanent memory." Frank recalls the taping to me: "Fertik was talking about how they manage reputation, using these huge words, and I was like, 'What the fahk does this guy do?' I hate highfalutin individuals. It really drives me fahkin' nuts."

But Frank also saw a flaw in Fertik's methods. "You can't

delete shit online. If you ask a newspaper or a blogger to take something down, that can backfire. It can be front-page news the next day. I realized, why not just create deception?" Fertik told me over the phone from the Bay Area, "Very emphatically, that"—deleting shit online—"is not what we do. We are a globally scalable business with two hundred people who are PhDs in math, computer science, and statistics. Frank is not a technologist," he said. "He seems like the kind of guy you'd see at the corner bar."

Corner bar or not, Frank has his method down pat. He manages his clients' reputations by essentially creating fake people who make fake websites, all with his clients' names. It's a variation on misinformation, also called "data pollution." For example, if Noah Schwarz made an amateur porn back in college, Frank builds websites for thirty other Noah Schwarzes, buying up every domain name, such as NoahSchwarz.net, NoahSchwarz.co.uk, and NoahSchwarz.org. One Noah Schwarz will be a juggler, one Noah Schwarz might be an accountant, but one Noah Schwarz (also fictional, but sharing certain traits with the real Noah Schwarz) will have gone to the University of San Francisco and will reminisce about his wild fraternity days when he and his buddies produced porn. The mostly fake Noah Schwarz, however, will live in Austin, Texas, while the real Noah Schwarz lives in New York. The mostly fake Noah Schwarz will be an insurance salesman, while the real Noah Schwarz is a professor. Ostensibly, the crime will be assigned to the mostly fictitious Noah Schwarz. "You can't rid yourself of the information," Frank says, "but you can use digital information to have somebody else take the glory or the misery, or just murk it up enough so it doesn't look like my client did the thing." Or more simply: "It's like high school. My goal is to make my websites more popular and yours less popular." He charges in the ballpark of $25,000 to build and maintain the websites for six months.

It seems to be effective, but some clients have objected to his method. Frank dealt with a wealthy horse trader whose former partner spoke disparagingly about him in a *New York Times* article. "He wanted me to get it down. He wanted me to pretext the *New York Times*! I told him, 'Look, you can't get rid of it.'" If the article exists on the *Times* website, it most likely exists on other aggregator sites, and locating every mutation of the article would be like ripping up a ream of paper into confetti, throwing it into the wind, and trying to recover every bit. Frank then gave a quick demo of how he would handle his client's predicament: by building ten fake websites, "with the stupidest stuff in the world," under the horse trader's name. When you typed his name into Google, you would find nothing but horses—clowns with horses, cowboys with horses—but nothing directly identifiable to the actual horse trader. Despite the fact that Frank managed to bury the negative article, the client was less than pleased. "He got pissed off at me. He was actually insulted. The problem I face with people is vanity. He didn't want to be attached to this dumb thing."

I asked whether any of his clients ever question the veracity of the search results they receive, whether it ever seems fishy to type in the name of a prominent person, and yet the top hits come up as jugglers and clowns. "Clients worry that someone is going to think it's bullshit," Frank admits. "But when was the last time you said 'This Google search is bullshit'? And who goes past page one or two on a Google search? If I can dump the damning thing on page eight, people most likely aren't going to find it."

Despite Frank's insistence, this strategy has been criticized as ineffective when the websites appear too tawdry or haphazard. Still, it's clever. As Frank put it, "You don't even have to disappear anymore. With digital deception, you can create the *illusion* of disappearing." I thought about this for a moment. Could you make it seem as if you've started a new life in Los Angeles while you're actually going about your business in New York? It seems impossible. In a city of eight million, I'm ashamed to recall the times I've found myself hiding behind cars to avoid ex-boyfriends or ducking into Duane Reade rather than engaging in awkward conversation with a vague acquaintance. And what about bill collectors? They're a pretty plucky bunch. Could I potentially avoid these confrontations without uprooting my life?

"You're using the deception to create whatever world you want," Frank explains, "to let people believe you're here rather than there. You can move from Upper Manhattan to Lower Manhattan and give the illusion that you've moved to East Jabib." Frank made it sound as easy as Photoshopping a picture of me in front of the Space Needle and writing a status update such as "Love it here in Seattle!" But what about my friends and family? Wouldn't I have to let them in on it, lest they think I am suffering from multiple personality disorder or delusions of grandeur? And how would that help me on the student loan front?

It began to occur to me that just as there are many layers of intimacy and connection with the people in our lives, there are also multiple layers of our manifestation in the world. Our selves are fluid, and we shift seamlessly between the physical and the digital. Integrating our physical being with its digital shadow—the unseemly events of college, or rumors, true or not—makes deception inevitable, whether you consider with-holding information deception at all. People can live one life but change age and gender online. "Deception" is just another name for "avatar," "casual encounter," or "Facebook profile." "Technology allows us to be who we want," Frank says philo-sophically, "and it's not always ourselves."

Deception has fascinated Frank since he was a kid, because he saw the power it gave the liar. Frank Sr. ran illegal gambling clubs in the Bronx, and, as a boy, Frank Jr. was impressed with what lying could get him. "I must have been six or seven years old, and one of my sisters had her first communion or some-thing like that, and my father took us out for Chinese food. There was this little lobster fork my dad got with his meal, and my father said to the Chinese waiter, 'We're tourists visiting the city. Can I keep this fork?' We lived a couple blocks away! But the guy said, 'Okay, no problem.' That story has always stuck in my head. I said, 'Wow! If you lie, you get things.'"

Maybe some people are just better at deception and even consider it a means to an end in the first place. I'll tell a white lie to make someone feel better ("That bolero jacket does not em-phasize your midsection!") or a lie of omission (I do not speak of my Meat Lover's pizza and Bravo reality-TV marathons), but telling out-and-out whoppers (like that I am dead) is daunting. What if Frank is right, and deception is just a move toward per-sonal liberation? Do we have a right to disappear? Or is shirking our responsibilities—the debts, the marriage, the tedium—the ultimate in human hubris?

Maybe evaluating one's motives can answer those ques-tions. From Frank's descriptions of the queries he fielded, most of the potential clients sounded less like nefarious conspirers or lazy deadbeats and more like everyday cogs in the wheel: "I have people who email me 'I'm thinking about disappearing,' so then I email them back and say, 'Tell me what's going on.' And they say, 'Nothing, I just don't really like my life.'"

Dr. Ze'ev Levin, a New York University psychiatrist and professor who specializes in personality disorders, tells me just how widespread this impulse is: "There's this fantasy that many of us have that if we moved to a different place, our lives would be different. It's not unusual for people to say that things are terrible in New York, so if I moved to Australia, things would be better. I think there are universal fantasies we have about wishing we were somewhere else, and someone else. Taken to an absolute extreme, erasing your life assumes you will then be reborn as something different. If I died while I was alive, I could come back as something other." Dr. Levin sees this tendency of avoidance cloaked in a daydream as an evolutionary trick that prevents us from confronting and examining the uglier parts of ourselves. "We are structurally designed to not want to look at what's upsetting," he observes. Actually going through with such a deceit and making the fantasy concrete would indicate antisocial and manipulative behavior, but as Dr. Levin says, "Fantasizing has nothing to do with being a sociopath." Dr. Laura Gold, a clinical psychologist in Manhattan, echoes Dr. Levin. "I have certainly heard people fantasize about the power of the credit card, to just go to an airport and get on a flight far away from their lives," she says.

This sentiment resonates with many people. Says Frank, "I think we've all dreamt about it at one point in our lives. There's a cathartic thing about it. It's like going for a long walk, or looking at apartments in Paris online, which I do every day. You can envision yourself there. Go to Google Earth, you can see the front of the building. No matter how good our lives are, there's a part of us that would just like to leave the whole world behind." Even Frank, whose occupation allows him to live out the fantasy of beginning again with each client, finds himself underwhelmed. "I'm so fahkin' bored. I've had my fill. I need to find something to occupy my time, but I hate hobbies. You can only write so much, you can only dream so much. I've been thinking about my own escape plan, and I think it's coming soon." I ask him why he thinks the urge to dream yourself away is so universal: "We all have wants. Unfortunately, life doesn't let us have those wants." Maybe fantasy can take you only so far; maybe a real erasure and revision offer the only solution.

———

SAM ISRAEL AND I struck up a correspondence in the form of very long emails and letters to and from Butner Federal Prison in North Carolina. Like faking death and disappearance itself, Sam's story, too, was much more complex than it seemed at the outset. He's infamous for the "suicide is painless" message, but, at least according to the man himself, he simply wrote it as a flip response to his mother's question of what he planned to do now that a court had handed him a twenty-two-year prison sentence. The newspapers didn't report the IDs that Sam was able to score in record time, or the other contingency plans he had set up. And there was still another part of the story missing, about how he managed to angle his jump off the bridge to land in the construction nets below—designed with high-tensile strength to catch chunks of falling concrete—and crawl hand over hand to the other side, and scramble unseen up the shale banks of the Hudson River to Hassan's getaway car. Even though the *New York Times* ran a story five days after Sam

went missing, announcing that the search for the convicted financier was "going global," the feds didn't catch him. But the
triumph was brief. He turned himself in to a police station in
Southwick, Massachusetts, almost one month after he appeared
to have jumped off the Bear Mountain Bridge. Why?

"You know how they got Sammy?" Frank asks me. "They
squeezed his girlfriend and told her she'd get indicted." Frank
invokes a rule: "Never become attached to anything you can't
walk away from in five seconds." Summoning the will to walk
away is not a possibility for most people. They're thwarted not
by carelessness but by caring.

===

I WALKED OUT OF Frank's office into Friday rush hour in August,
the heat from the sidewalk radiating up my legs and the smoke
from a deliveryman's cigarette blending with the fumes of his
idling truck. Pushing through the tides of people, I thought
about escape plans. Maybe some of the faces in the crowd had
already left one life behind. Once Frank had registered the fact
that I was not going to serve him papers, he offered up so many
insights about disappearance that he complicated my glib ideas
about what leaving it all behind really meant.

Is faking death really as impossible as he made it sound?
It seems that pseudocide becomes troublesome when it comes
to trying to commit life insurance fraud, or when you already
have the feds watching you. But what if you maintain a low
profile? How long could Sam Israel have pulled it off if he'd
never turned himself in?

Faking death still held a much deeper emotional resonance
for me than disappearing—if you were going to do it, you'd
really have to do it. In a cultural and technological moment when

we are neither ever fully present nor totally detached, when we can scroll through thousands of potential suitors on our phones and meet none of them, when we can curate a feed of foreign lands we will never see and aspirational gurus doing life far better than we are, pseudocide means surrendering potential desire for actual gratification. We live in a world of limitless options, commitmentphobia, and half measures. Disappearing, even as Frank described the benefits, felt like yet another way to hedge. It sounded a little wishy-washy. Pseudocide, instead, was all backbone, total investment. Besides, it was just sexier than disappearing.

If I'd learned anything about Frank, it's that he made a living off bullshitting. Maybe he had hypnotized me with his stories, bawdy jokes, and laser-like attention. He'd shown me how people can get lost, vaporized, obscured, hidden. And sifting through new permutations of life-on-the-lam fantasies and exit strategies, I felt more confused than ever. My fantasy of getting lost was shifting into a great big question mark. I needed a second opinion. I needed to be found.

2

HOW TO BE FOUND

Hector Mendoza wore a Rolex on his wrist to flaunt the success of his various business ventures. Although he'd lived and worked in Los Angeles for decades and was an American citizen, he hailed from the Philippines originally and cultivated influential government contacts. In the winter of 2001, he got a phone call from one of his Filipino associates. It was time.

Mendoza checked into a hotel in Manila. A few days later, he was gambling in a coin-toss game and was stabbed in a dispute over winnings. He bled out in a dusty park lined with doorless shacks and mangy dogs prowling for scraps.

The body was brought to a local morgue. His wife flew in from LA and identified his corpse. She organized the funeral, presided over by a priest. Mrs. Mendoza had her picture taken next to the open casket but covered her face with her hands, too distraught to look at the body inside, which was cremated and shipped back to the United States immediately after the service.

Later that evening, Mrs. Mendoza met her husband for dinner in a Manila restaurant.

———

SOMEONE DIED THAT DAY, but it wasn't Hector Mendoza. As Steve Rambam, who investigated the death, explains, "When I went to the tiny little restaurant where witnesses said they saw Mendoza get stabbed and showed them a picture of him, they all laughed! The person who was actually killed was the local drunk. His idea of a good day was scoring a bottle of rotgut whisky, playing a couple of twenty-five-cent dice games, and passing out in the bushes." Rambam arrived in the Southeast Asian country to conduct his investigation on behalf of one of the half dozen life insurance companies that had questioned the veracity of Hector's death when Mrs. Mendoza attempted to cash in six policies her husband had bought recently—worth several million dollars in all. Rambam has been investigating fraudulent death claims like Mendoza's for three decades now, so he's inured to the macabre theatrics. But he still can't resist snickering when he tells the story.

Rambam is an elite private investigator. A big part of his business involves contracting for life insurance companies. When fishy death claims that exceed a certain amount get filed (think seven figures), Rambam hops aboard a plane, treks out to the scene of the crime, and finds where the bodies are not buried. His job is not so much proving that a claimant is alive as it is demonstrating that the person is not dead.

He's telling me the Mendoza story in the pressroom of the Marriott Marquis in Times Square, during the annual Open

Web Application Security Conference. Earlier that day, Rambam was on a panel and dispensed some stern words to his audience: privacy is forever dead and we should get over it. In this world of hackers and security experts, he's a bit of a celebrity. As we were grabbing drinks at the bar, a bespectacled fellow recognized him. Rambam stands out a bit in this crowd, or "nerd convention" (his phrase), because he is over six feet tall and looks as if he wasn't dressed by his mother. But it's not just his appearance.

A few years back, FBI agents physically removed Rambam from the HOPE (Hackers On Planet Earth) Conference in Midtown Manhattan for exposing their malfeasance in a case that involved an impostor claiming to be the prince of Austria. He's now the star of his own TV show entitled *Nowhere to Hide*, a reenactment-heavy drama that re-creates his most famous cases. The show's fan base is mainly middle-aged women. He inspired a character named Rambam in writer Kinky Friedman's Masters of Crime series. Whereas Frank Ahearn is the rough-and-tumble Bronx boy, Steve Rambam flies all over the world in a tailored suit, keynoting conferences like this one. His face is arresting, he lumbers more than he walks, and he has massive hands like paddles. He seems to have been teleported from another era. Frank can find anyone with charm and a telephone, but Steve pounds the pavement in overseas investigations, going undercover, working with local law enforcement. Frank told me that if you faked your death and tried to collect on an insurance policy, there are guys who get paid to check you out. Steve is one of those guys.

Back in the Marriott Marquis, I'm trying to get a handle on what, exactly, Steve is telling me about Mendoza. How does a dead homeless guy have anything to do with the rich American businessman with an ostentatious watch?

"Mendoza was actually highly organized, because he worked with a very senior administrator in the local government in the Philippines," Rambam explains. "He'd been planning to fake his death and collect on a policy for a while. They waited until some local guy died of violence, not old age. And the guy had to fit Mendoza's physical description—a person of roughly the same height and weight—and then the family could go to the local morgue and claim the body. The wife came in and identified the drunk as her husband. But the body was always this homeless guy's." Mendoza had claimed the knife attack as his own.

Without a death certificate, insurance companies wait seven years to release money, and you need a body in order to get the paperwork. So Mendoza procured a corpse to expedite the process. For life insurance fraud, this peculiar practice is not exactly out of the ordinary. I'd heard rumors of so-called black market morgues where you can buy a body, cheap and easy, for your pseudocidal intentions. In 1986, Equifax Insurance spokesman John Hall told the *Wall Street Journal*, "In one Southeast Asian country, there's a private morgue that picks up dead derelicts, freezes the bodies, and sells them for insurance purposes." Based on Rambam's tale, it sounded as if mismatching bodies and identities is still a flourishing business.

Frank had reiterated again and again that faking your death was a stupid thing to do because, compared with simply disappearing, it's a whole lot easier to get caught. But since collecting a payout is one of the most obvious and frequent reasons people fake their deaths—at least as evidenced by the six o'clock news—I wanted to know what kind of chase a company will deploy. What are the big considerations to take into account if you want to get rich and *not* die trying? While Frank helps people go off the grid and can skip trace from behind a desk, I wanted to know who gets on the plane and digs up the bodies. And, of course, how do people get themselves busted?

And black market morgues?! Really?

Steve says it's not even that the morgues are illegal: "You can just go into any city morgue in almost any developing country, ask to see the unclaimed bodies, and cry, 'Oh, it's poor Uncle Marco!' They'll be happy to get a body off their hands."

So how would a fraudster like Mendoza, who wants to go to great lengths to set up a realistic fraud, obtain a body?

"A private morgue picks up any body that's not claimed," Steve says. "They take custody of this body, and they roll the dice. If the family comes and claims the body, obviously they charge storage. It's like towing a car. If no one comes and claims the body, it's their problem to cremate and bury it. I was in the Philippines a few months ago, and it's still going on. It's ridiculous," he says.

I ask how much it would cost to commit a death fraud in the Philippines, like Mendoza did. The figure is less than I would have imagined.

"I think everything, from soup to nuts, including your body, is about five thousand dollars," he says.

"Including a look-alike corpse?" I ask.

"You're doing them a favor! You're paying for the storage charges, and you're paying for cremation. They're not building you a body like Frankenstein in a lab! Okeydokey, then! Here's your body! Now they've got an empty slab they can refill. Their investment has come through."

Though attempting to pass off a deceased stranger's body as your own does add a flourish of grim verisimilitude, it turns out that acquiring a cadaver is usually not necessary to fake

your death for an insurance payout. Death fraud, in most instances, is conducted primarily with documents. In Mendoza's
case, his paperwork—his death certificate, and the accompanying police and coroner's reports—all checked out. "All the
documents were legitimate," Rambam explains, "because they
were obtained by the governor of the province." All of the seals,
watermarks, and signatures were authentic.

Rambam brought his guys to the local Quezon City Scene
of the Crime Operatives (SOCO) Unit, the Filipino equivalent
of CSI, and showed the crime scene investigators Mendoza's
passport photo. "They all said that the photo didn't match the
body that came in," he says. "So I interviewed his wife, and she
broke." Mrs. Mendoza recalled this interview in her grand jury
testimony four and a half years after the crime took place:

INTERVIEWER: What did Steve Rambam ask you?

MRS. MENDOZA: That he needed to talk to me in regard to
Hector.

INTERVIEWER: What did you tell him?

MRS. MENDOZA: I told him the truth.

INTERVIEWER: And the truth is?

MRS. MENDOZA: That Hector Mendoza is alive.

Mendoza was hiding out up in the north of the country, and
Steve spoke with a few of his co-conspirators. "The problem
Mendoza didn't anticipate is that everyone had gotten sick of
him. He was a real hustler, always into some kind of monkey
business," he says. All of the local guys with whom Mendoza
had colluded were eager to turn him in. They offered to deliver
him to Rambam on a plane to Hawaii for $10,000, whether he
wanted to be on the plane or not. They could get rid of their

problem and get paid at the same time. The fact that these double-dipping cronies offered to give Mendoza up for cold, hard cash illustrates just how difficult it can be to find trusted co-conspirators to help you fake your death. The deceased, unfortunately, can't collect without the right people to file on his or her behalf.

The investigation looked like it was going to come to a triumphant close: once on American soil, authorities could arrest Mendoza for a huge life insurance fraud. Rambam had even received the green light from the insurance company to collaborate with Mendoza's associates, whom he had managed to turn. He told them that they would get their money once they got Mendoza on the plane. The deal was in motion. But then the insurance company panicked and backed out at the last second. "They called me and said they spoke with their attorney and that this was kidnapping." Rambam tried to tell them that it was actually police ejecting him from the country; he would have paid them a finder's fee. "They said, 'We don't care how you package it, we're not going to do it.'" To Steve's knowledge, Mendoza is still in the Philippines, with an American warrant out for his arrest.

AS WITH FRANK, MEETING up with Steve Rambam in the flesh took a lot of time and massaging. I'd first encountered Rambam's name cited in a 1997 *New York Times* article headlined "Fake Deaths Abroad Are a Growing Problem for Insurers." Then I found the delightfully analog clip-art-spangled website for Pallorium, the investigation agency he founded thirty years ago. The number listed goes directly to voice mail, and he calls you back at his convenience, which I consider a boss move.

After a summer and fall of competing with Steve's hellish travel schedule, we finally organized a rendezvous when he phoned me from a blocked number and arranged the meet in military time.

I found him on a drizzly afternoon just before Christmas in front of the New York Public Library on Madison Avenue. He'd gone there to look up some files for a case he was working. He had dressed the part, in a tweed jacket with elbow patches over a sweater and tie. We walked awkwardly in the rain, and I kept bumping him with my umbrella. We popped into several establishments, which he deemed either too loud or too quiet, until we happened upon one that was just right. We took our seats and had a terse exchange in which he asked me sarcastically which sorority I pledged in college. Despite my pink dress, high ponytail, and the unfortunate Valley Girl twang I picked up God knows where (marathon viewings of *The Hills*, methinks), this lady neither rushed nor pledged. Taking offense, I rebuffed him with a testy "Guess again!" We spent several tense moments in near silence, punctuated by his commentary on the place setting before him—the tablecloth was filthy, the water glasses smudged—until, mercifully, the waitress came and took our order, and I proceeded to get day drunk on Chardonnay as Steve sipped his Guinness. Finally, lubricated, he asked me to explain myself and my interest in pseudocide again, and, in a fit of disappointment, guffawed, "You're writing a book on *what*?"

He would reprise this question to me over the next few years, and chastise me that it wasn't finished, and compare my publishing record with the many texts he's penned on British spies, practical privacy tips, and P. T. Barnum. The whimsical daydreams that Frank and I shared about the fantasy of disappearance and life's incompatibility with our desires didn't register with Steve. Instead, he'd lift one of his ample eyebrows in a doleful, pitying look that I became accustomed to absorbing and eventually relished receiving. If I got the lift of an eyebrow, it meant I was onto something.

Rambam describes himself as a "moving target." He is rarely in his home base of Brooklyn for longer than a handful of days at a time. The reason he is a moving target is because Pallorium specializes in overseas investigations work. By his description, his job is as hard as a spy's. "I'll get sent somewhere I've never been before, and I have to build up an intelligence infrastructure, develop contacts, and defeat local people. I have to do it all out in the open, and in a finite amount of time. I've got a few weeks to break a very sophisticated crime in a foreign country where I don't speak the language." James Quiggle of the Coalition Against Insurance Fraud says, "There is a certain Indiana Jones aspect to unraveling suspicious death claims in a foreign country." Richard Marquez, Rambam's longtime friend and colleague and the head of the Texas-based Diligence International Group, which describes itself as "global intelligence experts," believes that "Steve is one of a handful of people in the world who can do what he does." Marquez, too, has been at the helm of hundreds of death fraud investigations, and the two have worked dozens together. But where Rambam can be prickly and sarcastic, Marquez is easygoing and warm.

But what sets Rambam apart in the world of high-profile sleuthing is his tenacity. While Rambam is out in the far-flung corners of the world, working with local law enforcement, interviewing witnesses, and going undercover, a big part of the job is simply not going home when everybody else does. Beyond his brazen attitude and knack for subterfuge, Rambam credits his stunning success rate to sheer hardheadedness: "You know that old Woody Allen joke that ninety percent of life is showing up? Now, I'm not a Woody Allen fan. He's a lefty and he married his own daughter. But ninety percent of investigating is showing up. What most investigators don't realize is that just showing up counts for a lot. Just go and start investigating. These cases are daunting. Most people say, 'Oh my God! This case is in the Philippines! They have snakes there! And people disappear! And I'm never gonna find anything! And there's gonna be a language problem!' You can go on like that and paralyze yourself. But there's a real simple solution. Get on a plane and go to the Philippines. Start knocking on doors. Just go! Do it! You knocked on a door and you didn't find anything? Knock on another door. Then knock on another door. And even if you fail for ten days straight, on the eleventh day, you'll get something. Always."

Rambam's work is propelled by an ingrained sense of justice. TV journalist Mike Wallace introduced him on *60 Minutes* in 1997, saying, "The traditional cold calm of Canada has been shattered by a meddling American." As a personal project, Steve had located former Nazis living in Canada by scoring their information from survivor groups and documentation centers in Germany—he even "scammed some" out of the Simon Wiesenthal Center, the Jewish human rights organization. From a list of two hundred names, he winnowed it down to the most outrageous. "There was one Ukrainian SS guy who specialized in the murder of children. So he went on the list," Rambam tells me with a sinister grin.

"I said, 'I'm Salvatore Romano'—I didn't want them to know I'm Jewish, and I had a real Zairian passport made with that identity—'and I'm a professor at St. Paul's University of the Americas.' That's a bogus university, but I set it up as a business in Belize and made business cards and a sweatshirt. And then I'd say, 'I'm writing my thesis on blah blah blah,' until their eyes rolled back in their heads, and 'I'd like to talk to you about your wartime experiences.' And they would talk to me. A lot of them detailed the crimes they had committed, totally openly."

And what other kinds of jobs does Rambam handle, apart from Nazi hunting and surprising the undead?

"I do a lot of fugitive cases, a lot of difficult-to-find witnesses. Luis goes back to Guatemala after witnessing a shooting, I go find him. I do everything."

"What are your favorite kinds of cases?" I ask him.

"Whatever pays a lot."

And get paid a lot he does. Subcontracting for big American firms, when he is working a life insurance case somewhere such as India, Nigeria, or the Philippines (the same countries with the rickety governments and capricious extradition policies of my off-the-grid fantasies), he charges in the neighborhood of $1,500 per day plus expenses to track people. He always finds his guy.

It's oddly consistent work because there is often some industrious person somewhere who tries to die and get rich in his afterlife. When I first reached out to Richard Marquez, Rambam's colleague, he quipped in an email about the frequency of his jobs: "Our company specializes in foreign death fraud, and the problem is alive and well—excuse the pun." Steve told me that he personally takes on an average of twenty death fraud cases per year. In the context of all insurance fraud, however, death fraud is extremely rare, though exact statistics are hard to come by because of companies' tight-lipped policies. James Quiggle, whose organization documents and analyzes the panoply of insurance fraud—from Medicare to life to fire to flood—says, "Staged death is an outlier. I'd say it makes up less than one percent of the cases we see."

A typical life insurance fraud of the variety that Rambam and Marquez encounter might look something like this: You are summering back home in a bucolic corner of your native Mongolia. You die in a tragic oxen charging. A shepherd witnesses your pummeling and impalement and slow perishing on the side of the road. He sends for a doctor, who immediately pronounces you dead. The village holds a big country funeral, mourners weep over your coffin, and you are buried within a few days.

Your wife files to collect life insurance. She submits all the requisite paperwork: a death certificate, an autopsy report, a police report detailing your violent bovine disemboweling, and even photos and video from the funeral. But a claims examiner at the insurance company flags the application, delaying a payout. "Claims examiners know when they see a fraud," Rambam says. "They have a sixth sense." So when the policy is over a certain amount (they're not paying Rambam thousands a day for a piddly policy) and the company harbors suspicions (if, for example, you increased your coverage just recently), the company calls in their guy. Rambam gets on the plane, treks out to the obscure Mongolian village, interviews the shepherd, and takes statements from local police. If necessary, he will dig up the coffin. One time he found rocks inside.

What kind of person is cut out for this work? Rambam grew up in the Flatbush neighborhood of Brooklyn. "I grew up with a zillion different types of people," he recalls. "I was a guest in every kid's house: Chinese, Arab, every Caribbean nation you can think of. I had the most freakish bar mitzvah you've ever seen." He learned to live by an old-school code of loyalty and integrity: "You give your word, and that's it. There's no renegotiating in Flatbush."

In between his hardscrabble New York days and starting Pallorium thirty years ago, there's a long, cloudy gap in his biography, which he won't go into in great detail. Rambam will admit to earning his "sneaky training" working for a government locating missing persons. He also realizes the serendipity of entering the profession when he did. "I came into the investigative field when it was the real deal," he recalls. "You weren't just tapping on the computer. You had to go out and knock on doors. You had to learn film cameras, so you had to understand the light. You understood how to interview people, how to position yourself in the chair." He has led over five hundred overseas death fraud investigations. "Everyone has been either extremely easy or extremely difficult to find," Rambam says. "There's no in-between."

———

EVERY TIME I MET Rambam, he tried to discourage my civilian's fascination with faking death. He has dealt with too many incompetents to be captivated by its allure anymore. "You can separate yourself from the world without faking your death," Rambam explains. "You need a real reason to fake your death: either a nefarious reason or exigent circumstances. I've never found a case where somebody faked their death for an acceptable reason." But more than just finding an acceptable reason (and I still maintain that student loan debt and ennui are perfectly valid), Rambam echoes Frank's misgivings about the effectiveness of such a complicated plan.

"Faking your death almost never works," he says. "You

have to be devoted to staying disappeared like it's your job. It takes a lot of effort and aggravation. Everybody I've caught on life insurance fraud, I tell them, 'If you had put this type of effort, money, and dedication into your life as a law-abiding citizen, you would've made just as much money.'"

But how is the tedium of slogging through a dismal law-abiding existence to compete with the siren call of total freedom? And the temptation of a multimillion-dollar payout on your little life to underwrite all your yardstick margaritas, novelty T-shirts, and cabana boys in a lazy beachside town? I had yet to be convinced.

The people that Rambam and Marquez investigate typically fit a certain profile: they are foreign-born nationals who return to their native country and meet an untimely end. This is a different bunch from the white middle-class guys who fake their deaths Stateside, such as Sam Israel. And naturalized US citizens like Mendoza returning home and meeting a tragic death rarely make the news. "Faked deaths on foreign soil are very common in the overall sliver of faked deaths," Quiggle says. "A third-world country is far easier to negotiate, and the 'death' is far easier to set up in a foreign country than it is in the States. You have low-paid bureaucrats you can bribe. In societies where people are very poor and need money, a fraud can be seen as a desirable way to feed your family. Fraud can be considered a legitimate enterprise," he explains. Like Mendoza, the fraudsters will have strong local connections in their country of origin and know whose palms to grease and which fixers to charm in order to score the requisite documents. The countries in which the investigators pound pavement (or dirt roads) change often and go through cycles, but lately there has been an uptick in death fraud originating in the Philippines, Mexico, India, and China. "You have a lot of expats from these countries, people who are traveling back and forth," Rambam explains. "And you have a robust, centuries-old tradition of corruption." Typically, the accident gets staged in the boonies, and fraudsters don't anticipate the lengths to which a company will go to avoid paying out a hefty policy. "A lot of people think that once the insurance company has the documentation, they will just pay the claim," Marquez says. "And since a lot of these people are from remote towns, they think no one will ever bother to send anybody to investigate."

Death fraud can be big business in many of these obscure locales, not just for the claimant but also for the local economy. A small but thriving infrastructure exists to assist you in your tragic accident. A witness's testimony is for sale, as is a doctor's signature on your death certificate. In countries such as Haiti and Nigeria, enterprising middlemen streamline the operation for you. There you can buy what is known in the biz as a "death kit." Marquez elaborates what you can get for a few hundred bucks: "A death kit includes a copy of the fake death certificate, a burial permit, photographs of the actual burial plot. They will often make a video of the funeral Mass, of people crying and wailing, and the funeral procession down the street. They are basically performing the ceremony." Rambam sums it up: "A death kit is basically, 'Step right up and buy your all-inclusive fraud package!' It's a shell corporation for fraud."

How much you are willing to pay will sometimes determine the quality of the amateur dramatics at your funeral, such as how many mourners you can cast. Marquez remembers one video from a Nigerian case: "They had the body lying in the middle of the bed, and mourners were chanting in a circle.

When they came onto the screen, it looked like there were hundreds of people. But when I paid closer attention, I noticed that the mourners were the same villagers, circling in and out of the frame, and just changing clothes each time." He laughs. "There were probably around fifteen people there instead of one hundred." Sometimes, he adds, you can see the corpse sweat or the deceased's chest rising and falling in the coffin. Most often, and more conveniently, the body will be cremated.

So will a company ever conduct DNA analysis on the deceased's remains?

"You can't do DNA testing with cremation," Rambam says. Caitlin Doughty, the author of *Smoke Gets in Your Eyes: And Other Lessons from the Crematory*, has worked in Los Angeles crematories and funeral homes for nearly a decade. She explains why not: "DNA is organic material, and all organic material gets destroyed. Once a femur bone has been cremated, you can see right through it and crush it in your hand."

Rambam and I discuss the DNA question over dinner on an unseasonably cool summer evening, sitting at a sidewalk table in the Hell's Kitchen neighborhood of Manhattan. He flirts with the Ukrainian waitress, correcting her pronunciation of menu items. He gets distracted momentarily by the disproportionately sized head of a young man at the next table and refers to him as a pumpkin head. A middle-aged woman at the table next to ours gets her chair stuck in a crevice in the sidewalk and shouts, "I might fall in!" Rambam snickers. "Here's hoping," he mutters under his breath.

Pumpkin heads and clumsy co-diners notwithstanding, Steve gets back to business. While burning a body in state-of-the-art machinery might destroy all organic material, the investigations he has conducted abroad reveal different standards.

"In third-world countries, their idea of cremation is not our idea of cremation," he says, describing a coarser powder.

"Say no more." I push my burger to the other side of the table.

Before digging up the coffin to see who's inside, Rambam and Marquez always begin by following the paper trail. "Sometimes just checking the documents on their face," Rambam says, "they're going to be false. Sometimes you have to check the supporting documents. Think about what's involved in a death: you have the body, you have the recovery of the body, you have the examination of the body, and you have the disposition of the body—whether it was buried or cremated. You can look into all these things."

When he breaks death down this way, it's kind of stunning. I had never considered this perspective on dying, authentically or fraudulently. When I think about dying, or what it would take for me to fake my death, I see the faces of the friends and family I would abandon. As Frank described, I would relinquish enjoying the small delights that make me me, and make me traceable. In my case, indulging in $7 manicures; visiting museums on Friday afternoons after the school groups have departed; twirling on the dance floors of dive bars. These are the things you must surrender when you disappear. This is the way most of us approach death: from the perspective of life—of love and work, of connection—the little moments that make the slog to the end worth it. Rambam's concept of death, though, transforms it into boxes to tick off. He itemizes, indexes, and catalogs with bureaucratic efficiency. But that is what happens when your job is to try to divine the dead from the living. The juicy pulp of life gets replaced with documents, stamps, and official signatures. His workplace, in a way, is the DMV of death.

Not all people whom Rambam has investigated can cut ties and operate in the austere ecosystem of a second life. Some commit pseudocide precisely to pursue relationships begun in the first. In other words, they have mistresses. Rambam tells me about one of his favorite cases. He went undercover to stalk a Canadian with too many women. I thought back to what Frank told me about the different reasons that people fake their deaths: money, of course, either coming into it, owing it, or trying to get rich with an insurance scheme; violence; and then love, the bronze medalist of motivations.

"He had a wife and a girlfriend," Rambam remembers, "and he dumped them both. I interviewed them, and it was incredible. They were like clones of each other. Anyway," he says with a shrug, "I told them each about the other, and they spilled. They gave me everything. They said he'd told them both that if he could run away and hide, he'd go to Aruba and be a scuba instructor. So I went to Aruba and checked out the different scuba agencies. He was under a different name on a French passport: his name was Jack, and his passport said Jacques."

Rambam saw an opportunity to mingle business with pleasure. "I was already a rescue diver, and to get my master certification, I needed ten more dives. I kept telling the insurance company, 'I'm not sure it's him, I need to take more dives!' I was talking to a claims examiner, and she said, 'As long as you're not billing us for your dives, you've got a deal.' I went scuba diving with him every frickin' day. I stayed at the Marriott and got Marriott points. It was awesome."

After racking up dives and watching the Canadian lothario from afar, Steve eventually made contact. "I asked him where he was from, and he said, 'Canada, but I lived in California for a while.' He told me a lot about his real life. Then I went out with him for a drink. When he went to the restroom, I took his glass in case we needed to do fingerprints. I took pictures with him. The girlfriend was the beneficiary on his policy, but she didn't know where he was. The wife thought he was dead at this point. So I sent her our picture together, and she ID'd him. Then I went to him and said, 'Look, I gave you my real name, but what you don't know is that I'm an investigator. I've been investigating your death, and here's the identification from your wife.' He said, 'So what happens now? Do I get arrested?' I asked him to give me a video statement. I told him if he gave me the statement, I'd leave him alone, which was a lie. He gave his name and Social Security number and held up a copy of that day's paper, just like in the movies, and he said, 'I have no idea why people think I'm dead.'"

"So what happened to him?" I ask.

"I think the company didn't bother with him," he says with a shrug. Translation: the company rejected his insurance claim but didn't file any criminal charges.

If you fake your death abroad and then attempt to claim life insurance, the crime you are committing is under the jurisdiction of the insurance company's country. So if you attempt death fraud in Japan and then collect on an American life insurance policy, you are subject to American penalties. And since each state's Department of Insurance is responsible for monitoring fraud, charges are rarely levied against death fraudsters. Nor do the local governments where these crimes are committed seem compelled to make examples out of no-goodniks. Marquez explains why:

"A lot of times, law enforcement will not readily act on these cases. Say you detect a fraudulent case here in the U.S. of a person who has traveled to China. It's very difficult to get American law enforcement to prosecute a case. Even if we provide them with a lot of good evidence, they still have to conduct their own private investigation. Law enforcement would have to have the resources to send people to China to interview those involved, then bring them back to the U.S. to testify. It's a very expensive and time-consuming process. The insurance companies are mandated to report fraud to the states; then it's entirely up to the states to investigate and prosecute. A lot of states have budgetary problems, and pursuing life insurance investigations is complicated and expensive. Once we investigate the fraud and no money is paid out, there hasn't been a financial loss to the company. Law enforcement usually doesn't have the grounds to pursue 'attempted' fraud."

Rambam counters his colleague's claim, saying pointedly, "I try to get all my cases prosecuted. I'll push the state's Department of Insurance." Quiggle maintains that insurance carriers are reluctant to bring death fraud cases to the forefront, but for a different reason: "Some companies are happy as clams to quietly pursue the case and let it be adjudicated through denial of the claim rather than bringing it into the public [sphere] and giving others tips on how to commit the same crime." Ahem, others like me. With prosecution unlikely and a whole lot of earning potential, even Rambam realizes the appeal. "Life insurance fraud is very attractive," he concedes. "A bank robber, on average, only gets about five thousand bucks, the money is traced with GPS, then he gets a gun stuck in his face, and he'll get time in jail. In an insurance fraud, you probably won't get caught, no one will stick a gun in your face, and you can collect from a hundred thousand to a million dollars. The problem is, people get greedy. But if the policy is under a certain threshold, it probably won't be investigated."

What cases like Mendoza and the Canadian scuba diver

show is that if you are brazen enough to attempt life insurance fraud, the likeliest scenario does not involve spending time in the slammer. You just risk the humiliation of having your claim denied and being busted on your extended vacation.

So why doesn't death fraud for insurance purposes take place as much on American soil?

The greatest obstacle is staging the accident. To be viable, you typically need a scenario where no body can be recovered. And drowning, which is most people's go-to method, almost never passes the sniff test. "Ninety-nine percent of faked deaths are water accidents," Rambam says. "In most drownings, the body is recovered. So why was *this* body not recovered? You happen to fall in on the only spot on the shoreline where there's a riptide? And you didn't wash up anywhere?" This demystification really blew my mind. I'd seen *Sleeping with the Enemy*, and besides the montage of Julia Roberts trying on adorable hats in the mirror, my big takeaway was that (spoiler alert) one must stage a drowning. No body, no problem! But Rambam sorted me out: this amateur understanding of death fraud is one of the biggest misconceptions and a common way that would-be death fraudsters get themselves caught.

Even attempting a more complicated accident can prove troublesome. Marcus Schrenker, a thirty-eight-year-old money manager from a flush Indianapolis suburb nicknamed "Cocktail Cove," bilked clients out of $1.5 million by investing their money in a foreign currency that never existed, and was eventually reported to the state securities board. When, in January 2009, he realized the jig was up, Schrenker flew his single-engine propeller plane south toward the Gulf of Mexico. Nearing the Florida panhandle, he radioed air traffic control and reported turbulence, saying his windshield was cracking. He was hoping the plane would crash into the Gulf but it ran out of fuel about a hundred miles away. He put the plane on autopilot, opened the hatch door, and, at two thousand feet, parachuted out, and landed in the serpentine branches of an Alabama swamp. He wriggled out of his harness, splashed into the water, and made his way to a storage unit in Harpersville, Alabama, where he had stashed a motorcycle with cash and supplies the day before. But authorities apprehended Schrenker two days later as he hid out in a tent in Quincy, Florida, after he'd emailed a friend and detailed his plan.

Other innovative death fraudsters have attempted elaborate bait-and-switch schemes with crude methods. Jean Crump, a mortuary worker in her sixties who was employed at the now-defunct Simpson and McGee Mortuary in Lynwood, California, collaborated with a few friends to defraud several insurance companies out of $1.2 million. They held a funeral for one Jim Davis, who never existed. The casket they buried was empty. When insurance fraud investigators started nosing around, she realized she'd have to act fast. Exhuming the coffin, Crump and her associates filled it with cow parts and a mannequin, and then had the casket cremated. Investigators quickly unraveled the clever ruse, and Crump was charged with mail and wire fraud for filing a false insurance claim.

Rambam has investigated very few cases on American soil. Those types of death frauds are typically like Schrenker's, people who get caught mere hours later. Staging the fatal accident is where pseudocides go awry. What you need is a disaster, natural or otherwise. Turns out that one of the greatest tragedies in American history, with the greatest loss of life, also resulted in some of the most shameless scams.

I MET JOE CROCE, a sandy-haired retired New York City Police Department detective and father of three, at an Applebee's in Rego Park, Queens. Joe is one of those storied people who missed the September 11, 2001, attacks on the World Trade Center by mere minutes. He was slated for a nine o'clock meeting with a Secret Service agent in the North Tower. They were working a case together. But Croce didn't like the guy so he blew it off. He remembers seeing smoke billowing over Manhattan as he commuted in from Queens on the train.

Around 2001, Croce was a part of the Special Frauds Squad, an elite group of senior detectives who handled white-collar crime. Sergeant Dan Heinz, a third-generation cop from Staten Island, headed the operation. But once the towers went down, it was all hands on deck. Special Frauds was assigned to run one of the city's many ersatz morgues that popped up to sort through the carnage from the Towers. "I drew the short straw," Heinz explained to me over the phone from Texas, where he retired. Special Frauds ran a morgue and a center to report lost loved ones. It was on the West Side Highway, near TriBeCa, and the squad soon became the Missing Persons Liaison Unit. They set up a trailer in a parking lot adjacent to the World Trade Center site, where first responders dumped heaps of excavated corpses from the wreckage.

In charge of collecting as much identifying information as possible, Special Frauds detectives took exhaustive inventories from friends and family of features that might help distinguish a loved one trapped under the rubble. Croce explained, "Usually a missing persons report is a page or two long. These were like books. We asked, 'What was your relationship with him?

Does he have tattoos? Does he have rings? Does he have an inscription inside the ring? Does he have a hairbrush or a comb or
a razor that we could get DNA from?' Everything and anything.
These reports were so thorough. We took all this information,
and the computer crime squad entered the data."

Collecting this data—from birthdays to birthmarks—was
the easy part. "Our second job was to work at the morgue and
to identify these persons. So if they came across a ring with an
inscription, they could go into the database to see if there's a
match," Croce explained. "We were weighing body parts and
ID'ing each part in a system. So parts one hundred ten and one
hundred twelve might be the same guy—"

"So you were, like, sorting through arms and legs?" I asked.

He smiled in a moment of hard-earned gallows humor.

"Everyone thinks a body part is a hand or a leg. But a body
part can be a piece of your back, or just a hunk of flesh," he
said. Often, less than a pound of human flesh would be all that
remained of a person. When family members came to collect
their loved ones, Croce improvised a method to obscure this
harrowing truth. "Sometimes you'd just have a little piece, and
you'd have to throw it in a body bag. It looked like there was
nothing there," Croce said. "I remember blowing up plastic
bags to fill up a body bag to give the impression that there was
something in there."

This was the bleak backdrop against which Sergeant Dan
Heinz received a phone call from police in Oklahoma. It was a
tip. Cops who had worked on the 1995 bombing of the Alfred P.
Murrah Federal Building in downtown Oklahoma City advised
him to be on the lookout for bogus death reports. "We noticed
the first suspicious claim three or four days after 9/11," Heinz
told me. "Then a week or two after, we realized there would

be more. We could have ignored it at first. But after a while, it became impossible."

Missing persons reports in the immediate wake of the attacks climbed to over 6,000. But the official lives lost totaled 2,801 at the first-year commemoration. Of those more than 3,000 misidentified deaths, 44 were claims for either people who were still alive or people who did not exist. But no one knows how many weren't caught. More, of course, could have evaded law enforcement. Imagine coming up from the subway, recognizing the tragedy, immediately computing it as an opportunity, an opening, and slinking away? Nothing filed, no attempt at life insurance—just a split second's decision to vanish.

Most of the people Special Frauds ended up investigating didn't fake their own deaths. Rather, they invented a fictional relative, saying that he or she had been killed in the attacks, and then tried to fleece money from charities and insurance companies. It was easy to spot the hucksters. Heinz remembers how blatantly transparent these charlatans could be. "You know something is up," he said, "when people are very descriptive about certain things, like tattoos and appearance, but they can't give fundamental information, like date of birth. People who commit fraud aren't prepared for the simplest questions."

Cyril Kendall was one of those people who had trouble producing the requisite documents. In the immediate aftermath of the attacks, Kendall reported his youngest son (he had fathered twelve children), twenty-nine-year-old Wilfred, killed during a job interview at the financial services firm Cantor Fitzgerald on the one-hundredth floor of the North Tower the morning of 9/11. Kendall collected close to $120,000 from the Red Cross alone and another $40,000 from other charities before Special Frauds grew suspicious.

Croce asked the virile gentleman to supply a photo of his son. "So he shows up," the detective remembered, "and he presents us with a photograph of himself, but much younger than what his son would have been. It's a black-and-white photo, and he's wearing clothes from the sixties." The cops realized that Cyril Kendall was trying to pass off a photo of his teenage self as his missing son. "We were like 'That's you!' " Croce said with a laugh. Kendall served a few years and was then deported back to his native Guyana, but he never repaid the thousands of dollars he'd stolen, saying that he'd spent it all.

A handful of ingenious fraudsters latched onto the ruse involving Cantor Fitzgerald for their stories. A massive lightbulb went off over all their heads when the news reported that, due to the company's unfortunate position at the point of the first plane's impact, 658 of Cantor Fitzgerald's 960 employees had perished.

Jilsey McNish, the invented wife of a man named Carlton McNish, was reported as a Cantor Fitzgerald employee who perished in the attacks. Her name was read from a list of the dead in memorial services in 2002 and 2003. Mr. McNish even held a fake funeral for his beloved. He collected over $100,000 from charities before it was discovered he never married. He served almost five years in prison for grand larceny after his fraud was discovered.

A mother-daughter duo from Milwaukee, Dorothy Johnson and Twila McKee, colluded to collect life insurance from two companies when mother Dorothy purportedly disappeared on 9/11. McKee was the beneficiary of both policies, totaling roughly $135,000. But Johnson's fingerprints were identified on one of the claims forms stating she was dead. She also submitted an automobile claim to another insurer less than two weeks after she supposedly died. They were both charged with insurance fraud in 2003 and served three years in prison.

While all the other 9/11 fraudsters invented people (or used their own quite-alive family members) to report dead or missing, Steven Leung is the only person known to have registered himself dead in the attacks. He constructed the story that he had been an independent trader at Cantor Fitzgerald and had gone missing since the attacks. Or so said Leung himself when he posed as *two* different nonexistent brothers, Jeffery and William Leung, in attempting to arrange for his own death certificate. The real Leung had been living in the United States on an expired Chinese passport for years and had been arrested in Hawaii for using a fake Social Security number. He was out on bail when the 9/11 attacks took place. By killing off his former trouble-laden self, he would be able to simply adopt a new identity, avoid jail time, and begin a new life as a fully enfranchised citizen rather than live the shadowy existence of an undocumented immigrant with an outstanding warrant. So instead of attempting to squeeze some money out of charities, Leung used the disaster to become a freer version of himself, even seeking citizenship. (Exactly how he was to obtain citizenship after he was dead was never adequately explained.)

After faking his death in the attacks, Leung lived on as a reincarnation, but only briefly. In February 2002, just five months after his "death," the twenty-seven-year-old Hong Kong man went to retrieve his correspondence from his commercial mailbox and was arrested on the spot. Had Leung received his original sentence only for passport and Social Security fraud, he could have served up to ten years in federal prison before being deported. At his trial, Leung admitted that the whole story was an elaborate hoax, saying he just wanted to get his passport case dropped.

"You were hoping," presiding federal judge Denny Chin said, "that if the prosecution and the court believed that you had been killed in the World Trade Center attack, that the criminal charges would be dismissed?"

"Yes, Your Honor," he replied.

Leung was sentenced to four years, including additional penalties for jumping bail and obstruction of justice. As we know, there is no explicit law on the books called "pseudocide." But enough people try to pull a Steven Leung and phone themselves in as missing for the New York City Police Department (NYPD) to have carved out the classification of "self-reported missing" within the Missing Persons Department.

The only thing more surprising than those numerous brazen frauds is the breezy manner with which the detectives on Operation Vulture Sweep—as the 9/11 frauds that Heinz and Croce investigated became known—reminisce about this emotionally devastating era. Every police officer lost colleagues on that day. But recalling this traumatic time of sorting through human flesh and fused bodies at the makeshift morgue while simultaneously dealing with clowns like Kendall, McNish, and Leung, the detectives are not bitter. Instead, they harbor a resigned acceptance of low-budget, lowdown schemes.

"People were looking to take advantage of mass chaos," Heinz said. "How could they not? It didn't surprise me."

Croce echoed Heinz's sentiment: "I don't think these guys are any worse than any other guys I've arrested for white-collar crime. They just try to take advantage of the system. Think about human nature. Do you want to pay for this, or do you want it for free? I almost don't blame people who don't have a pot to piss in. The weaknesses in our government and charity systems almost light up for them."

Their nonchalance was hard for me to grasp, but maybe after a decade and a half they had simply found whatever sliver of light they could let in. I still felt queasy as Croce told me these stories. And I had trouble sifting out the most egregious aspect. Was it the fact that these schemers aligned themselves with people who had lost loved ones, therefore trivializing the memory of those who actually died, as well as the grief of widowed spouses and children? Or was it that they took advantage of the deep compassion that stitched together the wounded country? Death fraud, writ large, requires some instinct to deceive, to walk away, to bilk. When you fake your death, you make fools of the family members who grieve your loss; and, if you commit insurance fraud, you exploit a system intended to provide financial security to the bereaved. Maybe the backdrop of 9/11 serves only to highlight the darkness already at the heart of pseudocide.

I'd like to think that maybe these fraudsters were truly desperate, and they weighed the risk-reward equation. Given the grand scale of destruction, maybe Leung thought his crime of becoming documented was peanuts compared with terrorism. Maybe, since he was killing himself, he saw it as a victimless crime. But I was beginning to wonder if we can really pick and choose whom we harm and whom we protect.

=====

AT THIS POINT, I'D spoken with people who had investigated death fraud but not yet someone who was considering committing it himself. So when a friend told me about an unsettling conversation she remembered having years ago with a cagey older co-worker at a happy hour, I asked her to put me in touch.

Todd put me on Bluetooth when he called from the road on a Friday afternoon. He was on his way to a campground in Northern California. He had left work early to beat traffic and get a few hours to himself before his wife and his two daughters, ages ten and eight, arrived. A forty-nine-year-old software manager from Lafayette, California, an affluent suburb in the East Bay, Todd spoke in a soft, nasally voice that skewed more surfer bro. He called me from the car with the windows rolled down because he couldn't talk to me at home or at the office. He couldn't talk in front of anyone else because we were talking about how he thinks of faking his own death.

"The only way to do it is at sea or to get blown up," he told me. "You do it on a boat and find someone to witness it. First, I'd take out an insurance policy so I'd be gone but would know my kids could get a college education. I would arrange a sailing trip somewhere in Southeast Asia and make it seem like there had been a drowning. I'd head to Thailand because you can live in Thailand for nothing. I've traveled there, and I know how easy it would be. You don't need anything, not even papers. I wouldn't want to take any money with me, but I'd have some on the side, a few thousand. Now I'd have to make money, and I would do it online. I know I could make enough money to support myself under the radar—untraceable internet ad sales or something. It'd only make about ten thousand dollars, but I could live off that, just me, in Thailand, easy."

Todd described himself as "a cog in the wheel." In Silicon Valley, where baby millionaires are made overnight, Todd is uncomfortably in the middle. "The area isn't great for my career, and technical jobs are hard to get," he said plaintively.

Depending on how hellacious the traffic, he spends fifteen to twenty hours a week commuting from the eucalyptus-lined suburb to his office in Marin County. As he sees it, "I will never be able to retire. Every penny goes into mortgage, family, bills. I have no plan for retirement because we will never be as comfortable as my wife wants." Todd would be happy to spend his golden years living on a houseboat, but it's not an option. "I mentioned that once to my wife, and she went ballistic," he said. Todd has the life he thought he wanted: two healthy children, a wife, a house in the suburbs, and a good job. But he feels trapped. The idea of faking his own death provides fodder for his imagination during his commute and in front of his computer as he fantasizes about lazing on a Thai island, away from his responsibilities. Once, he Googled "faking your death" and was directed to the site wikiHow, on which someone had posted crude steps a person might take. Step one of the article instructs: "Decide whether you really want to do this."

The thing that surprised me most about Todd was not that he wanted to fake his own death. (I'd done the same Google search). And his plan didn't surprise me either. He sounded pleased with himself, like he had thought of everything—the drowning that would eliminate questions about a body, the insurance policy, the "untraceable" business model—but my research had taught me that his plan was really a pretty standard pseudocide. He'd likely get busted before he could even order a Singha beer.

But what did surprise me about Todd was his lack of sentimentality. I kept expecting him to qualify his plan somehow, to say something like, "Of course, I would never actually go through with it because I love my daughters too much." Sure, he'd accounted for them, mentioning the insurance policy that was to pay their college tuition. During our conversation, as the wind muffled his voice over the phone, as he drove by himself on a highway three thousand miles away, I kept waiting for the hesitation. But I didn't hear any.

———

STEVE RAMBAM HAS CAUGHT so many people that he knows what it takes to get dead and stay dead. But he requires a hefty burden of proof. "I don't believe somebody is dead unless there's an acceptable level of documentation, and by that I mean the New York City coroner took fingerprints, there's a DNA match, and there's a video of the person being run over by a car." Todd's brilliant idea of drowning and collecting life insurance without a body definitely would not cut Rambam's mustard.

So how does a girl on the run—whether from debtor's prison, from her psycho ex-boyfriend, or from the rote monotony of her life—evade the Rambams of the world?

Most of us cook up ideas like Todd's.

And as I was learning, that skeletal plan is far from foolproof. While both Ahearn and Rambam discourage faking death as a means of disappearing, I couldn't shake the feeling that simply vaporizing one day seems to lack the necessary narrative. If you don't leave behind a body, why would anyone stop looking for you? Think of Etan Patz, the original milk carton kid who vanished in Manhattan's SoHo neighborhood on his way to school in 1979. Based on new evidence, FBI agents excavated a building on Prince Street thirty-three years after the six-year-old went missing. Enthusiasts still hunt for D. B. Cooper and his money. Granted, I'm not an adorable kindergartner or a folk hero airplane hijacker, but I have enough connections (and outstanding debts) to think that I'd be chased were I simply to go off the grid one day. Corpses, or at least documents suggesting the existence of them, seem much more satisfying than a gaping, unsolved mystery. But I'm having trouble communicating this to Rambam, perhaps because he's just seen so many cases that they all blend into one lackluster fraud, or maybe because *me* faking my death successfully is simply inconceivable to him.

One night, as Rambam is power walking up Broadway to interview a witness on a local case, I jog behind him with my recorder. I throw out a hypothetical:

"Say a bad ex-boyfriend is looking for me. Is it better to fake my death or to disappear?"

"The restraining order isn't working," Rambam assumes. "What other resources does the bad ex-boyfriend have? Is he gonna come looking for you if you move to another city?"

"Of course! He's obsessed with me!"

Rambam looks unconvinced.

"If you don't have someone looking for you, isn't it better to fake death because it creates a story? Just disappearing seems too open-ended," I say.

"You have to understand the ramifications of faking your death," Rambam replies, becoming a little annoyed with my obstinacy. "First of all, you're faking your death! You're committing multiple crimes!"

"But what if I did it without collecting insurance or assuming another identity?" I ask, thinking back to Judge Procaccini's specifications about how you could theoretically stay on the precipitously narrow right side of the law.

"So you leave your wallet in a car next to a waterfall . . ."

"Exactly! That's not a crime."

"You could argue that," Rambam says wearily. "But it depends on what ultimately happens. Faking death might not be illegal, but the mechanics are. You'd have to lie to the police,

and file a false police report and death certificate. You would
have to bring people in on your disappearance unless there's
nobody in the world you care about. What about your mom,
your dad, your pet? Would you give up your pet? Are you putting Fluffy in the gas chamber?"

Well, when he puts it like that . . .

"A lot of people who fake their death think that five or six
years from now they're going to reintegrate into things," he
says. This reminds me of the 1946 film noir classic *Gilda*, in
which Ballin Mundson (played by George Macready) stages his
death in a plane crash at sea to evade his pursuers. He returns to
Buenos Aires, Argentina, three months later, only to encounter
new problems. Many would-be death fakers opt for the Mundson route—like Sam Israel in his getaway RV—believing that
staging their deaths can allow them to get out of a bind temporarily and then return home once their troubles have sub-
sided. Rambam recognizes the shortsightedness of this plan:
"Some people think they're going to go away for a while and
come back to be with their children. What are you gonna do, go
see your kids and say, 'Look, it's Mommy'?"

———

OVER DRINKS IN THE pressroom that day at the Marriott Marquis, I ask Rambam to walk me through each and every step
that a potential life insurance fraudster should take into consideration. And I ask him to start at the beginning.

"Can you leave your life behind?" Rambam asks first. Amateur hour, I think. Just like Todd's wikiHow article. Isn't that
the whole point?

"Are you capable of never seeing family and friends again?"

Okay, so that's not for everyone.

"Are you in good health? Do you require any special medications?"

I'm healthy as a hambone.

"Do you have sufficient funds to live independently for at least one to two years while you wait for the insurance claim to come through?"

Here's where it gets tricky.

"How much money are we talking here?" I ask.

"I say a minimum of fifty thousand dollars a year to live in Thailand. If not, what's the point?"

I think back to Todd's plan to live in Thailand on a few thousand a year. "What about a shack in Nicaragua?" I ask. My standards are subterranean.

"You might as well stay alive, then," Rambam says, raising his substantial eyebrows at me yet again in a combination of charity and weariness.

"Okay, what about if your budget is more like ten thousand dollars per year? Or twenty thousand?"

"You just need more than that," he says. "You've got to get a place, and you've got to get a place where nobody will spot you. Fifty thousand dollars. But that's me. There are people who can live in a campground like a homeless person for two years."

Jeez. I might be a pauper by New York standards, but living in abject poverty for two years might not work for me. Moving on!

"Do you have a trusted co-conspirator to file the claim?" Steve asks.

Now, who would do that for me, and how much would I be willing to give that person on the back end? Still, an accomplice to your crime isn't always necessary, because, as Rambam explains, "If you gather all the information and documents you need, then the co-conspirator is gravy." Besides, Mendoza's henchmen turned on him.

Next!

"Do you have an alternate identity prepared?"

I have several working identities at any given time to avoid certain nemeses and to ingratiate me to others. With a few bourbons and on the right night, I'll introduce Daphne Huckabee of the Savannah Huckabees. But what Rambam is getting at is something much deeper than the alter egos I bust out when drinking. What he means is the raw matter and material to operate in the world. Identity, I learn, is more than a whimsical character you put on at a bar to see how far you can get and to impress your friends. Identity today constitutes papers, documents, and a unique digital footprint traceable and peculiar to you. So what exactly do you need?

"You don't need a passport if you're not leaving the U.S., but if you want to fake your death, you'd be stupid not to have one," Rambam says. "First of all, if you want to do a good fraud, you want to make it international. You want to have the fake identity in one country. You want to have the insurance policy in a second country. You want to have the accident in a third country. You want the beneficiary in a fourth country."

Why?

"Most people don't operate real well multinationally. Most investigators won't go. And not only that, let's say they catch you. It's way harder to get all the evidence and all the witnesses and all the bad people from all the foreign locations."

He continues, going over the list:

"You need a driver's license, a Social Security number, a car you already bought." The car thing is a big deal. So many people I'd read about got busted because of their cars, like Bennie Wint and his broken light. In *How to Disappear*, Frank Ahearn cites people being unable to part from their cars as the number one giveaway that gets them caught. Perhaps if you want to fake your death and remain in obscurity, the best move is to relocate to a metropolitan city and enjoy the wonders of public transportation.

You can get a fake passport and a working Social Security number easily enough. "Frankly," Rambam says, "you can go out and buy a Social Security number. If you're in Los Angeles, you go to MacArthur Park. There used to be a guy who sold Social Security numbers by the food carts in Queens." But the stickiest part of constructing an identity on paper is fabricating your financials in a believable way. Rambam first told me that you would need to spend at least a year using the new bank accounts and credit history in your false identity. But then, when we discussed it further, he said you would actually need closer to a decade of recorded transactions under your proxy to make it believable. That's some serious foresight.

There was one person I had read about who knew a thing or two about disappearing and leaving not a mark in the world. In 2009 Evan Ratliff, a co-founder of *The Atavist Magazine* and author of the *Wired* article "Vanish," set up an interactive game wherein he would disappear for one month, and eager participants would try to locate him for prize money. It was hard to imagine that he could stay obscured for very long. Ratliff is devastatingly handsome, even with the strange half-bald haircut disguise he donned while he was off the grid. He rented an apartment under the identity J. D. Gatz (in homage to *The Great Gatsby*), used prepaid gift cards and burner phones, and psyched out his trackers with disinformation. He evaded his pursuers until the final week. Surely he would have some insight into how one lives under an assumed identity.

On a humid Indian summer afternoon, Ratliff and I sat by the East River under the Brooklyn Bridge while I perspired through one of the three professional polyester H&M shirts I owned, with a sweat mustache accumulating on my upper lip. I asked him, "If you really needed to get out of Dodge, what would you need to consider?"

"If I was going to jail for the rest of my life for a crime I hadn't committed, I would fake my death. The thing is, you need so much time," Ratliff said, just like Rambam. And this rang true across the pantheon of guys who had gotten caught. The Wints, the Schrenkers, the Mendozas—all seemed to have botched already hasty jobs. But perhaps with the right amount of planning and care, you could get away with it.

"Money is the number one thing," he continued. "Transferring tens of thousands of dollars into a crooked bank account is hard, because it can easily be traced back to you. So do you get it out in cash? I would spend a lot of time thinking about money. You can get a fake passport, and a fake Social Security number if you stay in the U.S. You can stay offline. You don't have to get a smartphone. But what are you going to survive on? Are you going to work as a migrant laborer? Money is where it starts to hang up for me."

I felt the same way. I can come up with all the creative costuming and backstory, but establishing the cash flow necessary to sustain oneself is where things get hairy. Coming up with the funds and then finding a way to obscure them while waiting to commit another financial crime—insurance fraud—means going from MacGruber to Jason Bourne with a touch of Gordon Gekko overnight. And given that so many low-rent con men fake their deaths because they've gotten themselves into hot water financially, perhaps compounding the problem would not yield the most desirable results.

Fine. My dreams are dying. But what else?

"You can't have any significant internet presence," Rambam tells me that day at the Marriott. "If you've got a Facebook profile with eight hundred pictures, I can start matching that to anybody else who pops up." I think back to my conversations with Ahearn about managing information on the internet once it's already out there. Even if you delete photos from your social media profiles, there's always a possibility they never truly get erased; people take screen shots, report to other sites, bandy them about as they will. Not that I've ever Googled myself (ahem), but if I had, I might admit that an image search still brings up unfortunate photos of me from years ago, from profiles long deleted (which, sadly, coincide with the dawn of MySpace and a more experimental phase in my personal style, which included two-tone hair and low-rise jeans). Isn't extracting your digital life nearly impossible?

"If you start a year or two in advance, you can do it. Stop tweeting, posting photos, all that," Rambam says. And like Frank said, you can clog the search engines through tagging yourself as just about anyone, to create disinformation.

"Do you need to build up a presence as your new identity? To, like, make yourself more believable?"

"No, just stay the hell off completely."

"Even if you use Tor?" I ask, referring to the software program that claims to obscure your browsing information and IP address.

"Tor is bullshit. There are ways around it. Like I said, just stay the hell off completely!" Rambam sucks down another Corona. I'm wearing his patience thin. Next!

"Do you have fingerprints on file?" he asks. Strange, I hadn't yet considered this line of inquiry. Who has fingerprints on file? Hardened criminals, of course, and I vaguely recall an ominous elementary school project where we dipped our hands in blue paint to impress our tiny digits on cardstock, lest we get kidnapped on our way home from the school bus.

Then it dawns on me.

Of course I have fingerprints on file, from back in my teaching days. In order to pass a background check, the state fingerprints you to ensure that you are not a pedophile. Fingerprints on file, of course, means that you can be tracked that much more easily. Your unique loops and whorls will give you away if you plan on employing a stand-in corpse. If you want to hold a stately wake with keeners, processions, and a viewing of the deceased, like the kind that Marquez investigated, the body's fingerprints can readily be cross-referenced.

"Do you have an intelligent method to fake your death?" Rambam asks.

"What's an intelligent method?" I ask. Drowning has been unilaterally eliminated. (Ratliff and I shared a little chuckle over the conventional wisdom around faking death. Laypeople always offer the same solution: "Fake a drowning!") "A shark attack? A plane crash?" I posit.

"There you go; there you've got a lot of variables," Rambam says.

What about hiking? I ask.

"People disappear hiking all the time, legitimately," Rambam says. "In my opinion, that's a great way to disappear. Especially if it's a young or middle-aged female, because women are snatched off hiking trails all the time for real, and raped and killed and the body hidden. That's semibelievable." Yikes. As a young(ish) woman who has gone on a solo hike or two, this point gives me pause. One of the glorious aspects of pseudocide, to me, was the autonomy I could exert over my story. But to be believable in Rambam's eyes, I'd still need to summon the lurking madman out from the shadows to brutalize me. I couldn't just slink off intact. For me to be reborn, it would have to appear as if my life had been taken. The thought frightens and depresses me.

At this point, Rambam's longtime friend comes in maneuvering four Coronas, two for each of us.

"Yes! Please give her another drink! Maybe she'll stop asking me all these goddamn questions!" Rambam shouts. But I am insatiable, fueled by beer and free cocktail wieners.

"Do you have a guilty conscience?" Rambam asks. This strikes me as odd. Obviously, people who are willing to abandon their families, debts, and obligations are categorically not handwringers.

I ask him to elaborate.

"A couple times people have given themselves up, but it happens very rarely. They go to the insurance company and give back the money. They don't get prosecuted." How odd.

The next few questions Rambam implores me to consider seem pretty straightforward: Do you have problems with drugs and alcohol?

(Loose lips sink ships.)

Is there any other way to get the money without committing fraud?

(I mean, I could infiltrate Sallie Mae and wipe clean its computers, but cyberterrorism seems a bit out of my wheelhouse.)

Have you increased your coverage in the past two years?

(Insurance companies consider a death within that time frame as a "contestable period" and will automatically scrutinize the claim.)

Are you willing to risk disgrace and imprisonment if you're caught?

(I think part of the problem with someone who would consider pseudocide in the first place—me included—might be delusions of grandeur. How could I ever get caught?)

Then: "Can you justify insurance to make it worthwhile?"

Come again?

"A guy working at a hot dog stand isn't going to get six million dollars in coverage," Rambam explains. Mendoza's net worth, for example, was approximately $200,000, yet he had policies in the millions, which immediately looked suspicious. "You have to make a lot of money, or you form a bogus company with your co-conspirators, and you both get key-man insurance." He's referring to certain business policies with greater coverage for important higher-ups in the organization. "There are a million ways to justify key-man insurance, but one of the reasons why I caught this guy in Mexico was because he was working for his brother-in-law's garage, and he took out a million dollars from six different companies."

Okay, so I'm worth about forty bucks and a scratch ticket. Gotta up my value. Rambam's next question catches me by surprise: "Have you considered suicide?"

Back when we first started going over the viable motives for faking death, Rambam said that you had to have a legitimate reason, and he has yet to come across one. Which means that your problems have to be big: bigger than financial misdealings, bigger than love affairs, bigger than the average mortal mishegoss. What Rambam is getting at, I think, is that if killing yourself might also solve your problem, it might be a better option than faking your death. I thought about Hector and Todd and whether this option ever crossed their minds.

"So that's where it all ends?" I ask. "Kill yourself or stay alive?"

"You ask yourself all the tactical questions, all the moral questions, all the strategic questions. If the stars align, you kill yourself. There are other questions you ask if it's an emotional reason. Have you tried to resolve the problem? Have you considered murder?"

Whoa! Not sure how we went from pretending to take your own life to actually taking the life of another, but this is where the road leads: to annihilation, to blotting out. For Rambam, it seems that taking your own life is more honest, somehow nobler, than staging the exit. But if actually killing yourself or committing murder still won't solve your dilemma, and faking your death remains the only option on your road to glory, then Rambam (thank you, ma'am) has one last question for you: "Does Steve Rambam consult for your insurance company? If yes, *stay alive*!"

SHOULD YOU FAKE YOUR OWN DEATH ☠ COLLECT LIFE INSURANCE MONEY?

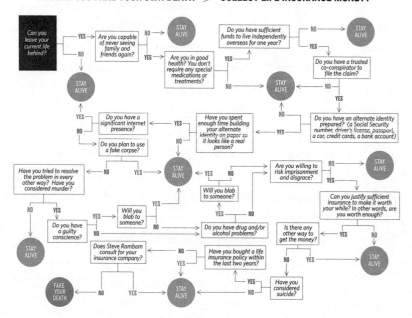

In Rambam's entire career of tracking down fraudsters on the lam, he says that only one person has ever evaded his capture: a Mongolian woman whose good friend was married to the local police captain and used his connections for her plot. She has been hiding out and avoiding extradition in France ever since. She sounds like a smart lady. "If she ever goes back to Mongolia, there will be a bunch of angry cops there waiting for her," Rambam says. You can tell he harbors a teensy bit of ire at not being able to claim a totally flawless track record. But it's pretty damn close.

After he's laid down all the different questions, big and small, that a carefully considered pseudocide would need to address, I feel wrung out and crestfallen. Clearly, pulling off a hoax on your own mortality involves some serious planning.

"Don't you think there's anything romantic about faking your death? Daydreamy, even?" I ask him. He looks at me as if I am insane; as if I'd had wads of cotton lodged in my ears for our entire stiff conversation; as if I've just blatantly disregarded the lengths to which he goes to smoke out criminals from their garrets, and the shame leveled upon them when he does.

"It's not colorful," he says in a voice quieter than I've heard him use yet. For a moment, his bravado is gone. "It's actually pretty cowardly."

Ahearn, Rambam, and even Ratliff agreed that, logistically and in terms of its success rate, faking death is not the way to go. And now Rambam was refuting my poetic notions about fresh starts and clean slates in exchange for the image of an invertebrate con man slinking away. But I still wasn't convinced. Is it cowardly to renounce problems that feel so deeply entrenched to the point of total despair, or is opting out entirely the ballsiest move one could make? It was time to hear from someone who knew firsthand.

3 | THE CANOE MAN

John Darwin hadn't kayaked in some time, but on the afternoon of March 21, 2002, he felt inspired. Neighbors recalled seeing him crossing the street with his bright red kayak—or "canoe" in local parlance—hoisted over his head. When the fifty-one-year-old corrections officer failed to appear for his shift that evening at the Holme House prison in Stockton-on-Tees, England, Anne, his high school sweetheart and wife of over thirty years, reported him missing. Authorities kicked off a search party, with helicopters from the Royal Air Force swarming the gray skies over the North Sea, hundreds of rescuers combing the rocky beaches, and coast guard boats hunting for Darwin. After scouring the area for sixteen hours, they discovered only a paddle a hundred yards offshore. Police canceled the search. Rescuers noted that the water had not been especially rough the day Darwin disappeared.

In the months that followed, no corpse washed ashore. Anne mused on her unique predicament to reporters: "People die, have a funeral, they have a headstone, there is something to mark the fact they existed. I want to bury his body, enabling me to move on," she said. Her sons, Mark, twenty-six, and Anthony, twenty-four, returned home to care for their mother. She tossed rose petals out to sea at the spot where her husband vanished. But no bloated body would wash up to provide the family with closure or to make Anne an official widow.

No corpse would materialize because for a great deal of the time he was considered dead, John Darwin was actually upstairs in his own home. He had colluded with his wife to fake his death and erase his debt by collecting insurance payouts. He assumed the identity of John Jones, a man born the same year but who died in infancy. With an authentic British passport in Jones's name, Darwin traveled the world while Anne sold off their properties in England. The couple used those proceeds to buy a penthouse in Panama City and a plot of virgin jungle. After Darwin turned himself in nearly six years after his initial disappearance, a photograph of Anne and John beaming in a Panamanian real estate office would surface. Mark and Anthony thought their father had been dead the entire time.

===

ON THE DAY I arrived in Seaton Carew, England, eleven years after John Darwin's legendary disappearance, the clouds hung so low in the sky it felt like being in a basement. Situated an hour southeast of Newcastle on the North Sea, the silvery water is the main attraction here. Seaton Carew has been billed as a seaside resort town since the mid-1800s, when the stately

Staincliffe Hotel was built. Since Darwin's return, the Staincliffe has renamed two of its restaurants the Darwin Room and
the Canoe Bar. And a few doors down and built not much later
sit two mammoth adjoining Victorian gingerbread homes that
John Darwin used to own. What led me here was the chance to
learn from someone who had successfully faked his own death,
at least for a while. I hoped that if I spent enough time with him
and learned the particulars of his strategy, his knowledge and
experience could seep into me via osmosis.

It's hard to overstate John Darwin's pop-culture cachet in
the United Kingdom. I first read about him in Frank Ahearn's
How to Disappear, as Frank thanked him for the uptick in his
business, mainly from UK media outlets that wanted him to comment on Darwin's plan. When Darwin wandered into a London
police station in December 2007, he quickly became the story
of the year. Maybe it was the slow holiday news cycle, or the
universal fantasy of leaving one's life behind, or the delight-
ful schadenfreude of the plan going awry, but readers couldn't
get enough. The former prison guard is still synonymous with
pseudocide in the United Kingdom—every time I've mentioned
my quest to a Briton, he or she immediately references the
Canoe Man. Darwin's death fraud has put him at the top of the
pseudocide survival-of-the-fittest heap.

He had recently been released from prison when I sent him
a letter. When I opened my email to be greeted by a message
from "johndarwin6969," a wave of adrenaline coursed through
my body. Having devoured all the salacious tabloid articles
about him, I felt like I was speaking to a celebrity. I was a little
taken aback, yet totally psyched, that he was so game to talk
to me. I didn't know if, having lost so much, he'd be offended
by the request. But it became clear pretty quickly that he has

embraced the throne of the man who claimed dominion over his fate and paddled out to sea. He said I could come to England, and that he'd show me the beach where the course of his life took a sharp turn.

Standing on the stretch of sand, if you squint, hold your breath, and focus your gaze on just a few inches of ocean horizon, the place looks pleasant enough. But inhale, and the olfactory system is assaulted with the stench of sewage draining into the ocean. Look to the left, and you see the old coal docks that serviced the underwater collieries. The beach is stained black from shale that still washes up onshore thirty years after the last mines closed. Industrious folks drive flatbed trucks down the shore and shovel the black sand to sell to the local power plant for cheap energy. Look to the right, and you've got the belching chimneys from the Petroplus Teesside Refinery and docks for shipping containers coming to port, flanked by giant turbines catching the relentless wind that slashes your face. Picture an off-season Myrtle Beach crossed with Pittsburgh, and you have Seaton Carew.

But the place does possess its own grim beauty. I found myself drawn viscerally to the winding old streets, the low-slung homes, and the wild elderberries that form canopies over the damp sidewalks. The land resonates with me in a primordial way. The rust-belt shit town where I grew up, Worcester, Massachusetts, boasts its own dreary downtown, much like Seaton Carew's, where the main beachfront drag is home to a video arcade, a fish-and-chips shop, and a burger joint that roasts the patties to the consistency of mulch, and everything closes at four in the afternoon. My neighborhood in Worcester, too, possessed a handful of loiterer-friendly businesses like the minimart, the liquor store, and the keno lounge. Neighboring

Hartlepool, a mile north of Seaton Carew, has a fluorescent-lit mall with the same hallmarks of my adolescence: dollar stores, a McDonald's with a long line, and lots of skinny boys in track pants with sunken cheeks and narrowed eyes.

The North of England also resonates with me because this is the land of my ancestors. They were part of the Puritan diaspora from Yorkshire in the sixteen hundreds; part of the great migration to America—which begat the Appalachian white trash and aspiring southern gentry who would earn the distinction of "good name, no money" after the Civil War and ultimately evolve into our current manifestation of WASPs who get drunk in drafty houses in lieu of emoting. I've always felt that I came from no place. "Northern English" does not a spicy heritage make. Even the Irish Catholics who populated Worcester seemed downright exotic in comparison. This is, of course, the agony of being a privileged majority, but weirdly, here in the North of England, centuries after my relations boarded ships to evade being burned at the stake, I see myself in the citizens: the ghostly pallor; the hooded eyes heavy with alcoholism, depression, and lack of vitamin D; the upturned ski-slope noses the Viking pillagers gave us; the pudding-soft bellies. I have found my people.

John Darwin's story struck me as an English story, but a Northern English story in particular. Many locals I talked to told me through gritted teeth that there are two Englands: the South and the North, or, more to the point, the rich and the poor. Industry has historically been located in the North, in the form of factories, shipbuilding, coal mining, and steelworks. Service and creative classes have always been located in the South. Prior to Darwin's caper, this town did not register in anyone's mind as a place with much to recommend it. But

adjacent big brother Hartlepool is synonymous with the "monkey hanging," a tale from the Napoleonic Wars that captures
the nature of the sheltered locale. Fearing an attack, fishermen
were on the lookout for invaders. They paid close attention as
wreckage from a French ship washed ashore. There were no
survivors save a soggy pet monkey, dressed in military garb for
the sailors' amusement. Having never met a Gaul, the fishermen
questioned the monkey in an impromptu beach trial, and determined him to be a French spy. They sentenced him to death,
and hung him from a fishing boat's mast as a gallows. Today
he is immortalized in a bronze monkey-hanging statue. Visitors
can toss coins into his open arms. You can buy monkey-hanging
key chains and mugs in the local history museum. "They really
thought he was a person," John would explain later. "The people are a bit backward here."

John's rubbery, expressive face betrays his British stoicism.
He gives sidelong twinkling glances when he's being mischie-
vous, typically about whichever titsy Russian pops up on his
cell phone—"women who want to meet me"—or when referring to "the pair of identical twins" who (you guessed it) also
seek a private audience with the Canoe Man. He suffers from
high self-esteem, which is what it takes to even conceive of faking your own death and getting away with it, outsmarting law
enforcement and insurance investigators. "John from England
with blue eyes" is how he describes himself to the women he
meets in online role-playing games, several of whom he visited
abroad when he was "dead." When we met, he was sixty-two
and balding, but in sturdy shape. He often goes for long walks
along the blustery waterfront in steel-toed boots. He finds people his own age, especially women, to be adventure-averse wet
blankets. Darwin speaks often of his acts of bravery: eating wild

mushrooms covered in live maggots, kayaking without a helmet ("crash hats are for wimps!"), drinking water straight from the tap in every far-flung country he has visited. In another life, he might have been an explorer.

In his 2012 memoir, *The Canoe Man: Panama and Back,* he presents himself as haplessly virile, seduced by a parent when he was a young teacher (a profession he entered because he "loved the idea of long, long holidays"): "[T]here was me, a good Catholic teacher, standing behind and making love to the mother of two of my pupils in my own classroom . . . The noise seemed extremely loud, the sound of my hips slapping against her flesh . . ." He has programmed his cell phone ring tone to play a Clint Eastwood Western melody. He refers to the period of adventure after his disappearance as "when I was dead." He lists foods that are aphrodisiacs and waits for your reaction. He says "women are my drug" and describes himself as a "randy old man" who, despite a six-year, three-month prison sentence, a divorce, and an estranged son who won't talk to him, still has a lot of vim, vigor, and joie de vivre. His devil-may-care attitude toward life is inspiring, if a bit troubling.

Since his dramatic return from the dead nearly a decade ago, John Darwin has occupied that sweet spot of D-list celebrity that tabloids are built upon: not famous enough to be insulated by handlers, yet still popular enough to garner fascination. "People ask for me autograph," he says with amusement. The British newspaper the *Daily Mirror* follows his goings-on with the same kind of train-wreck rubbernecking that *In Touch Weekly* magazine heaps on the likes of *The Real Housewives* reality stars in the United States. He went with a local radio host friend to see heavyweight champion boxer Frank Bruno give an after-dinner speech. Upon entering the banquet hall, Darwin was recognized instantly, and the audience began applauding for him in spite of the star onstage. He describes the encounter as a bit embarrassing—but also set up a makeshift photo booth for fans to take a picture with him for £5 a pop, the proceeds of which he says he donated to charity.

Such celebrity comes with rabid fans, such as a "stalker" (his word) named Lorraine Forbes. They struck up a correspondence when he was serving time. She wrote every few months, sealing her letters with lipstick kisses and promises of "Option 3." Darwin explains the options: "When I was in prison, we wrote, and she gave me three options: number one is a meal, number two is the cinema, and number three is a damn good night bonking!" The perks of celebrity are not limited solely to groupies like Forbes but also extend even to Her Majesty's Royal Mail. Forbes still writes Darwin, and, not knowing his latest whereabouts, simply addresses the envelope to:

> John Darwin
> "Canoe Man"
> His Bungalow
> Seaton Carew

And the letters always find him.

———

THOUGH FRANK AHEARN AND Steve Rambam had insisted that death fraud makes a poor exit strategy—for the sole reason that it's far easier to get caught—Darwin's story perhaps serves as the exception to their ironclad rule. I wanted to know what it felt like to be "dead" among the living, and what it is like to come back. But after getting to know Darwin personally and noting his refusal to obsess over having exploded his former life, a new question emerged: Can you ever escape the past, and can you ever escape yourself?

I suspect that Darwin's blustering and chest puffery are rooted in something much deeper than machismo. The man is undeniably a product of the British class system and what happens, in the words of his father, Ronald, when one "has ideas above one's station." To his neighbors in Seaton Carew, his "getting one over on the insurance companies, the banks, and the government," as some claim, is the stuff of folklore.

He describes his background as "working class with middle-class aspirations." His mother was a dietician, and his father was a bricklayer. He grew up in a small bungalow in neighboring Blackhall Rocks, one of the local towns that exist to service the mines. "You had three choices," he explains. "You could go down the pit at one colliery, or you could take the bus to another colliery, or you could go to the steelworks." Rather than accepting this fate, Darwin extracted himself from such bleak prospects and attended the University of Manchester, where he studied to become a teacher. He felt resentment from friends when he returned home. "When they think educated people aren't as good as them, it's a kind of snobbery," Darwin says.

He married Anne in 1972. They had known each other since high school. The couple soon had their first child, Mark. Anthony followed two years later. Anne came from a strict Catholic family, which John thinks drove a wedge between them from the earliest days of their relationship. In his memoir, John describes Anne's family finding out that she was on birth control before they were married and forbidding her from seeing him. He describes her worldview as somewhat limited. ("She'd never had cheese before she met me!" he says, incredulous to this day.) After they married, when Anne was working as a secretary and he as a math and science teacher, John wanted the young couple to apply for an exchange in Australia. But, by his account, Anne's provincial family forbade them from straying too far afield. So he dug in and ensconced himself in his role as a family man. "We were Mr. and Mrs. Average," he writes in *The Canoe Man*. After being denied a promotion at the school, Darwin worked briefly at Barclays Bank but quit because he was "quickly disillusioned by their sales methods." He then applied for teaching positions in London and for a job in the prison service. He received both, and opted for the prison because "there was a good chance that would be closer to home." But those "ideas above one's station" persisted.

He had grander aspirations to make money. "I don't care what anyone says. Money isn't everything, but it's ninety-nine-point-nine percent of everything," he tells me. He became involved in a number of endeavors to bolster his income, from trading stocks and shares (though he once got entangled in a pyramid scheme) to raising African snails to sell to local restaurants as escargot to crafting garden gnomes to peddle at markets. Darwin actually made money from these. He is quick to contradict the media narrative of his life: "It wasn't just fail, fail, fail, and then canoe into the sea! The newspaper said, 'Oh, he wanted to make a lot of money.' Well, the British media has to castigate anyone who's successful in this country. If you try to pull yourself up, they'll kick you in the teeth."

Turning his entrepreneurial eye to real estate was the financial decision that would forever alter the course of his life. According to his memoir, he saw buying rental properties as a way to provide Anne with security in old age, as her "piddly little job" would not provide a comfortable retirement: "We realized the rent from one tenant would make as much as her proposed pension, so the logical plan seemed to be to buy a house in Anne's name and kit it out under the guise of bed-and-breakfast accommodation."

John and Anne sold that first house and used the proceeds to buy cheaper properties to rent out. John describes his Donald Trump–like ascension: "Like a Monopoly player, I bought more houses, usually bank repossessions, finally only mentioning the fact to Anne in passing. She did not even know how many houses I owned or even their locations." Darwin cultivated capital to purchase these homes by consulting a book that advises readers in the art of "creative banking." Using a crafty system of financing deposits through loans (usually in the form of cash advances on credit cards), John steadily acquired a rental portfolio of a dozen homes over the course of two years.

In late 2000 the Darwins found the crown jewels of their portfolio at their friend's home one night in Seaton Carew, when he showed them an advertisement for nos. 3 and 4 the Cliff, a pair of conjoined Victorian guesthouses connected by a series of interior corridors. The couple fell in love with the properties: their vast size, their craftsmanly charm, their oceanfront views. They decided to make no. 3 their dream home and turn its Siamese twin into a rental property. Anne dug up a photograph of her taken opposite the houses when she was eighteen. John remembers the nostalgia the photo evoked: "This brought back memories of how she looked when we first went out with each other many years ago." They bought the homes at a decent price because they were fixer-uppers. "They seemed an incredible bargain," John writes in his book, "£150,000 for the pair. . . . Of course, we had to raise the money, which involved a fair amount of creative accounting. Once again, I had to take out personal loans." They now owned fourteen properties, an impressive feat in only four years.

Although they were living in the stately grandeur of no. 3 the Cliff, with its seven bedrooms, John was still shuffling funds from one venture to pay for another. And the income his rental properties generated turned out to be unreliable. Even though most of his rooms were rented out, the Darwins rarely received the rent on time because the majority of their tenants received a government housing benefit, which was often late. "The work was piling up," he writes, "acts of vandalism by tenants, and late or nonpayment of housing benefits from councils pushed us deeper and deeper into debt." He had not accounted for bureaucratic failings in his creative banking scheme. On the houses alone, he owed £240,000. Soon John couldn't keep up with the payments. Since the homes were rental properties, he had taken out a commercial mortgage instead of a personal residential mortgage. According to Darwin, because of the nature of his financing, he could not declare bankruptcy on the properties. He would have lost everything.

The boiling point came in the form of another bureaucratic failing: a credit card bill never got forwarded to his new address at the Cliff. After months of notices, the credit card company didn't just threaten legal action but also made charges imminent. Once the notice finally arrived, John opened the envelope to see that he owed £5,000, which would have to be paid within seven days. He writes, "Somehow, through juggling the house-move, my job, the upkeep, and maintenance of 14 properties and often just signing cheques for bills without looking properly at what they were for, we had never thought to check on this other card. . . . Think about it; does anyone remember to pay bills they have not actually received?" He called the credit card company and attempted to make a settlement, but it wouldn't budge: pay up within one week or face bailiff action, meaning that everything the Darwins owned, including their property portfolio, could be repossessed. Darwin says that laws have since changed, but at the time, the relatively small credit card debt resulted in an unfortunate domino effect. As he explains it, "We would've been out on the street, and there was no guarantee that we'd be out of debt, because the government would've just sold the houses for nothing. I would be homeless, Anne would be homeless, and twenty-six people would have been homeless." It was in this moment that he realized he was worth more dead than alive.

I'd read this account in his book, but it still hadn't clicked into focus for me. Faking his death seemed a pretty big leap as the only viable option. "Unless you write it out on paper, it's very hard for people to grab hold of," he admits. Darwin's life at that point had been constructed as a house of cards, with one precarious investment holding up the next, with all of their daily expenses, mortgage, and credit card payments hanging in the balance. And the law was not on his side.

I checked into this version of things with an English lawyer, someone more familiar with the systems of bankruptcy and foreclosure. He contradicted several of Darwin's principal legal claims. Regarding the credit card catastrophe, Alan Hodge, a solicitor from Bristol, said, "The notion that all the card company had to do was employ a bailiff, without first obtaining a court order, is not plausible. Credit card companies are (and were at that time) governed by robust consumer regulations. The tenants he mentioned would be protected from any arbitrary eviction by the simple fact that eviction from residential premises cannot take place without a prior possession order."

Darwin wouldn't have been able to sell off the houses without the bank's blessing. Hodge also questions the credibility of Darwin's point about not being able to declare bankruptcy: "Any individual who can prove their debts exceed their liabilities can ask the court for a voluntary bankruptcy order on a payment of fee." But according to Darwin, this kind of public bank settlement could have cost him his job. He explains: "Since I was a prison officer, if I was taken to court, not only would the bank hear about it, but the prison authorities would also hear about it, and I'd be in danger of losing my job. If you're a prison officer and you've got all these drug barons and they know you're in financial trouble, they'll put pressure on you. That's why the prison authorities have the rules that you have to report trouble to them so you don't get sucked in. If I was taken to court without telling them, then I would have gotten sacked."

Still, this is the point in the story where most people would take a different course of action. Dusting off the old kayak, packing a rucksack with camping essentials, and colluding with one's spouse to claim insurance money and pensions might not spring to mind as a first solution. It wasn't Darwin's first idea, either. Some of the options he entertained included robbing a gas station, mugging a pedestrian, and crashing his car for an insurance payout. He considered suicide, but claimed he wouldn't do it given the effect on Anne and his family. Plus, from his research, there was no money in suicide. He considered simply disappearing, but that wouldn't have solved the financial problem, either. So he gave the Walter White excuse: I committed the crime to save my family.

But beyond the problems with his prison officer job, beyond making Anne an accessory to fraud, there were two other people to consider: their sons, Mark and Anthony. That's the part that casts a shadow over Darwin's clever plan. How could you let your children think you're dead?

"How old are you?" Darwin asks me in an echoey restaurant on the waterfront by the stretch of beach where he'd staged the accident.

"Thirty," I tell him.

"The two kids were a couple of years younger than you. One was married. They weren't babies. They were adults who had moved away from home, leading independent lives. So in that respect, they weren't children," he explains. John is quick to make the distinction each time his sons' names come up: they were his kids, but they were not *kids*. He goes on to express, with exasperation, the thing he knows he is supposed to say:

"Yes, it was a terrible thing to do. You don't think of these things when you're under a lot of stress. In the cold light of day, you wouldn't do it. But under stress, you'll do extraordinary things," he says. Darwin often employs the second person when reflecting on his actions. The goal, I think, is to put me in his shoes: What would *you* do under such excruciating pressure? You would do the same thing. He makes a macabre comparison: "In this county, there are a lot of people under financial stress who end up murdering their wives and kids."

The plan was always supposed to be a temporary fix, as Darwin tells it. Rather than disappearing for life, he intended to collect the commercial mortgage insurance policy that would allow Anne to sell off the houses and then make good on his debt. The plan was just to "borrow" money from the insurance company and then pay it back once they'd liquidated their property assets. At the end of their trial in July 2008, he and Anne were charged with defrauding £250,000 total from Norwich Union and from John's teaching and prison pensions. Of course, he figured he'd pay a fine and do some jail time, but that seemed a whole lot better than putting his family and tenants on the street and living under the draconian rule of an unjust financial system. "It wasn't planned in the long term," Darwin says, "it was something done to meet a requirement. I wanted to release the equity in the houses. It doesn't matter how much equity you've got in the houses if you have to pay back the bank twenty dollars a month and if you can't, they foreclose on you."

The fact of his planned return is critical to Darwin's narrative. It supports his contention that he was not caught, nor was he about to be caught, but rather that he turned himself in when the time was right. But Darwin also cites his devotion to Anne as a reason for faking his death instead of just disappearing and shirking his responsibilities—a point that would make the inevitable prison sentence worth it: "I would still be married. We would be able to live together as man and wife."

Darwin writes poignantly in his memoir of the shame that propelled him toward the plan ("I don't want to be seen as a failure . . . the man who lost his home, who couldn't provide for his wife and family") and the anxiety he experienced when, on a cold March day, he made the decision to go through with it. "Can I do it? Should I do it? I went to the hall door and then, as I put the key in the front door to unlock it, my hands started to shake. 'Not again,' I thought as I turned to the toilet, feeling distinctly sick. Dry retches wracked my body, but as I had nothing left in my stomach, only yellow bile emerged." But the nerves eventually dissipated. A few pages later, he narrates, "Can I get away with it? Yes, I can." What comes next is the part of the story he unabashedly loves to tell: the problem solving, the logical turns. He kept the red kayak in what was once a chapel but had become a storage shed.

"What, you don't have a chapel in your backyard?" Darwin asks me as we stand across the street from no. 3 the Cliff. This is the great plan from the great man who got away with it. At least for a while. On a blustery day, he guides me down to the spot on the coal-flecked beach where he launched. The clouds are low and pregnant in the sky, threatening a downpour at any moment. The wind whips our faces, but Darwin is unmoved.

He carried the kayak out of storage in the chapel. Inside the boat, he had stuffed a plastic bag with a change of clothes, two T-shirts, a sweater, socks, underwear, two long-sleeved shirts, a money belt containing just over £150, a flashlight, matches, and a pair of sunglasses. He recalls his shoulders burning under the weight of the thing as he crossed over from his house to the beach, and pretending it was light as an empty shell.

"You've got to look down the beach," Darwin explains in his science-teacher voice. "You've got people walking dogs, then over here it's secluded." He points to the area a ways down the shore, closer to the chemical plant and away from the houses and shops lining the Cliff. "So you've got to be seen kayaking out. What I did was, I timed it, so by the time I got here, it had started to get dark. I went out around four, and I was in no rush. This was in March, so it gets dark quite early. Once it was dark, I tried to push the kayak out, but it must've been a woman, because it was very obstinate! It was very frightening and exciting going in. I quite enjoy paddling!" Setting out, he still hadn't made up his mind if he was going to go through with it or just turn back.

Once it was dark, Darwin crash-landed down the beach, away from his neighbors who often used binoculars to watch ships coming into port. He left one sneaker by the tide line for rescuers to discover hours later. The September day when we are standing on the beach brings the kind of English damp that just makes you sad. He says that day in March years earlier was even colder. He remembers wondering if he should just pack it in, go home, and take a hot shower. But instead, he paced around the sand dunes in drenched clothes with a pole slung over his shoulder so that he might be mistaken for a fisherman. He waited a few hours for Anne to pick him up and deposit him at the Durham train station, about twenty miles north. "The first place the police would look is the Hartlepool and Seaton Carew railway stations," he explains. "In the U.K., there are closed-circuit cameras all over the place. You've got to think ahead."

An older man walking a terrier passes us and does a double take and smirks. "He knows me! That one knew me!" Darwin whispers to me as soon as the dog walker is out of earshot. "You can always tell when they have a certain type of smile on their face. They recognize you."

When we reach the end of the beach, we turn onto a path through tall grass of North Gare to a parking lot bordering a golf course a short walk away. This is where Anne picked up the freezing, shivering John, whose night shift at Holme House prison was to begin in a few hours.

Anne is the big question mark in the story. I sent her several letters, but she never replied, and she has not spoken to the press since her now ex-husband's return. She seems eager to leave this chapter of her life in the past. Her only words are from a police interview that was made public. Explaining her role in the plan, Anne told investigators in December 2007, "I knew the day that John had gone missing . . . that he planned it. I got a telephone call from him at work that afternoon to say he was going out in the canoe and that he wanted me to get home by seven o'clock to pick him up and help him make his getaway. Eventually he came toward the car, and he said he had everything with him that he needed." In an audio recording posted on YouTube, her voice in this interview is slow and deliberate. To me it sounds as if she's recalling a really awful dream.

But even since their divorce in 2011, Anne still looms large in John's life. He often refers to her not by her name but simply as "she." As we walk along the gravel path to the almost empty parking lot, John offers, "She was really nervous; she's not as strong-willed as me." But when the couple's debt seemed insurmountable, she threatened suicide, saying that she would "walk into the sea." When he initially floated the plan of faking his death, Anne thought he had gone mad, he says. He convinced her that it was the only way they would be able to collect the mortgage insurance money that would allow them to release the equity in the houses, pay back their debt, and, one day, resume life as Mr. and Mrs. Average. When John broke the news to Anne of his plan the week before he staged the accident, she kept a stony distance from him until the morning he paddled out to sea, when she rolled over and, according to John, said, "I don't want you to do this, but if you're determined to carry it out, then I'll help you. But only on the condition you'll find a way to come back."

When he climbed into Anne's car, he was shivering, almost hypothermic. She told him he was a "silly old man" and forbade him from camping on the beach in Silloth, on the northwest coast, as he had planned. John had chosen Silloth because he knew that his accent gave him away as a northerner. He would stick out too much in the South. Anne had withdrawn the last £100 from their checking account and gave it to John to spend the night in a bed-and-breakfast once he arrived on the other side of the country. On the car ride to the train station, they discussed simply turning around and pretending the thing never happened. But as they took back roads to Durham, they kept driving. The plan was in motion. There was no turning back.

Somewhere between the Durham train station and the bed-and-breakfast in Silloth, Anne got a call from the prison that John had failed to appear for his night shift. Usually the couple might have grabbed a quick dinner before John headed out to work, but on this night, Anne told his supervisor, she had gone shopping and hadn't seen him all day. His car was in the drive-way, and his passport, credit cards, and phone were upstairs in the bedroom. The only thing missing from the house was the kayak.

"She must've had to act really panicky," I say to John.

"If you are panicking because you're doing wrong, you don't have to act. You're just panicking. She was scared stiff," he explains.

It begins to rain as we stand in the parking lot. This is where the plan truly commenced, where the couple committed to the fraud. I'm straining to understand how he actually feels beneath all the bluster and bravado.

I ask him if he feels bad for having had Anne lie on his behalf.

"We were both under a lot of stress," he explains. "Yes, you felt bad for putting her under the stress, but what's the alternative? It's not like the newspapers say: 'I blame everybody but meself.' I don't!"

"So what responsibility do you take?" I ask.

"I bought the houses for Anne's pension. This would be her security. For coming up with the plan, I suppose ninety percent."

"What about the other ten percent?"

"If she was telling the police about 'my dear departed husband,' then she must have some responsibility, don't you think? Or do you not agree with that?"

The thing I have noticed about John Darwin, as with so many of these other guys who fake their deaths, is that his ideas, while bizarre and demented, do possess a certain internal logic. It's not like he was ripping off the insurance company—he was simply "borrowing money" from it! And his kids were adults with their own lives; they wouldn't have cared if he'd died anyway! He was worth more dead than alive! If you allow John's rationalizations to wash over you, you can see how once the plan was activated, it seemed easier to stay the course. And Darwin's use of the second person is meant to help you see exactly that. So once you're tucked into your bed-and-breakfast in Silloth—having successfully made the cross-country journey without incident—and you turn on the TV in your room and see the news reporting the disappearance of a middle-aged man off the coast of Seaton Carew, well, you can't go turn yourself in now, can you? You absorb your own disappearance. You are officially on the run.

Lying low was critical those first few days of the investigation. John boasts that the police report (which was sent to Anne accidentally) stated there was not even a 0.1 percent chance he'd faked his death, but other investigators had their suspicions. In an interview during the initial investigation, the detective who led the inquiry said, "I am concerned that the absence of his body may lead people to think he did a Reggie Perrin." The detective was referring to the main character of the (very British) mid-1970s sitcom *The Rise and Fall of Reginald Perrin*: a middle-aged middle manager at a dessert factory who stages his suicide by leaving his clothes folded neatly on the beach.

John Darwin is just the latest in a rich legacy of Britons faking their deaths, and doing it with panache. Graham Cardwell, a Lincolnshire dockmaster, staged his drowning in 1998, only to be discovered eight months later living on the other side of the country. He claimed to have cancer, and hadn't wanted to burden his family. Richard John Bingham, also known as Lord Lucan, was a dashing titled graduate of tony Eton College who wrote a suicide note in 1974 after his children's nanny was nearly bludgeoned to death. His wife identified her aristocratic husband as the assailant. Lucan sightings have been reported in Switzerland, New Zealand, and Africa. In an ironic twist, one of the reported Lucan sightings turned out to be John Stonehouse, a British Labour Party minister who had managed to successfully fake his death. Stonehouse had been caught skimming money from charities he'd set up. He was imprisoned for seven years but was released early because he'd suffered three heart attacks. Upon his release, he faked a drowning in Miami, Reggie Perrin–style, with a pile of clothes and the image of a swim, in November 1974, and collected insurance and pensions totaling $382,500. He managed to vanish, but for only one month. He was found alive with his former secretary in Australia on Christmas Eve of that same year, living under the name of a deceased former constituent. Stonehouse died for real in 1988. Just a few years ago, MI5, the British intelligence agency, revealed that Stonehouse was a Communist spy. Some historians have speculated that his involvement with the KGB provides an additional explanation as to why he faked his death. "Lord Lucan and John Stonehouse used to be the most famous for faking death," Darwin tells me. "Now it's John Darwin," he concludes with a satisfied grin.

While authorities investigated John's disappearance, he camped out on the rocky, frost-covered shore of Silloth on the west coast of the country for almost two months. "Living rough" is how Darwin describes the time after his initial disappearance and during the investigation. He slept on a cheap air mattress in a tent on the beach. He ate canned beans and candy bars, and read paperbacks from charity shops. He always had a fire going at night, not just to stay alive in the freezing weather but also to boost his morale. He explains his false identity: "I told people I'm from York"—about an hour south of Seaton Carew—"I'm an ornithologist, and I'm working my way down the coast. I knew people would accept that." The secret to lying, he tells me, is "keeping as near the truth as possible."

John would call his wife from a pay phone daily to get the updates. Disguising his voice in a deep grumble, he would pose as a prospective tenant. "It's amateur dramatics," he explains. If the police were in the house, Anne would keep up the ruse.

She controlled the purse strings and had begun submitting paperwork with the mortgage insurance company that would fix their financial bind. "I would call, and she'd say, 'You trapped me!' But I had no money, and *she* wasn't going to contact *me*." From John's vantage, Anne was the one with the upper hand, not him.

Another part of the reason he camped in Silloth was to develop the pièce de résistance of his master plan, and what would actually keep him shrouded as he hid in plain sight: his disguise. He grew a long white beard, lost weight from "living rough," bought a pair of tinted glasses, and added a limp and a walking stick (very Father Time). He practiced his new gait down the beach. When Anne eventually picked him up two months later to drive him back to the Cliff, she passed him "without a flicker of recognition. I looked right at her through my dark glasses. When your own wife doesn't recognize you . . . I knew it was good," he says.

By the time Anne retrieved her gaunt and bearded husband, police and family members were still coming around. But the thought of those luxurious empty guest rooms in the Cliff was enough to drive John crazy. "It had come to a point where I couldn't take it anymore," he says. So, with his disguise intact, Anne dropped him off a mile away from their home, the scene of the crime. He walked in the front door of no. 4, where all their other tenants entered, and opened the door to the room for Karl Fenwick—his assumed identity. Anne was chatting in the hall with another renter when he entered. "Oh, he's a new one!" the tenant remarked. "Yeah," Anne said. "They're changing all the time."

It seems totally inconceivable that Darwin was able to return to his home after being presumed dead. But he slipped seamlessly between the guest side and Anne's side of the sprawling double house through a series of connecting stairs and corridors that had remained intact between them since they were built in 1924. When the story broke, the press made it sound as though he was hiding in a garret-like compartment behind a wardrobe. One publication cheekily titled the Darwins' story "The Liar, the Witch, and the Wardrobe." Not only did he live next door and sleep in the same bed as his wife ("king size," he is quick to point out), but he also lived in the house intermittently for five years.

This is the part that captures my imagination and somehow endears John Darwin to me, in spite of his Machiavellian scheme. His duplicity encapsulates the joy of faking death: things are not as they seem, and the mundane facts of life might hold a secret, an alternate reality, right under our noses. It's like training my gaze on the one tranquil slice of the Seaton Carew horizon line while neglecting to see the rest. Forget about the sons, and the wife, and the financial crimes for a moment and just look at the brains and the balls that faking death requires. It's nothing short of magic.

When John was "dead," he spent his days in much the same way as he does now: surfing the internet, tooling around the house making improvements, walking along the waterfront into Hartlepool to window-shop. The only problem was that police and detectives would often be inside the house when he was ready to come home. So he came up with a code for Anne to alert him to stay away that took him "fifteen seconds" to devise, he tells me as we walk along the ocean just across the street from nos. 3 and 4 the Cliff. Anne would signal to John that detectives were inside by hanging the parlor curtains straight down, and he would keep walking. But if he saw the curtains tied back in the window, it meant the coast was clear, and he could enter.

"Pretty devious!" I say as we gaze at the two homes, which look shabbier than they do in the photos that ran in every UK newspaper when Darwin returned.

"I would say *clever*," he counters. "Intelligent," he sniffs. "The point is, you could see the code from a long way away."

He recalls one day when he was out for his daily constitutional, in full disguise. Walking back home to the Cliff, he says, "My heart nearly stopped, because in front of me was my father and brother walking toward me." This wasn't the first time he had encountered people from his old life. He often passed former colleagues and acquaintances on the street. "I usually had my glasses on, so I'd look away, not make eye contact," he explains as we sit in the café section of a box store called Adsa, the English answer to Wal-Mart. So what did he think when passing friends and family? "Damn good disguise!" he says.

But Darwin is not always so flip recounting his time as a ghost. "You were more or less a spectator," he explains. Reflecting on his time camping in Silloth, he says, "You ended up being depressed because you don't know what's happening in the outside world. If you cross the street, you don't even look. Cars are beeping their horns. You say 'I'm already dead! What's the difference?' You get to such a stage where only one person in the world knows where you are. You want to trust that one person one hundred percent, but there's always a doubt in your mind of whether she's going to carry through with her part. You think, 'Who else in the world cares?' The banks do, because they want their money. You think about the children all the time," he says, and then stops himself. "But they were more mature. They were not the same as children."

The man likes to talk, so I imagine him fuming when forced to endure a stranger's faulty explanation of the details of his "death" without jumping in and correcting it. But John did have the proper foresight not to give himself away by making the common mistake of checking in on himself posthumously, like the compulsive self-monitoring that led investigators directly to Patrick McDermott's hideout in Puerto Vallarta. John followed reports on his whereabouts, but he was diligent enough to use software that pinged his IP address through several different countries.

John kept himself robust working outdoors most days. As Karl Fenwick ("You need a lot of aliases!"), he was the helpful handyman, whipping the Cliff houses into tip-top shape to be sold at the best price to pay back the insurance company "loan" that he and Anne had collected since his pseudocide.

He made repairs to the interiors, gardened, and painted the exteriors of both homes. As the handyman, he was very attentive and friendly to his landlady, Anne. "We walked around town together!" Darwin explains. "I was the workman! She would move me from one room to another room to work on the decorating. She worked me to death when I was dead!" he puns.

Was it really that easy?

"I would tell her to go in number four and ask me, 'Are you free tomorrow afternoon, because I need help at the hardware store?' and make sure she asked in a loud voice. You were two neighbors being neighborly, and nobody thought anything about it. I'm not pulling a fast one! These things did happen," he says, reading the skepticism on my face.

"Where is the best place to hide?" he suddenly asks me in a low voice.

"In plain sight?" I fill in the blank.

"Exactly!"

=====

SINCE SO MANY DETECTIVES, reporters, and grieving friends and family were still coming around in the months following his disappearance, John had the idea to get a passport and take vacations abroad to evade his potential captors. It took almost six months for him to construct his identity from scratch and to gather all the necessary paperwork. "When I turned myself in, the police asked how I got the passport. I told them I went to the post office and asked how to get one. They expected me to say I got it down on the docks."

The first thing he needed was a name. He found the name John Jones in the genealogy department of the Morpeth

Library. Like him, Jones was born in 1950. He then took the train to neighboring Sunderland's record office to retrieve Jones's birth certificate. It was perfect: "John," so he would never have to worry about responding accidentally if someone called his name, and the commonplace "Jones." One needs only to provide a birth certificate in order to file for a passport. The next step was finding a landlord to verify his address. So he printed out one of his own tenancy agreements from when he was Mr. Average and backdated it. He signed it John Darwin.

He also needed an official person to sign off on his identity. In the United Kingdom, the signature of a teacher or librarian suffices. So Darwin made it a point to cozy up to the local librarian, chatting each day about the weather and local goings-on, so that he could score her autograph and put all the pieces in place. Within six months, while still puttering around his properties as Karl Fenwick and still married to Anne, John had an official UK passport. After his return in 2007, lawmakers on the floor of Parliament referenced the ease with which he'd assumed a new identity as evidence of porous post-9/11 security.

Once Darwin had secured his John Jones passport, he began a series of monthlong trips to the States (unbeknownst to his wife) to visit women whom he had met online playing EverQuest, a role-playing game. The first woman he visited was Maria "with the raven-black hair," an Italian beauty who lived in the Bronx. This was less than two years after 9/11, when suspicious bewhiskered men were routinely questioned by authorities. Cops in Times Square once stopped John after they saw a bearded man recording the area with a tiny video camera. He showed the cops his passport, and, as he explains, "because it was from the U.K., they accepted it. I wasn't scared getting on planes."

Since finances were his chief concern, I ask him how he afforded these trips. "The flight was only about ninety-nine pounds," he says. And once he arrived, he stayed with his hostesses and enjoyed their hospitality. Like Blanche DuBois in *A Streetcar Named Desire*, Darwin always relied on the kindness of strangers. And what does one tell one's wife who is providing one's cover and conspiring to collect insurance while one is on an American romp with various women?

"When Anne asked where I was staying in New York, I told her I hailed a taxi at the airport, and we got to talking, and he invited me to stay at his place!" A New York City cab driver inviting one of his charges for a sleepover might be the most unbelievable yarn of Darwin's entire web of deception.

His real host, Maria, was unaware of John's wife. He says she wanted to marry him.

"Didn't you feel bad about misleading two women?"

"I was economical with the truth," he says.

"But what about Anne?"

"She was in one of her moods most of the time. I'm not trying to justify it. I wanted somewhere to stay, and Maria offered to put me up."

It's funny, his candor about his conquests. He chronicles each and every dalliance in his memoir with *Penthouse Forum* detail. In person, he showcases his gusto at least once an hour, as he whips out his cell phone to brandish photos of the buxom foreign women with whom he corresponds online. While he is telling me all of this, I'm feeling an odd sense of rancor on Anne's behalf. But more surprisingly, I'm also feeling a weird sense of protectiveness toward John. What if he was getting catfished? He once showed me a photo of an ass in a thong, with no face attached. Then and at times like this, I fear he is getting played, either by a bored internet troll or a woman who probably thinks he has more money than he does. I find myself wanting to give him a tutorial on Google image searches. But I didn't. The ass without a face was a form of companionship in those days, so it seemed better left alone.

To my surprise, I found out later that the ass did indeed belong to a face. Darwin made headlines again a few months after I left England. The siren call of the thong was too much to resist, so he violated his probation—which required him to stay put in the United Kingdom—to travel to Ukraine to meet several prospects. While abroad, he emailed me daily installments, the first with the subject line reading simply "Urgent":

> *UK newspapers photographed me with 3 girls near the russian border in an Ukrainian city called Sumy. fallout will be terminal because I have an international travel ban. Its the third time I have been abroad since July*
> *I think I may be in prison over Christmas*

But the rest of his travelogue lacked this urgent tone, and included commentary on his media coverage, his inevitable punishment, and the more lubricious details of his sex tour:

> *apparently it is in the UK papers today. Wonder if it has a pic of the 3 girls I was out with that night. They threatened to follow me around Ukraine, but I lost them in the Crimea and this is why they have printed the story. I am 63 and the total ages of the girls was just over 70)))*

In spite of all the Olgas and Natashas he bragged of, and the international notches on his bedpost that he has recorded in his self-published book, he claimed that he would still get back together with Anne if she would have him. "It's difficult for a woman to understand." He's got me there.

In the years between his 2002 disappearance and his move to Panama in 2007, John bounced back and forth between women in the United States, visiting ladies in Kansas and Oregon. But he also took vacations with his wife to sun-drenched destinations such as Greece, Cyprus, and Spain. In airports, Anne would go ahead of John Jones in case there was any trouble. But they never found any.

I thought back to my first meeting with Frank Ahearn. I was so excited to talk shop and impress him with my knowledge of death fakers. (My friends were growing weary of my niche expertise.) Frank and I had talked about Sam Israel, of course, and Marcus Schrenker. Frank said those guys were "morons and idiots," but that Darwin was different. Unlike Israel and Schrenker, whose bad business ventures had already caught up with them, Darwin's financial troubles didn't offend the UK securities commission and angry investors. His crimes were smaller potatoes. "He was a regular guy," Frank told me. "Nobody figured he had anything to hide, so nobody thought nothing of it. Schrenker and that Israel guy faked their deaths because they were afraid of going to jail. John Darwin and his wife tried to get out of a financial crime, but they're a whole lot smarter."

I passed along Frank's compliments to John one brilliant afternoon. It's a good thing I stuck around to see Seaton Carew in the sunshine. Those rumors of the place being considered a seaside resort town made a tad more sense.

"That's his business," Darwin said, looking down at his boots, with a small smile curling his lips. "But I do remember reading in the paper that Ahearn said he would give me a job."

So what are John Darwin's Rules for Disappearance? Over a plate of shiny fried fish and mushy peas, the Canoe Man relays a few cardinal rules:

"Keep near enough the truth," he says. "Use your first name. That's a must. A disguise is another must, initially. If you don't change your appearance, it's because you're daft. You've got no brains. And it can't be just one thing, it has to be a number of things. I grew a beard, I wore glasses. I never used to wear a hat, so I put on a hat. I wore a different sort of coat than I would normally wear. Then I had a walking stick, a stoop, and a limp. You would look like a vagrant if you were dirty, but I was clean. Changing me appearance was easy. If you can think logically, anything is easy."

An interesting proposition, because faking one's death hardly seems logical. It actually seems like the ultimate whimsy.

So what else, Professor Canoe?

"Be vigilant." Stick to the story and anticipate obstacles.

John's experience violates one of the cardinal rules that Frank and Steve had hammered home: if you are going to disappear, you must be prepared to cut all ties. Anne was his wife, helpmate, financier, and accomplice. But filing an insurance claim puts the death faker in a catch-22, as one also needs a trusted co-conspirator. Darwin kept her on because, besides the fact that he loved her, he also needed her to collect the mortgage insurance on his behalf. And he knew that she was a safe bet: "Anne wouldn't tell anybody because she was implicated in it. It was self-preservation on her part."

Part of that protective instinct was to relocate to another country once they had sold off most of their property portfolio. "I couldn't hide under the bed when visitors came," John jokes. He researched options for the couple from his laptop while upstairs in the Cliff house. Choosing their safe haven became a process of elimination: "You've got to move abroad. You've got Spain and France close, but if we moved to France, people could use the Chunnel, fly over, take a taxi. My sons could have knocked on the door and, 'Oh my God! It's me dad!' You've got to go farther afield so it isn't in the range of a casual visit. So you choose the United States' Spain," he says, referring to Panama, a country that uses the dollar as its national currency and is increasingly popular with gringo retirees. Anne told colleagues, friends, and their sons that she wanted a complete change, to move somewhere free of association with her dead husband. That's why she decided on Panama. Quite the exotic move for the woman who'd never tasted cheese until she was in her twenties. Darwin credits the Northeast's provincialism as protection from nosy neighbors: "Panama is an obscure little country. Most people here can't tell the difference between a monkey and a Frenchman!" So Panama was the plan. He'd encountered no trouble traveling abroad for the past few years. Why would Panama be any different?

They began looking at houses to buy on their first trip to the country in July 2006, which is when the infamous photo of the couple in the realtor's office was snapped. They look happy and affectionate, and grin at the camera like satisfied pensioners. After John surrendered voluntarily in December 2007, claiming amnesia, a curious neighbor typed the search term "John Anne Panama" into Google, and the happy tableau turned up, the smoking gun proving that he had indeed faked his death.

But even despite this irrefutable photo evidence posted online, John still believes firmly that the technologies of the twenty-first century assisted his disappearance rather than hurt it.

"The internet helps people disappear," he explains. "You can find out what the culture's like, what the climate's like. I bounced my IP signal to change the address. The downside is if you don't change your appearance, there are multiple TV sets all over the world. That's why I changed my appearance so drastically." Given his likeness in the realtor's photo, perhaps he should have stayed in costume longer.

The first piece of property they purchased was a penthouse in Panama City for $90,000 in March 2007. The second was a five-hundred-acre plot of virgin jungle, which they picked up for $387,760 that same month. After John turned himself in, multiple newspapers reported that the two of them were planning on opening a bed-and-breakfast for kayakers. John says this rumor is false, and resents it. "We had around seven hundred thousand dollars in the bank, all from the sale of houses," he says. "So why, with all that money in the bank, earning a high interest rate, would you then open a B and B?" Darwin doesn't want you to get the idea that he was a petit bourgeois businessman. He wants to advance the image of himself as landed gentry. Really, he eventually planned on building a tropical courtyard house, hiring a gardener and a maid, throwing in a hundred head of cattle, and luxuriating in obscurity. But the couple never got the chance to build the hacienda of their dreams. Instead, they spent their time in Panama taking day trips to jungle spots and beaches, horseback riding and trekking. "It was like *Pirates of the Caribbean*," he says. "It was like a second honeymoon."

Anne had sold the first Cliff house in April 2007, and the

second in October. She went back and forth between Panama and England, settling their accounts, and John stayed. The couple had set themselves up in their retirement villa. But there was that unsettling fact of still owing money to the insurance company, and of their two sons still thinking their mother was a widow while she was riding horseback down the beach with their most sentient father. Now, with a healthy figure in the bank and a home established in Panama, the moment seemed opportune to make amends.

It was the end of November 2007, and the couple had crossed over to Costa Rica to renew their visas. On the way back, John asked Anne if she thought the time was right to turn himself in, which he claims had always been the plan. "As normal, she wouldn't give me a straight answer," John says. "I asked her if I should come back. She said, 'It's up to you.' I told her if I left, she would be in Panama all alone. If she'd said no, I wouldn't have gone. I wanted input. I'm not trying to pass the buck or anything. That's just fact."

John decided that it was time to face the music and turn himself in. I recalled what Steve Rambam had told me about investigating death fraud scams: that the odd fraudster will occasionally come clean due to a gnawing guilty conscience. When he named that obstacle as a consideration when one decides to fake death, it seemed ridiculous. Wouldn't the hubris of the act and the rush of getting away with it stamp out the sentimental bathos of returning to the drudgery in an attempt to make good?

But maybe it isn't hubris that is required to pull off a successful pseudocide. Maybe it's actually humility. Staying dead in the long run means keeping a low profile, without any audience to receive the story of your clever caper. Relating the tale is totally off-limits. If, as Frank described when he told me about helping people disappear, you become a humble landscaper working off the books, you can be *only* that. You cannot *also* be the humble landscaper who was once a would-be entrepreneur but faked his death instead. Hubris might propel the plan but it is humility that sustains it. And that might be the tallest order of all.

If John Darwin felt invincible, he had reason to. Through his death at sea, he had been reborn into a swashbuckling international man of mystery. And his relationship with his wife had grown stronger than ever trekking around the backwaters of an exotic land. So much for Mr. and Mrs. Average. The Darwins were living the dream. John had successfully faked his death, refinanced his problematic mortgages, and reorganized his mundane life to a shape that better suited him. He had flouted immigration and customs, and was leveraging a financial system that had screwed him to underwrite his adventures. So why wouldn't he be able to make good on his "loan" with the insurance company and repair his relationship with their mourning sons?

He didn't realize that circumstances wouldn't quite jell the way he had dreamed. John had expected to do some time and pay a fine, sure, but he didn't know that returning would cost him everything: all of his worldly possessions, not to mention a relationship with one of his sons and his marriage.

Anne stayed behind in Panama while John flew back to England. Once he cleared customs at London's Heathrow Airport, he ripped apart the John Jones passport page by page and scattered the evidence in different trash cans. Walking toward a police station in central London, he had mixed feelings: "I wanted to see the two lads again, but wondered if I was making a big mistake." He wandered into the station, saying that he'd lost his wife while shopping at Harrods department store. He also couldn't account for the events of that afternoon, that week—and really nothing prior to the year 2000. He had no identification on his person, just a few pound notes that Anne had given him from her last stay in the United Kingdom.

So how does posing as an amnesiac missing person square with paying back insurance money obtained fraudulently? "The amnesia bit was rigged to get a foot in the door into my sons' houses without putting them under suspicion as part of the crime. I know the police. If I had personally contacted my sons, they would accuse them of concocting a story," John explains as we walk along a busy highway in the late-afternoon sun. "I knew that's what would happen; that's why I did it the way I did. It was done for a reason," he says, bitter at how the British press made his story sound like a careless lark.

The police summoned his sons that night when they genuinely believed their father might be an amnesiac. I asked him what it was like seeing them for the first time in years, even when he was often just on the other side of a wall, unbeknownst to his grieving children.

"It was very emotional. They came to the station. They saw me in an office. It was very emotional," he says, his eyes cast down at the sidewalk as we trudge back to Seaton Carew. "I'll say in my defense, it's complicated."

For a few days, doctors and investigators examined the befuddled man who drifted in off the street. Trying to verify his lack of memory, they asked him what 7/7 (the day of the 2005 terrorist bus bombings in London) signified. He said 14. And 9/11? He told them 20.

I ask him if it was hard keeping up the act during his interrogation.

"It was second nature. I knew what they were going to ask me before they asked it."

But John didn't anticipate how things would shake out for him. As he imagined it, he would spend a few days with his sons and then be assigned to a community care officer, like a social worker in the United States. He knew this procedure from his time as a prison guard. According to his plan, after a day or two with his sons, a lightbulb would flash on in his head with the memory that Anne might have claimed some insurance money, and that they would pay it back. Darwin expected to go to prison but didn't imagine Anne would get charged.

The community care officer was appointed but never showed up, and the police realized that Anne had already received a hefty sum from the commercial mortgage payouts and John's teaching and prison guard pensions, totaling around £400,000 altogether. John said the police froze Anne's HSBC bank accounts, which, though opened in Panama, were under the jurisdiction of the British bank. John was arrested for fraud. The press got hold of the tale, and the "Canoe Man" emerged as the story of the year. Anne came back from Panama and turned herself in nine days after John had ambled into the Oxford Circus police station. Reporters were already on planes to Panama. Using the Proceeds of Crime Act, typically reserved for organized crime and terrorist organizations such as the Irish Republican Army, the court seized all of the Darwins' money and possessions. Eventually the couple would give up everything in exchange for shorter prison sentences. In the judgment of the Darwins' appeal, from March 27, 2009, the High Court judges Stephen Irwin and Wyn Williams wrote, "Anne and John Darwin are a married couple of previous good character. Together they set up a fraudulent conspiracy. The deception worked. . . .

Their return was not the consequence of remorse or a sense of guilt. What they were trying to do was to make up for the impact on themselves of the consequences of their own criminal activities."

=====

THE SUBJECT OF JOHN Darwin is a charged one around Seaton Carew and Hartlepool. I met up with musician JB at the Seaton Carew Social Club on a Saturday night to get the local read on Darwin. The front room was filled with older couples playing bingo under fluorescent lights, while in the back bar, men watched the Sunderland-versus-Arsenal soccer match. A rock band played covers upstairs. You can't smoke inside anymore, but the place still contains the heavy smells of decades of butts, stale beer, and disinfectant. I settled into a booth with JB and a couple of pints and asked him about Darwin.

"The irony about his faked death is that it turned him into a celebrity," he said. "He has two rooms named after him at the Staincliffe! People who have gone to jail for fraud wouldn't be too amused. I got heavily fined for fraud in the nineties, but I didn't become a celebrity. It cost me me marriage," JB said. One can understand the resentment. When I stepped outside for a smoke, I asked a middle-aged couple for a light, and they asked where I was from. We got to talking, and they were impressed that I had kept such close company with the Canoe Man all week. The woman was clearly tipsy but offered a drunken poetic insight: "When you meet people and really spend time with them, you realize they are good and bad, just like anyone."

Rumors about Darwin are rampant. That's what happens when your town becomes known as "Seaton Canoe." "I heard he knew the person whose identity he stole. It was a person he knew in a coal mining village who did something he didn't like," JB said ominously. I couldn't bring myself to tell him that the truth of John Jones is far more prosaic. I'll bet John Darwin would prefer this strongman version anyway.

"He was a prison officer. That's where he got the idea for the crime," a white-haired patron offered. JB thought that there were also positive feelings about Darwin around town: "A lot of people I know think he got one over on the system, and they like it. You've seen the news. The government is ripping people off and getting away with it, and profiting off it. In a nation where an ordinary guy like that carries out an act of fraud, they think he got one back on the system."

Over breakfast the next morning, my mustachioed inn-keeper echoed JB's sentiments: "That's a funny thing what he did, innit? The nerves to do it! I think he got overpunished. He didn't hurt anybody, he just fiddled away some money. You look on the news, and you see MPs doing that. The big insurance companies just wanted to make an example of him."

I am all for getting one back at the system. One day at lunch, I told Darwin of my own debt, the six-figure student loan that not even bankruptcy can absolve. "I'll show you a place where you can buy a canoe," he quipped, and we laughed. I reveled in the idea, and when JB framed Darwin's faked death as a jus-tified act of terrorism against an unjust system, I was tempted. But would it be worth the personal price?

John's return from the dead in 2007 set off a media feeding frenzy in the sleepy seaside town. Every hotel and bed-and-breakfast in the area was booked with reporters who stalked the Darwins until their trials ended. John was sentenced to six years and three months because he pled guilty. He served three years of his term. Anne pled not guilty ("because she's daft and listened to her solicitors," according to her ex-husband) and got six years and six months. Now John would be not the guard holding the keys but the crook locked up inside. He recalled his first day in Durham Prison, a stone building from the eighteen hundreds with "green slime on the walls."

"The first day I went out on exercise with the other prisoners, a group of inmates walked by. One of them called out, 'Hey, boss, do you remember me?'" Prisoners call guards "boss" in the United Kingdom, or "screw": one Victorian punishment was to set an inmate to run on a treadmill, which guards would turn up, or screw, forcing the prisoner to run faster and faster. "The guards were going crackers!" John remembered. "They shouted, 'He's not a boss, he's a prisoner!'" But John said he always felt more at ease with prisoners, although the *Hull Daily Mail* reported that Darwin was attacked by another inmate who recognized him from his time as a prison guard. This happened just days after Darwin was transferred to Everthorpe Prison in East Yorkshire. "I was never friendly with the other prison officers. Their idea of fun was getting blind drunk and ordering a curry. I didn't drink, I didn't swear, I didn't gamble. I'm quite well educated. As a prisoner, they wouldn't have lasted five minutes." John described his sentence as not so bad. Because he was a former corrections officer, he got his own cell. He wasn't lonely, because if he "wanted to have a sensible conversation, I just looked in the mirror and started talking." He spent a good deal of his sentence writing his memoir.

But it was in prison that John and Anne's relationship ultimately dissolved. If the Panamanian plot rekindled their marriage, serving time and becoming the press's pet pariahs broke them. It seems to me that Anne got it worse in the papers than John did, but he disagrees. While we are used to fathers bowing out on their responsibilities, Anne, as a mother who deceived her children, got painted wickedly. Headlines such as "Canoe Wife Is Guilty of Heartless Betrayal" and "Canoe Wife Disowned by Sons" were splashed daily across the tabloids. Between the relentless dissection of their lives and serving hard time, their thirty-five-year marriage ended in 2011.

While John was in hiding at the Cliff, Mark and Anthony often visited Anne for weekends. I don't broach this subject directly until our last day together. Darwin has been most criticized over this point—the one aspect of his caper that seems to get to him despite the constant justifications. If you knew your distressed children were on the other side of the wall, how could you not break through and embrace them?

"Let me put it this way," he explains. "You're on a slippery slope. You're at the top of the steepest ski jump in Wyoming. You can't just put the brakes on and stop. But it's very emotional."

John's boasting usually eclipses his subdued murmurings about the emotional tax, but there was no denying the sadness in his eyes. I think that, like so many of the men who fake their own deaths, he has found a way to compartmentalize the pain and make up for it in adventure and women. I wonder whether it is easier for a father to listen to his sons' voices and not respond than it would be for a mother.

As a middle-aged, middle-class heterosexual white man with a family, John represents the person most likely to fake his death. Indeed, an uncanny number of them are named John. I'd noticed this disproportion in the demographics, and I wondered if there was anything to it. Frank told me that the majority of his disappearing clients were men, and J. J. Luna, author of *How to Be Invisible: Protect Your Home, Your Children, Your*

Assets, and Your Life, told me that "far more men than women!" seek his "invisibility" services. In the 1996 guidebook *How to Disappear Completely and Never Be Found*, disappearance enthusiast Doug Richmond writes, "To a man of a certain age, there's a bit of magic in the very thought of cutting all ties, of getting away from it all, of changing names and jobs and women and living happily ever after in a more salubrious clime!"

But why do these seemingly privileged men, who enjoy every perk that DNA has to offer, feel so hemmed in that they must go off the radar entirely? Perhaps it's because although men still outearn women, they then entangle themselves in financial trouble trying to enhance their fortunes. Maybe they shrug off because they feel less responsibility to see their children grow and flourish. Women shoulder the burdens of family and community—they take care of dying parents, snotty kids, shut-in neighbors—anyone before themselves. Though that might be relying too heavily on conventional wisdom about gender roles, the numbers speak for themselves: faking death seems to be a heavily male phenomenon. After combing through the stories and examining the traits that men like John share, I noticed that they all seemed to feel emasculated, made impotent, by their mundane lives. So, not earning enough money, they invest in a harebrained scheme. Underwhelmed with their monogamous sex lives, they take up with other women. Faking death seems to be not only a way out but also, counterintuitively, a way to be brave.

In the rare cases that women do get caught faking their deaths, violence is sometimes a motivating factor, just as Frank had said. In the summer of 2015 a twenty-nine-year-old Pennsylvania woman feigned a fatal seizure while her abusive boyfriend whaled on her. Thinking he'd killed her, he called 911 to report her unconscious. Once safely with the paramedics, the woman admitted to faking her death to save her life.

Not that the circumstances are always tragic. To avoid jail time for shoplifting $2,500 from Macy's, Sarah C. Moretti of Nashville procured a fake death certificate stating she had overdosed. These two cases straddle the margins of life-threatening urgency and small-potatoes crime. Neither assumed the white collar mantle of Israel or Schrenker, or attempted an insurance fraud like Darwin.

Since John is a man who faked his own death, and since he has a lot of theories about women, I ask him why more men than women do the deed.

"Women don't have the gonads to do it. I've done the research. They don't seem to have them! Anatomically." He pauses. "I'm just trying to be funny. Men are normally more reckless, more adventurous than women. Women are more cautious and careful and think things through," Darwin opines. Or maybe women fake their deaths just as much as men. They just don't get caught.

While John routinely boasts of his relationships with various women one-third his age, he still holds a tender place for Anne. He resents the fact that she was the one to file for divorce. "She hasn't written or spoken to me since November 2010, when she said it was all over." She wanted the divorce on her own terms. "So much for the little woman who's under my thumb," he says.

"Do you think that's the way it's been portrayed?" I ask.

"Yes. When she talked to the papers, she said she was under my control. You've seen the photo of her on horseback in Costa Rica! Let's face it, she didn't look like my hand was up her back pulling the strings to make her smile. The other thing is that she had all the money from all the houses. I'm in Panama with a passport in the name of John Jones; no money at all except for what she's giving me. If she didn't like me that much, what's to stop her from going to Australia and taking all the money?"

It's hard to have it both ways: the cool strategist and the vulnerable husband.

John has another theory as to why Anne divorced him in prison.

"She befriended Tracie Andrews," a woman who'd been incarcerated for having stabbed her fiancé forty-two times in 1996. "I said to my son, 'I hear your mother's got a new friend. Are you inviting her to carve the turkey?'" He laughs to himself.

The tabloid press, of course, had a field day with this story.

"So the reason she wanted to divorce you was because she became a lesbian?" I ask. It seems totally ridiculous. She gets imprisoned because of her part in the plan he concocted, but she divorces him because she's suddenly gone sapphic?

"It seems funny that once she met Tracie Andrews, everything changed. She stopped writing, she wouldn't accept my calls. The reason she wanted the divorce was because of"—he mimes a stabbing motion and mouths the high-pitched background music to the shower stabbing scene in *Psycho*: *"Eee! Eee! Eee!"*—"but she's always been peculiar. If she came back tomorrow, I'm daft enough to say, 'Okay, I'll marry you.'" He then takes out his phone and pulls up a photo of a scantily clad woman. "She's thirty-eight years younger than me. But if Anne came back, I would still marry her."

———

TABLOIDS HAD REPORTED THAT Anne works at a charity thrift shop in York, a university town, and I intended to ask her a few questions. John was not thrilled when I mentioned it. He opposed my visit because he said it would make things tense between him and Mark, the son who still speaks to him; he does not want John talking to reporters; and surely Anne would let Mark know I'd been sniffing around. But it would be insane to come this far and not try to find Anne. If I couldn't speak to her, I wanted to at least see where she lived.

This is a woman who allowed her sons to think their father was dead for nearly six years, going so far as to throw petals out to sea and keep a single rose on his pillow, which I imagined John removed each night before resting his head. She profited from his pseudocide. But a part of me sympathizes with Anne. After all, John said that his wife really had no idea how many properties they owned at any given time. So maybe she's the woman who decided to stand by her man and bail him out, and ended up going to jail for him. Or have I fallen for the narrative that John claims is utterly false: that she was under his control?

I took the train on a classically drizzly English morning. Having come from Seaton Carew, stepping onto the platform of the York station felt like entering a thriving metropolis. It's a postcard-perfect university town, with art galleries, a Ferris wheel along the riverbank, specialty cheese shops, and ethnic restaurants enclosed within the ruins of a Roman wall. There's even a Topshop. When I saw it, I knew instantly that Anne had moved up in the world. Walking over a bridge and through the crowded, curving streets, I had the naive hope that I might spot her. According to the tabloids, Tracie Andrews gave Anne a makeover before she was released from jail, dyeing her white hair a fetching shade of chestnut brown. I searched the face of every woman of a certain age.

The charity shop where she is supposed to work is on a

street lined with cobblestones. I walked up and down the block four times before finally crossing the threshold of the shop, hoping she was scheduled. It seemed like a cozy place to work, full of the residue of well-loved things: scuffed handbags, board games missing pieces, junk jewelry, printed blouses, teacups, paperback romances. A teenager who looked like he should have been in school was working the register that day. I lingered by the mismatched china plates to eavesdrop on people in the back office. I ran my fingers over a cow-shaped saucer as I glanced over my left shoulder to see if Anne was there. I felt a mild nausea. It was a bit like stalking a celebrity. She wasn't there. I left a note and my card with the young man and went to the café down the block to wait with a mint tea. It rained softly on the window, and the whole town felt like a pleasantly drowsy afternoon nap. Anne never showed up. Still, I couldn't help but picture her peaceful here. This seems like a place where one could find a life of contentment, walking in the manicured parks and popping into bookshops, a few hours but worlds away from Seaton Carew.

BACK IN THE SEASIDE town, I meet John at his bungalow before having dinner at his local radio DJ friend's home in Hartlepool. "I hate the place," he says about his current residence. It's a bit damp and the ceilings hang low, but it's quaint. "It's a big shock coming from a house with seven bedrooms!" he says, remembering again his home at the Cliff. It doesn't seem polite to point out that his last residence was actually prison.

His home is a classic bachelor pad: dirty dishes in the sink, a hodgepodge of vinyl sofas and armchairs, computer cords and electrical wires strung across the floor, laminated photos

printed from the internet taped up on the wall. A photo calendar of his grandson is displayed prominently. He has rigged
a projection screen to occupy one of his living room walls, on
which he watches pirated movies throughout the night. Darwin
needs only four hours of sleep to feel refreshed. He pulls out
his laptop and shows me a live countdown clock ticking down
the seconds until his probation ends. Then he opens a painstak-
ing PowerPoint he made when he was dead to sell nos. 3 and 4
the Cliff, complete with clip-art seagulls flapping perpetually
in the breeze. The photos show a handsome middle-class home
and the back garden he designed. He looks proud as he shows
me what good work he did to the houses, the bourgeois life he
achieved.

I ask him how he feels at the moment, living here and waiting out his probation.

"Like a tiger on a leash," he says. "But I could disappear
tomorrow if I wanted to."

"But do you even have a passport, and wouldn't it get
flagged at the airport?" I ask.

"There's more than one way to leave the country."

John has always managed to get things done by his own
accord, to which he credits his charm. "I've found that whatever country I'm in, I must look like little boy lost. People want
to be friendly and help." He describes flirting with the clerk
who did his paperwork for his ID when he got out of jail. And
he projects this confidence into the next phase of his life, after
the liminal moment of his probation ending: "I'm sticking it
out here until March, and then I'm off. I've already booked my
plane ticket. I've got offers in the States. Wherever I go, I seem
to fall on my feet."

His local radio DJ friend, a barrel-chested real-life Alan

Partridge, picks us up in a black sports car and ferries us to his modern home on a cul-de-sac in Hartlepool. His girlfriend serves a delicious meal from her native Thailand. John asks the wife if she has a sister no fewer than three times. The bathroom is wallpapered with framed photos of the local radio DJ with reality-TV stars from *Big Brother*, contestants in singing competitions, provincial politicians. It's better to eat in, the DJ friend says. When John goes out, he often gets bothered by fans wanting his autograph. The other guest is a quiet but affable guy in local soccer promotions. He and John get into a heated debate about reopening the mines. John tells us it would be impossible because the tunnels have been flooded, and does a science teacher demo with his cutlery to illustrate why. They both agree that things in the Northeast went to hell after the mines lost their subsidies and closed. But the soccer promo man makes a good point: "I wouldn't want my kids going down the pit."

John recounts a memory from when he was young. He was playing outside, and saw two children roughly his own age walking home from a day at the mines. They were stained black from head to heel from the coal they had sorted all day. Their faces were covered in soot, and he could see only the whites of their eyes. It's an image that has lingered with him for almost sixty years, maybe because they are an example of what he has refused to be.

And who can blame him? For a man of John's generation, to struggle against such a rigid class system is to rebel. Having been born into the shambles of postwar England, to reject his working-class station is to dismantle the norms with which he grew up. But there are more pernicious ways in which class aspiration can wear you down, when striving alienates you from your peers and severs you from the middle class you seek to join. The Darwins' story was made into a BBC Four TV movie, which aired to healthy ratings in 2010. It also inspired the 2009 novel *Return from the Dead* and a plotline on the popular British soap opera *Coronation Street* and again in 2015 on *EastEnders*. Can it be that people relate to the pressures that propelled his pseudocide? After all, when your own father tells the tabloids that you have always had aspirations above your station, it becomes apparent just how immutable "stations," for some, remain.

For our last day together, John and I meet on a crisp morning. John asks if our Thai hostess had given me any cooking tips. He notes that I ate so much, my plane back to New York would likely not go aloft the next day. He says he doesn't like tattoos and then asks me about mine. If I didn't know better, I would say that John is attempting the misguided flirtation technique of "negging," where men lob insults at women with the intent of making them feel insecure. But maybe he is just weary of my questions by now. We walk along the waterfront to Hartlepool, retracing the journey along the front he often traveled when he was dead. I ask him what he considers to be common misperceptions of his story.

"Only the stupid people believe the police were onto me. If they were looking for me, why would they wait six years? Why didn't they just phone Panama?" And he never collected the £1 million the newspapers cited; it was really only about £260,000.

It must be an extraordinary thing, leading multiple lives: one as Mr. Average, one as the bearded ornithologist camping on the beach, one as Karl Fenwick, one as John Jones, and now one as the Canoe Man.

"So why did you decide to move back to Seaton Carew?" I ask him.

"Because I live here!" he answers.

Despite how much he complains about the crap English weather and conservative attitudes toward May-December relationships, for John, for now, this is home.

We walk around Hartlepool for most of the afternoon and then loop back to the Cliff, in front of his former houses, which are now in a state of disrepair. It's hard for John to see them this way. "They've gotten grottified," he says. The new owners have hung a stained-glass sailboat decoration on the front door. John does not approve: "It's tat, cheap, common," he says. I ask him about his plans for the future. He'd like to leave the damp fog of England. He knows he will marry again. (He did, in 2015, to a Filipina woman, Mercy May Avila, in her thirties.) "I'm nearly sixty-three, but I forget how old I am. I've got about twenty years left. I'm not going to sit around the house moping, I'm not going to live the life of a hermit. One son won't talk to me, but I'm not bothered."

"Do you think he's being unreasonable?" I ask.

"Put it this way, he changed his surname from Darwin. What name would be the biggest slap in the face?"

"Stephenson," I say, giving Anne's maiden name. He's surprised I know.

"That's the biggest slap in the face, which is to basically say he agrees with the Stephensons' side, which is: I'm scum."

"Do you feel angry about that?" I ask, though the answer is written on his face.

"It's his choice. He's an adult. When all of this happened, he was an adult."

We are accustomed to the narrative of bad behavior, apology, and redemption. I suspect that if John Darwin had been a Silicon Valley striver and paddled off into the San Francisco

Bay, he would have given a teary jailhouse interview with Diane Sawyer, and all would be absolved. I want him to say it. I want him to say he's sorry. So I set him up. I decide I will help him make the apology.

"Do you have regrets?" I ask.

"I'm not a demon! I came back to see me sons! Of course you've got regrets. I would have done many things differently. There are people I would have avoided like the plague. For one thing, don't do the crime." He pauses. "And if you do, don't come back. It's easy to fake your own death. It's damn difficult to come back."

"If you could go back and give your twenty-year-old self life advice, what would you tell him?" I press.

I'm ready for it: money isn't everything, family first, savor each moment, cherish your health, be grateful for what you have because you don't know when you'll lose it—the usual platitudes.

"I would have told myself how to make a lot of money."

I am shocked at first. What about the kids? What about Anne? But then, after thinking about it, I'm not shocked. You do need money. It's just that no one wants to talk about it. As Darwin said on our first day together, "Money isn't everything, but it's ninety-nine-point-nine percent of everything." I think he's right. Money and debt are what propelled me toward my fascination with death fraud and put me here with Darwin in the first place. When you have money, and especially when you come from money, it's easy to say that money isn't everything. Because money is just a fact of life.

But money is security, and security is a prerequisite to happiness. Money doesn't solve every problem, but it solves many problems. To negate the import of money is something that rich people do to feel better about themselves. I thought of a guy I dated for five minutes who had a trust fund. "I hate money," he said once. "Now, that is some shit only rich people say," I thought. Growing up with a single mom and always feeling on the precipice of ruin, I never had any big philosophical ideas about money, loving it or hating it. But I've always had a visceral instinct that I needed it, needed to make my own, and would always need to squirrel it away. So when that guy said he hated money as he enjoyed the home that money bought, the education it afforded, and all the questions he'd never have to ask, I just stayed quiet. I felt I had no claim on how to talk about money—and my craving for it—without sounding gauche or naive.

Maybe John's desire to accumulate didn't necessarily grow out of greed but rather out of a desire for stability. Greed is easy to see in others when you have enough. But when your origins are more humble, the goalpost of "enough" moves constantly. If John had socked away some savings, or had a fat inheritance in the works, he might not have turned to creative banking and put down payments on credit cards. Maybe, with a little more, he would not have felt so compelled to make risky wagers to get more. Maybe, comfortably enjoying bourgeois life, he would have felt as if he belonged rather than always feeling like an impostor. Money means membership. Money means safety. Money means never having to descend into the coal pits.

John left a trail of destruction in his wake. He hurt people, namely his family, and, like the 9/11 fraudsters, made fools of first responders and the loved ones who mourned him. But when you fake your death, you must go all the way. To turn around now and repent for the sins of abandonment and unburdening is to betray yourself, the choice you made when you realized you were worth more dead than alive. To admit wrongdoing would be to contradict not only the bold act of resistance but also the outlaw image of the Canoe Man. Before faking his death, when he attempted his minor business plans such as breeding snails and crafting garden gnomes, John Darwin was pure potential: an intelligent guy who had yet to fulfill his aptitude. In faking his death, he crystallized that capacity into something real.

What is clear to me about John's position now, back from the dead, is that he has to cling to his story. And whether the cost-benefit analysis of such a trade-off reveals John to be on the wrong side of the balance sheet is hard to tell. It seems like he has made the best out of the bad situation he created. Whether that is optimism or opportunism is harder to decipher.

"It's going to wee down," he says, pointing up to the black clouds rolling in from the west. The forecast predicted gale force winds and hail. "We better get inside before it begins."

He holds open the mahogany door for me as we enter the Staincliffe, in all its Victorian majesty: heavy wooden banisters, burgundy-colored drapes, floral-printed Oriental rugs. He points to the engraving on the door to a large banquet hall. It reads "Darwin Room."

A freckly teenage girl is sitting at the small reception desk. She will be visiting New York for the first time in October and asks me for some recommendations. We chat for a few minutes. She is lovely. Before we go into the Canoe Bar, John leans in and asks her, "Who is that room named after?"

She looks around, a little embarrassed by the peculiar yet obvious question, but answers anyway.

"You," she says.

He smiles, and we sit down to lunch.

4

THE BELIEVERS

At 1:14 p.m. on June 25, 2009, an unconscious fifty-year-old man under the alias Soule Shaun was checked into UCLA Medical Center. Doctors attempted to resuscitate him, without success. At 2:26 p.m., he was pronounced dead.

But Shaun's death isn't a cut-and-dried DOA. Establishing the true identity of the person who died that day and accounting for events in the twenty-four hours leading up to that afternoon prove difficult—and there are also some who have patched together the following underreported events to point to a death hoax conspiracy of the highest order.

When Shaun's bodyguard called 911, he never stated the name of the man going into cardiac arrest. When police took his live-in physician's statement, he stated that he had attempted to administer CPR. But instead of transferring the body to a hard surface, per standard operating procedure, he had begun chest compressions right on the bed when the man's heart stopped.

Relying on hard documentary evidence to establish basic facts also proves slippery. The two security cameras on the perimeter of the Holmby Hills estate where Shaun resided in the last years of his life show nothing: one of the cameras was inoperative, and some claim footage from the other was mysteriously destroyed by the Los Angeles Police Department. Some have noted that the ambulance that departed from the Carolwood Drive mansion transporting the body is not the same vehicle that arrived at the hospital. In a grainy video captured on a phone, you can see two figures jumping out of the back of the ambulance in the hospital parking garage and stealing away into the shadows. One news outlet reported that Shaun had actually expired six minutes before he was supposed to have died, at least according to the coroner's report. The photo of Shaun on the stretcher looked phony. And the body that was transported from the hospital to the coroner's via helicopter also shows peculiar discrepancies. Leaving UCLA, the body is secured with straps. But when the corpse is pulled out after arriving in downtown LA, those straps are gone.

Shaun had been dropping hints that he might be up to something for the past few years. He referenced *Gilda*, in which a man stages his death and later returns triumphantly, in one of his last public presentations.

At his eventual resting place, he wouldn't be listed in the cemetery's database. There would be no name engraved on his tomb.

And days before the ambulance carted away his body, a courier rang the doorbell of the mansion on Carolwood Drive. He was dropping off $2 million in cash to Soule Shaun.

Soule Shaun is the alias under which Michael Jackson was checked in at the hospital that fateful day.

For some, puzzling out what happened since has become a life's work.

=====

"I'M JUST GIVING YOU the facts," Pearl Jr., a regally stunning African American woman, tells me. "It's up to the interpreter to decide." To understand Michael Jackson's death hoax, she argues, one must look at the "accumulation" of "evidence." Isolating a mere trifle, like the fact that, say, Michael Jackson has not been seen by any human eye or camera lens since June 25, 2009, is insignificant when you look at all the "clues" he has delivered to fans that he is alive. "As a stand-alone thing," she explains, "it would sound ridiculous. But when you accumulate a thousand things, then it makes sense." Which is why Pearl says she doesn't waste her time proselytizing to people who won't invest in examining the myriad anomalies surrounding his death. She'd rather not sound like a fool.

While Steve Rambam and Frank Ahearn approach death fraud as skeptics—they both believe it is nearly impossible to pull off, despite John Darwin's success, albeit temporary—Pearl occupies the opposite end of the spectrum. She and many Believers, a fringe group within the complex and sprawling fan base of the King of Pop, trust with all their hearts that Michael Jackson faked his death with panache and aplomb, and that he even communicates with them from beyond.

As the public face of the Believers, Pearl is deft at marshaling and arranging her facts. I first stumbled upon the self-proclaimed "Michael Jacksonologist" while combing Netflix one night in 2011, when her homespun documentary *Alive! Is*

Michael Jackson Really Dead? was one of the most popular ti-
tles streaming at the time. I was mesmerized by the way she
peppily narrates the peculiarities around Jackson's death with
a broadcast-news smile on her face, all to the creepy, haunted-
house background music of straining strings. She walks her
audience through what she considers an insurmountable heap
of evidence that Jackson is alive. Her exhibits range from the
compelling (conflicting autopsy reports and discrepancies in
legal documents); to the less compelling (brother Marlon Jackson wearing an FBI hat the day after "the death announcement," to signal that the family and feds are in cahoots); to the
absurd (if you examine closely Jackson's face on the cover of his
posthumous release *Michael*, you can make out the message "I
Live" on his lips).

Pearl was just as chipper when we spoke on the phone
the first time, pleased that someone in the mainstream media
was interested in this bombshell of a story. She is evangelical
about spreading the good news that He Lives and will return
in a Christlike second coming. But oddly, I didn't sense that I
was speaking to a wackadoo with too much time on her hands.
She'd done the work. She had an answer prepared to counter
my every quibble. At the time, the Jackson family was still
in litigation over his "death," and she told me there would be
big reveals coming soon. When I said that I'd love to tag along
and watch her at work piecing together her clues, she said she
would gladly show me how it's done. I had already encountered people who were intimately enmeshed in the world of
death fraud: those who had considered it, attempted it, or investigated it. There must have been others out there who had
succeeded at it, though I hadn't been able to track down any. I
never got that anonymous phone call in the middle of the night

from somebody assumed dead asking me to meet him at a Starbucks. But what about those who thought they'd done what I couldn't and solved a mystery?

=====

IT WAS IN THE Polo Lounge of the Beverly Hills Hotel that I witnessed just how profoundly Pearl's belief colors her worldview. With the hotel's decades-long no-cameras policy, stars can sip martinis in repose without fear of swarming paparazzi. As a result, you can't swing a Birkin bag in the lush mahogany-and-glittering-gold dining room without hitting a star, whether brilliant or burned out. We selected the overpriced restaurant for an early dinner this evening because Michael (first name only) used to take a lot of meetings here. We had Michaeled all day long ("Michaeling" is a verb, you see, which means something like half sleuthing and half stalking), and we were famished.

All three female onetime cast members of *Friends* were sharing appetizers in the crescent booth to our right. Lionel Richie was holding court at the bar. Even by slovenly LA standards, Pearl and I skewed casual in our sensible Michaeling attire: she, statuesque in a tropical pink floral dress, and me in jeans and heels (out of character for this hobo, but we were driving instead of walking, since hell*looooooo*! This is LA!). We acted like we belonged. And in turn our waiter treated us, somewhat skeptically, like we belonged. Pearl's self-possessed swagger was infectious. She exuded this plucky aplomb no more than when she accosted Cedric the Entertainer, who was outfitted inconspicuously in a lime-green polo and straw fedora.

"Hey, Cedric! How you doin'?!" she cooed as the comedian ambled past with his entourage.

They exchanged pleasantries, while I was simultaneously thrilled and mortified. Living in the haughty, nose-in-the-air celebrity climate of New York, I've learned to pretend to ignore movie stars in the wild. But Cedric the Entertainer! Enjoying a low-stakes nosh? In the words of *Us Weekly*, "Stars—They're Just Like Us!"

Pearl, however, was unfazed by the encounter. After bidding Cedric good night, she leaned over and whispered, "Once you think you're talking to the King of Pop every night, anyone else is like, 'Who are you?' "

Earlier on our Michaeling itinerary, when we were crawling on the 405 freeway in rush-hour traffic on our way to Jackson's last residence, Pearl revealed that she regularly communes with "a close friend" who goes by the name Peter Pan. The night before, when we confirmed our Michaeling plans, she mentioned that we might have occasion to rendezvous with this Peter, and that he is "very important." She believes Peter to be Michael Jackson.

Though they have never met in person, they have spoken on the phone for "over a thousand hours," and regularly watch movies together over the wire, pressing the Play button simultaneously. They talk about ordinary things such as work and family. He opened the Twitter account @PeterPanPYT one day before the "death announcement" and he predicts big Michael Jackson reveals. "I haven't pinched his skin," she admitted. "But the voice, how sweet he is—it's him."

If you are a Michael Jackson fan (and if you think you are a Michael Jackson fan—like, you throw your hands up when "Don't Stop 'Til You Get Enough" comes on in the club—then you haven't met a Michael Jackson fan), enjoying virtual hangouts with your idol would be the pinnacle of your earthly existence. And since Michael Jackson died (or didn't, depending on whom you talk to), chittychatting with him on the phone would be a transcendent ecstasy. Given the squeals of unmitigated joy that pour forth from Pearl when discussing her love for Michael, it's hard to overstate just how much his attention means. No wonder enduring boring, old, fully sentient Cedric felt anticlimactic.

It's not that Pearl doesn't realize how crazy all of this sounds. "I'm not the kind of person who believes in death hoaxes! I'm a very sensible, logical, feet-on-the-ground type of girl," she says. She is so pragmatic that her nom de plume (or nom de guerre, as she is also the target of much vitriol), Pearl Jr., doesn't include her surname. She keeps her Michaeling life and her professional life in sales in two separate hemispheres. "I don't want to be the Michael-Jackson-Is-Alive lady!" she said.

And how did Pearl and Peter become acquainted? "I believe that Michael has been watching me from afar for years and years," Pearl explains. In some ways, everything in Pearl's life—all the divinely ordained synchronicity and coincidence guiding her to be in the right places at the right times—has been propelling her toward Jackson. And Pearl is one of the most vigilant Believers. Michael would be remiss not to reach out to his staunchest defender.

Eight months after Jackson's "death announcement," Pearl saw the evidence mounting that he had actually staged the greatest caper of all time, and she could be silent no longer. Since February 2010, she has been on a mission to spread the good news. She is the auteur behind her own multimedia lifestyle brand, which is equal parts freelance detective, investigative journalist, and Twitter provocateur. She is the author of the first-ever "emoviebook," which is entitled *Pseudocide: Did Michael Jackson Fake His Death to Save His Life?* and available on Amazon. Released in May 2010, it is a 442-page stream-of-consciousness tome chock-full of links to her You-Tube videos.

Listen to her, and the world starts to look like one big scavenger hunt. Forget about banal, everyday life. Take, for example, the spate of previously unreleased songs made public since the so-called death announcement. Michael's 2013 single "A Place with No Name" is a wink to his alleged final resting site at Forest Lawn Memorial Park, where his grave is unmarked. Pearl urged me to look at this in chorus with other oddities: "You need to ask yourself, why is there no name on his grave? Why does Forest Lawn not have him listed in the database? Why are all his death documents in the wrong name?" She was referring to the fact that his death certificate was made out to "Michael Joseph Jackson," when legally he was only "Joe." To Pearl and the Believers, that holy trinity of peculiarities—no name on his grave, no listing in the cemetery's index, and the wrong middle name—are the crux of his death hoax.

Pearl was not always "the Michael-Jackson-Is-Alive lady," but she has always been an agitator. She has an unrelenting can-do attitude and supports several causes. She described herself as "an activist, first and foremost. I'm flighty, but I get things done!" The mother of two adult children, she lives in Palmdale, California, a dusty suburb an hour north of Los Angeles. In 1989 she graduated with honors from California State University at Northridge, having majored in broadcast journalism with a minor in African American studies. She is the author of three non-Michael books: *The Climate: A Perspective Unvisited*, which argues that "the prehistoric climate created racial mentalities"; the dating advice book *How to Tame a Dawg: The Pussy Kat Ain't Doin' It!*; and *Black Women Need Love, Too!*, which "exposes the conspiracy to keep Black

Women single." The writer and pundit Dr. Earl Ofari Hutchinson mentored her when Pearl hosted her own local TV show *TRUtalk: Straight Outta L.A.*, which is how she initially fell into the Michael world. Hutchinson had served as a TV commentator on the 1995 O. J. Simpson trial and hoped to lend his insight into Jackson's 2005 molestation proceedings. He sent his protégée Pearl Jr. to the Santa Maria courthouse to pass out flyers.

She was less than impressed. She had no desire to lurk around, but said, "Earl had helped me so much, he was one of those people I couldn't say no to." Her videographer, Cecil Rhodes III, suggested that they tape an episode of *TRUtalk* reporting from the trial. Unexpectedly, she gained full press access and attended the trial almost every day until Jackson was acquitted of all charges. Pearl and Cecil went on to self-produce a documentary film about the trial, called *Michael Jackson: The Trial and the Triumph of the King of Pop*. And thus a Jacksonologist was born, or, rather, anointed. "God made all these things work," Pearl said.

In the years between her up-close-and-personal access at the 2005 trial and the "death announcement" in 2009, Pearl became more enmeshed in the fan community. In the months when Jackson was living with his three children in a French château–style mansion on Carolwood Drive in Holmby Hills while rehearsing for This Is It!—his fifty-date residency at London's O2 arena, scheduled to open on July 13—Pearl hung out by the gate, listening to music and chatting with other hard-core fans. A handful of those ubiquitous fans were known as the Followers, who trailed him across the globe and camped out wherever he slept. Pearl got a tip from a friend who sells star maps and happened to be in front of Jackson's home when the ambulance arrived on

June 25. She says she issued the first tweet alerting the world to the trouble. Pearl then drove to UCLA Medical Center to see what was up. "I was there at the hospital when I saw his mother rush in, I saw the SUVs, I saw the ambulance," she said. She spent the next eight months in a trough of depression, mourning her idol. "I cried every day," she said. "Every day. I took it as a personal insult. I said to God, 'How could you bring me so close to him and then kill him on me?' I didn't deserve it."

Pearl would eventually become a spokeswoman for the Believers, but she was not the first to suspect that he'd faked his death. She started receiving tips from fans who had liked her work on the 2005 molestation case. She had been a sympathetic, "independent" journalist, unlike the other media hounds, who, in the fans' opinion, had been out to crucify the singer just to sell newspapers. Soon fans across the globe were sending her daily clues pointing to suspicious circumstances. Such as: the ambulance that arrived at UCLA had different hubcaps than the one that left Carolwood Drive; the photo of Michael on the stretcher looks suspiciously Photoshopped from an earlier image of the artist lying onstage; and Jackson's name was never mentioned in the 911 call. But under a heavy blanket of mourning, Pearl could easily explain away these speculations.

Then one afternoon Pearl happened across the book *Is Elvis Alive?* by Gail Brewer-Giorgio on Cecil's bookshelf. In the 1988 book, which has sold over a million copies, Brewer-Giorgio examined the fishiness surrounding the King's death: his middle name, Aron, was misspelled "Aaron" on his grave; mobsters were out to kill him for collaborating with the FBI; funeral attendees reported a dummy body with pasted-on sideburns in the casket. Reading this book was Pearl's epiphany. She remembered "throwing it across the room" when she realized

"Michael had followed Elvis's plan to a T." The truth could no longer be denied.

Since that fateful day, Pearl has spent the bulk of her leisure time piecing together the codex of clues Michael left behind for devotees to solve. "Evidence, proof, conjecture, coincidence, synchronicity, and facts. That's all we have," she said. Some might be troubled by the wide chasm between "conjecture" and "proof," but that does not dampen Pearl's intrepid investigatory spirit. The Forest Lawn cemetery, where Jackson is *not* buried, is a main target for her ire. Because after years, there is still no name on the side of the Great Mausoleum where he allegedly dwells, alongside actors Elizabeth Taylor, Jean Harlow, and Red Skelton. All of those other names are emblazoned proudly across their tombs. But if you search the cemetery's interment records for "Michael Joe Jackson," nothing shows up. Pearl finds this highly suspicious.

The majestic Disneyland of death was key on our Michaeling itinerary. We drove through the strip malls, manicured lawns, and big-box stores of Glendale in Pearl's comfortable black Chrysler up to the Forest Lawn security booth. The man inside, a bored twentysomething in an ill-fitting gray suit, asked if we needed assistance.

"Excuse me!" Pearl shouted. "We are here to see Michael Jackson! Is his name up there on Holly Terrace yet?"

"Uh, no, not yet."

"Well, *why not?*"

"I don't know, it's just not there yet. Do you want a map?"

He handed us a photocopied key to the stars' graves, and we drove up the crest of the hill to the mausoleum where Michael isn't. "*They still have no name!*" Pearl exclaimed, punching the steering wheel and pressing on the gas. Earlier in the day, we had driven out to the Jackson family estate in Encino, where we lingered outside the gate until security came to shoo us away. A delivery truck carting pink and purple petunias arrived, and we stood aside to behold the gate opening onto the compound of show business's greatest family. "Those were dinky little flowers! Someone is moving in soon!" Pearl said definitively. Could that someone be the King of Pop? Later that night, she tweeted this "clue" to her 9,600 followers.

We parked outside the Romanesque mausoleum at Forest Lawn, where fans from all over the world have left behind a shrine of stuffed animals, flowers, and construction paper cards. Pearl declined to have her photo taken. "I don't want to be associated with that," she said, waving her hand over the trinkets. "Still no name!" she muttered as we climbed back into the car.

We were on to our next stop: the afternoon court session of the negligence lawsuit Katherine Jackson filed against AEG Live, the promotion company responsible for the This Is It! concert series. The Jackson family matriarch charged that the company did not properly investigate Michael's physician, Dr. Conrad Murray, before hiring him. I had watched all of Pearl's YouTube videos, in which she collages together granular pieces of evidence like this, and yet I still hadn't quite figured out some more plaguing fundamental questions, such as: How did he do it?

"Cryonics," Pearl stated plainly on our way downtown. "Michael was obsessed with the process of cryogenic freezing, like Walt Disney. All he would have to do is find a cryogenically frozen body around the same height and weight, a body of a person who had died from a drug overdose, and switch them out." That's all! Picturing MJ dressed as a cat burglar, I imagined him sneaking into a climate-controlled vault and holding up a cryogenically frozen corpse (three hundred or so exist in the entire world) as if he were considering an expensive Italian suit.

One imagines that Jackson could not single-handedly carry out all of the preparations to fake his death. So who was in on it—other than the FBI, of course? "It's kind of like a terrorist cell," Pearl explained. "One cell has a job and a duty, but they don't know what the whole plan is. I don't think Michael shared his plan with many people. Everybody had roles, but nobody had the perfect plan."

And where might he be today? "He could be on Marlon Brando's private Tahitian island! It would be his payback for making Michael pay him a million dollars to appear in the 'You Rock My World' video." Brando predeceased Jackson in 2004, but perhaps they are relaxing in the South Pacific sun together?

And how would Michael Jackson negotiate airport security?

"His passport doesn't expire until his birthday this year," Pearl said.

"But wouldn't customs or immigration flag it?" I asked.

"The FBI! Now go back to Marlon Jackson in the FBI hat! The FBI is in on it."

"He must have had a very high security clearance," I said skeptically, yet trying on the cockeyed logic.

"And lots of people are named Michael Jackson."

"But if it's a picture of *the* Michael Jackson on the passport—"

Pearl cut me off. "I don't know. I'm just here to tell you he's doing it."

When we arrived at the 111 North Hill Street Courthouse in downtown LA, Pearl briskly led the way up to the courtroom. She tries to come to the Katherine Jackson versus AEG Live trial whenever she can, which often means using a vacation day from work when she knows a high-profile witness will be testifying. I thought for sure I would need some kind of press credential to get into this trial, which was receiving national coverage, but we breezed right in. Seated in the front row was Katherine Jackson herself, in a long floral skirt and blue blazer. Several other Jackson family members flanked her. Paul Gongaware, co-CEO of AEG Live Concerts West division, was testifying, and he didn't seem to recall much of anything. But I was not interested in the particulars of this lawsuit, or the brash attorneys up front billing thousands of dollars a day for the duration of the months-long proceedings.

What enraptured me were the dozen or so fans in the gallery. One birdlike white woman crocheted the whole time. An African American woman with a bleached buzz cut like SisQó's took notes in a small diary. And there in a white fedora was William Wagener, CEO of the M.J.J. Innocent Forever Foundation. Its mission? To prove that Jackson was a "singing, dancing saint." Pearl and I sat next to an attractive younger woman who, I later learned, harbors perhaps the most peculiar theory about Jackson's untimely demise: that he was kidnapped and is being held hostage by his record label, which is forcing him to pen songs for other artists.

Pearl rolled her eyes when Taaj Malik entered the courtroom with long, colorful scarves trailing behind her. Malik, a Pakistani-British woman with kohl-rimmed eyes and *Love* tattooed across her knuckles, is the leader of Team Michael Jackson, which supports the Jackson family's desire to hold AEG accountable for the singer's murder and wants to preserve Jackson's good name. Larry Nimmer, a videographer who testified at the 2005 molestation trial for Jackson's defense team and subsequently earned minor fame in the fan community, described Malik lovingly as "a passionate Michael Jackson fan" and "a gangster girl with an English accent." Pearl was visibly annoyed by her dramatic entrance. "I'll tell you later!" she mouthed to me as court carried on.

Most of the Jackson superfans I talked to agreed that prior to his death/"death," fans were united in "clearing his name" and protecting him. They remain deeply troubled by the unfounded molestation accusations tainting the singer's reputation and blame "the media" for twisting Jackson's innocent, childlike nature into something much more sinister in the name of a salacious story. *Bullying* is a verb they use often to describe the treatment "Wacko Jacko" got in the press. The fans seek to undo the media narrative popularized by British journalist Martin Bashir in his 2003 *Living with Michael Jackson* documentary of Michael sharing beds with children. Jackson cooperated with the documentary (though Bashir was accused of manipulating Jackson by pretending to revere his lifestyle) and sat for extensive interviews over an eight-month period. Instead, fans want to emphasize his charity work and benevolence.

When I asked Pearl what "clearing his name" would look like, she said it would involve retractions from journalists like Bashir and raising awareness about Jackson's good works. For several years, William Wagener has been trying to raise money to fund a full-length feature film to educate laypeople on the graft and political corruption he claims caused the Santa Barbara County District Attorney's Office to put Jackson on trial in the first place. One Jackson fan, who wished not to be named, likened the impulse to clear his name to protecting a loved one. "Imagine a family member," she said. "A father, brother, or son was accused of child molestation. Wouldn't you do everything in your power to bring the truth to light?"

Since June 25, 2009, the formerly tight-knit fan community has splintered into factions (though Malik told me later, "There have always been fights over who is a better fan"). As soon as the ambulance left Carolwood Drive, fissures erupted, and even some years-long friendships dissolved. Every fan asserted that she (hard-core Jackson supporters are almost inevitably female) alone had the right story. Larry Nimmer walked me through the schisms at the time of the 2013 trial: "Some individuals think it was murder, because Michael owned the Beatles catalog. Most fans think it was really AEG's fault, and that Conrad Murray was negligent." It was Dr. Murray who administered the lethal intravenous dose of the general anesthetic propofol.

Nimmer identified two main groups that polarized the fan community: "One group defended the estate, and the other group defended Katherine Jackson." The estate group believes that the executor who carried out Jackson's will, powerhouse entertainment attorney John Branca, acted within his rights and had Jackson's children's interest in mind. The Katherine Jackson supporters, led by Malik, vociferously seek to punish AEG for his murder and to reveal Branca as a criminal. In Malik's words, the estate side "sees Michael as a product. We are the only ones who see him as a human being, as a man, as a father, as a son, as a sibling." The estate group declined to comment.

To an outsider, these distinctions might seem like splitting hairs: Jackson, whether dead or alive, is gone (for now), so why can't they all just get along? But within the über-fan community, owning the right narrative is a matter of grave consequence, so to speak. Most of the infighting happens online, in the form of websites, blogs, Twitter accounts, and Facebook groups. But the differing online opinions have real-world outcomes.

Malik described the vitriol that opposing fans lob her and Team Michael Jackson's way: "They call us conspirators, they call us crazy people. There is a lot of adversity against me in the community. There are a lot of hate blogs against me. People target me with daily attacks. In the last three days, I've had four people calling me a thief and a con artist." A Jackson fan from a warring faction nabbed photos of Malik's daughter from her Facebook page and edited them into several videos posted on YouTube under the pervy title "Aspiring Model to Be." The videos were receiving thousands of hits a day, and Malik had to involve the police in order to have them removed. Because of Malik's active support for the Katherine Jackson camp—she attends court and purchases transcripts with fan donations to post on her website, and was the subject of a profile in the *Los Angeles Times*—she has become friends with certain members of the Jackson family, which does not sit well with some fans. "When I started associating with Joe," the Jackson family patriarch, Malik said, "the fans accused me of having sex with him." Proximity to their idol is everything, and jealousy runs rampant.

But as contentious as the estate versus Team Michael Jackson division is, no group within the fractured fan community is more reviled than the Believers. Fans are quick to condemn Believers leadership for propagating what they see as a bogus story for personal gain. "I think Pearl Jr. is a horrible person," Malik said plainly. "She's exploiting fans and using their grief, and benefiting from it financially."

I asked Pearl if she profits from her death hoax products. She said she doesn't, explaining that she got a bad distribution deal for *Alive!* and that her self-published "emoviebook" only "sells a few copies here and there." She keeps up with her Michaeling as a public service. "It's a sacrifice," she said. "I just want to get the information out there." Whether Pearl profits from her efforts or not, many in the fan community find her work distasteful. One fan expressed concern for Pearl's devotees, saying, "If Michael Jackson was your whole life, you can't let go of him. I'm actually worried that those people who are following Pearl Jr. will hurt themselves when they realize he's not coming back."

Larry Nimmer remembered a contentious scene at the 2013 Conrad Murray trial, where Michael Jackson's doctor was found guilty of manslaughter: "Pearl Jr. was reporting at the trial, and she got into a lot of arguments with people because they felt what she is doing is cruel. She's giving Michael's kids hope that he's alive, and other fans think that's hurtful." Debbie Kunesh, the creator of the Michael Jackson site *Reflections on the Dance*, added: "In some ways, I feel the hoax makes a joke out of his death and the mourning his friends and family have gone through." I think another resentment Pearl's detractors hold on to is that she espouses a counternarrative, and there is no room in the estate versus Team Michael Jackson debate for another, far more extreme story.

=====

"THERE WERE A LOT of anomalies around June 25, 2009," William Wagener, the fedora'd independent journalist, was telling me as we stared out at the sun going down on the Pacific. "Things were weird, and I'm not talking about the fans this time," he added, laughing. I first spoke to Wagener at Larry Nimmer's birthday party at his family beach house in Carpenteria, California. Wagener that day was wearing a polo shirt emblazoned with a print of the Constitution. He has the light eyes and sandblasted tan skin of a Californian, and looks like he could have been a Beach Boy. He became enmeshed in the Michael Jackson world during the 2005 molestation trial, when he claims to have seen widespread corruption originating in District Attorney Tom Sneddon's office. Like Pearl, he too had a local cable-access TV show. He received full press access and attended the trial every day.

When it comes to the myriad "anomalies," as he describes them, around Michael's death/not death, he does not believe the fans are asking the right questions. "Why did Dr. Conrad Murray call Michael's assistant instead of 911?" Another thing he told me that I had never heard before: "A courier delivered over two million dollars to the house just days before" on June 25. "And I talked to that courier. Nobody has talked about that money: not Conrad Murray, not La Toya"—Michael's second oldest sister—"who claims to have gone to the house shortly after Michael was declared dead. Nobody."

But Wagener has a different theory from Pearl about Michael's motivation for faking his death. Rather than simply laying low to recoup time to "clear his name," Wagener suggests that Michael was at the center of a plot orchestrated by defense contractors and other evil sorts. Because Wagener reported each day from the 2005 trial and always contended that the star would be acquitted, he received a call from Michael himself one day while he was driving down the freeway. "Michael called me on the phone and wanted to know who was behind Tom Sneddon," he said. "I told him his enemies are in London, and if you go there, they'll kill you." Coincidentally or not, London is where the This Is It! engagement was to run.

I asked him who Michael's enemies were.

"His real enemies are the people making profits from wars, while he's singing about healing the world. Michael is trying to stop the wars. Princess Diana isn't talking about stopping wars anymore now, is she?" He paused to let that sink in. Then he continued. "There's a great motivation for a hoax. When you know you can't win, and they're going to kill you anyway, and you know they killed Princess Di, and now you're going to die . . . maybe it's time to disappear. This is about Michael trying to stop World War III and the people who continually gain more control over us. And that is the key that the fans are continually missing."

When I asked Wagener if he believes that Michael did indeed fake his own death, he is a bit more temperate. He hedged, saying, "In this kind of world, you ask me to prove if Michael is dead or alive based on official records? The only way I would know he's dead is if I saw the autopsy, if I saw them peel back his skull. When you're dealing with a system that's this corrupt, how can you believe anything you don't see with your own eyes?"

Total distrust and disenchantment with the official narrative is a grievance that all of the Believers—and, really, everyone I spoke with from Sam Israel to Frank Ahearn to Steven Rambam—agreed on. Things are not as they seem. But Wagener sees the problem as much more sinister than simply Michael's self-exculpation. He sees uncovering the truth about the plot against Michael as arming himself with authentic knowledge. "It's like *The Matrix*," Wagener contended. "Do you want the truth, or do you want to remain ignorant?" Wagener also takes a keen interest in the "truth" behind 9/11 and President Barack Obama's birth certificate. He explained the real reason why the government gets away with such malfeasance.

"They're doing things that are patently illegal because people are too busy watching *American Idol* or *The Voice* or *Dancing with the Stars*. Women are busy doing their lesbian porn, and men are busy doing sporn."

"I don't know what that is," I confessed.

"The substitute for real porn is sports. Men get all thrilled on basketball and football games, and then a month later it doesn't matter."

Now, I agree with him regarding the epidemic of amateur lesbian erotica sweeping the nation. Lately I can barely get any of my lady friends to keep dinner plans, so consumed are they with creating sapphic cinema. But men obsessed with sports? Not ringing any bells.

Wagener listed some of the more outlandish Believers theories he encountered while attending the Conrad Murray trial, although ranking them as to their weirdness was beginning to seem a fool's errand. "People have made allegations that they saw pink elephants and toys around the judge, and indicating that this was all a hoax by Michael. I had dozens of fans tell me that when Murray is convicted, before he's sent out in handcuffs, Michael is going to walk into the courtroom and say, 'See how easy it is to get somebody convicted of something he didn't do?' So that would teach the non–Michael Jackson fans a lesson."

I asked Wagener what he thought of Pearl Jr.'s work around the death hoax, and some of the critiques in the fan community against her methods. He's known Pearl since the 2005 molestation trial, and she interviewed him for her documentary *Michael Jackson: The Trial and the Triumph of the King of Pop*. "When you start talking to Pearl Jr., the moon might indeed be made out of green cheese," he said. "She is trying to make money.

She was selling her DVD about the '05 trial for thirty bucks a pop, and it didn't tell you anything. I don't dislike the woman; I just think she does real shoddy journalism." (Pearl maintains firmly that she is not making money from her Michaeling. "I'm not earning a living off it, though I wish I was," she told me.)

Because Pearl Jr. has positioned herself as the public face of the Believers, she bears the brunt of antipathy. But the theory that Michael Jackson faked his own death extends far beyond Pearl Jr. Olga, an elfin young Uzbek woman with doll-like features and a dry sense of humor, explained Jackson's death hoax to me as a portal into an alternate reality that unlocks doors to wisdom that far transcends squabbles in the fan community.

"I don't follow Pearl Jr. much," she told me at a chain café one Friday afternoon after clocking out of her office job. "Basically, she's the last person I would look to." Olga doesn't consider herself a fan but rather "an admirer." When Jackson's death was announced, she was surprised that she "didn't feel anything." But a few days later, she found herself overwhelmed with grief—and questions. "It felt like such a huge betrayal of universal law," she said. "He's such a great person; how could it be this way?" She found her way to a website devoted to pseudocide theorists known as the Michael Jackson Death Hoax Investigation. Poking around the "facts and evidence" culled by investigators from all over the world, she was floored by how many things seemed prestaged. There were website domains for the hoax registered on June 23 and June 24, mere hours before he supposedly died. There were two different helicopters transporting him, with two different bodies inside. "It was like a Russian doll," she said. "You can open it and open it."

The secrets nestled inside surpassed even the hoax itself.

Like Plato's cave, like Wagener's matrix, Olga sees Jackson's faked death as a warning to question what we accept readily as fact. "It's not just an escape from reality," she said, countering a common dismissal of hoaxers. "It's opening up to a new reality."

Because if Jackson could pull off this elaborate plan right under our noses, what other subterfuge might be waiting to be revealed? In her understanding, and similarly to Pearl, Olga believes that Jackson left behind a series of clues for fans to crack. But they can decode his messages only through educating themselves in "psychological, philosophical, metaphysical, New Age literature," as well as the histories of the Egyptians and the Maya. According to many Investigators, guiding people to this wisdom was Jackson's most profound gift to his fans: "He had a humanistic interest in mind, not just to be the greatest of the great. He wanted to affect society, to make them believe, and to shock them," Olga said. The clues that Jackson is leading his fans to, then, are actually tools for survival. The death hoax is not just the set of coincidences and conjectures that Pearl puts forth but rather a sacred text. "It's not about Marlon wearing an FBI hat; those are silly things. It's about life, history, art, religion," Olga maintained. "You don't just discover the death hoax of Michael Jackson. You discover yourself."

But while discovering the death hoax was a momentous breakthrough for Olga, she doesn't discuss it with friends. Like Pearl, she keeps this area of her life cordoned off. Believers find respite and kindred spirits online. Using complex numerology equations, they calculate the next "Bamsday," an acronym for Back Again Michael Day. As one Believer put it, " 'Bamsday' means, like, *bam!* He's back!" Many death hoax investigators pointed to June 25, 2013, as Bamsday, because in his 1995 ballad "Earth Song," Jackson sings, "We've got four years to get

it right," which would be four years after the death announcement. Pearl Jr. predicted that his return would be on December
21, 2012, to coincide with the end of the Mayan calendar, which
to some also heralded the end of the world. As soothsayers, they
continually forecast the second coming of their King—like the
Millerite Christian movement in the nineteenth century, which
waited for the rapture to come sometime between March 21,
1843, and March 21, 1844; or more recently, evangelist Harold
Camping, who foretold that the Day of Judgment would come
on May 21, 2011. Camping quickly pushed the date back to
October, then suffered a stroke. When October came and went
without any apocalyptic activity, he gave up on his predictions.
His personal Judgment Day came on December 13, 2013. You'd
think Believers, too, would have been disappointed that Bamsday has thus far failed to arrive. I asked Pearl if these false leads
felt taunting—even cruel. "It can be frustrating, but I've gotten
used to it by now," she said. "He sets up many comeback dates,
but that's to keep you on edge. He's giving you intervals of time
so you stay engaged and hopeful."

All Believers seem to take quite a beating in the court of
public opinion, even among friends and family. Natalie, a Believer from England, described the derision she has received
when describing Jackson's death hoax to outsiders: "My mum
thinks I'm daft, and most of my friends do too." Diane, a British
grandmother, echoed these sentiments. When discussing her
death hoax theories with non-Believers, she has "been laughed
at and ridiculed. It hurts, and makes me feel very silly and im-
mature. So I say very little. I am not a confrontational person
and can't think of how to answer. They all bombard me with
the same questions, and I can't cope with it. They believe the
media and don't look deeper."

If you want to "look deeper" than the mainstream media's story, Google is the go-to place to find "facts and evidence" that, say, the 9/11 attacks were part of a US government conspiracy; or that the Beatles' Paul McCartney was killed in 1966 and replaced by a look-alike (and prodigious talent–alike) known as "Faul"; or that the 2012 Sandy Hook Elementary School shooting in Newtown, Connecticut, was orchestrated by President Barack Obama to make the case for imposing gun control laws. But instead of seeing them as a web of readily manipulated stories as pliable and subjective as those they condemn in the mainstream media, many Believers view the shoddiest sites as immutable canons of fact and fear. The words we string together as search terms inevitably turn up information that supports our own confirmation bias—the tendency to give more weight to data that support our beliefs rather than ideas that run contrary to our personal assertions. With its limitless resources to help people "look deeper," and the support groups that can form over laptops and across oceans, infinite online information is what has made the Michael Jackson death hoax theory as popular and developed as it is today. The auspicious timing, with social media's vise grip on our consciousness, has made this particular death hoax theory one of the most prominent in history.

———

BUT CELEBRITY DEATH HOAXES have always captured our imaginations. It just doesn't seem fair that people who are so talented and usually at the peak of their careers can be snatched from us so soon. Like Olga said, it feels like a violation of universal law. Infamous figures, too, refuse to die. For a TV special, Steve Rambam once conducted an investigation of Adolf Hitler's suicide (he shot himself while longtime mistress Eva

Braun bit into a cyanide capsule) as if it were an insurance fraud. He examined all the documents and interviewed witnesses in South America who claimed they had spotted him. Hitler death fraud fascination, though, remains fringe compared with the Believers.

When Tupac Shakur was shot to death in Las Vegas at the age of twenty-five in 1996, theories swarmed about his faked death and escape to Cuba. According to *Icons of Hip Hop: An Encyclopedia of the Movement, Music, and Culture*, edited by Mickey Hess, Shakur read *The Prince*. On his posthumous album *The Don Killuminati: The 7-Day Theory* (released two months after his death) he assumes "the name of Makaveli and [foreshadows] his own death. . . . The album was an homage to Niccolo Machiavelli . . . who spoke of staging one's own death in his book *The Prince*." Following a familiar formula, proponents claimed he used numerology to clue in his fans, and that he was wanted by the FBI. But in 1996 these theories had no place to go save a few primitive GeoCities. Today a few flimsy websites discuss his pseudocide, but because Tupac's death preceded the advent of social media, there's no real steam behind the movement. But it was reinvigorated in 2015 when retired LAPD officer David Meyers claimed from his deathbed that he was paid $1.5 million for his part in the cover-up the night Shakur was shot four times while sitting in the passenger seat of a BMW.

The death hoax theory that provided a template for Tupac and Michael is, of course, the one spun around Elvis Presley. Fans simply would not believe that the King died unceremoniously from a drug overdose on August 16, 1977. Writer Gail Brewer-Giorgio has penned four wildly popular books on certain discrepancies surrounding Elvis's death, including the novel *Orion*, about a masked man who bears a striking resemblance to the King, as well as the nonfiction volumes *Is Elvis Alive?* (which inspired Pearl's conviction that Michael Jackson lives), *The Elvis Files: Was His Death Faked?*, and *Elvis Undercover: Is He Alive and Coming Back?* Brewer-Giorgio pointed out suspicious circumstances in Elvis's death that Jackson fans co-opted in their theories: his middle name was misspelled on his gravestone, and he later communicated with loved ones, and even the writer herself. If Michael Jackson "followed Elvis's plan to a T," as Pearl told me, then she has also followed Gail Brewer-Giorgio as a model, including claims of fielding phone calls from the stars from beyond the grave.

The business of the middle name has been paramount to both Brewer-Giorgio's and Pearl's arguments. "Elvis Aaron Presley" is on Elvis's grave at Graceland, but this was not how he typically spelled his middle name. Brewer-Giorgio tried to find evidence to support the double *A* spelling: "I went through all the documents," she told me over the phone from Georgia, "his birth certificate, his RCA contracts, his army discharge papers, everything. Even Priscilla Presley sent out thank-you cards from their wedding with 'Aron.'"

So why, and how, does a misspelled middle name equal a faked death?

"Originally, I thought if you're alive and you have your own tombstone, it might be a hex to have your own name there. But Elvis told me I was wrong. Elvis liked numerology, and he thought our whole system revolves around numerology. So by adding an extra *a*, he was able to change his numerology feeling from an eight to a nine," she said.

Michael Jackson's mysterious "Joseph" rather than "Joe" has been fodder for Pearl's campaign. But Jackson's misspelling his middle name is for reasons more practical than spiritual.

"California law says that you must use the legal name on a death certificate," Pearl acknowledged. "Then he released a song posthumously with Barry Gibb called 'All in Your Name.' So he's giving us clues, and he's finding these loopholes. I think he hired lawyers to help him go through these uncharted territories."

Elvis might have inspired longtime impersonator and avant-garde comedian Andy Kaufman to fake his death. Comedian Bob Zmuda has spent a good part of his career advancing the theory that his friend and partner in crime Andy Kaufman did not die of lung cancer in 1984 at age thirty-five. Instead, he committed pseudocide as part of his performance art, or as Zmuda put it, "to pull off the ultimate prank." And according to Zmuda, Kaufman talked openly about his plans to do so. "I remember right around the time Elvis died, and the rumor went around that Elvis faked his death," Zmuda told me over the phone from Burbank, California. "Kaufman was a huge Elvis fan. That's when the idea started to jell in his head. He said, 'Can you imagine if he did fake his death, and he returned one day? This would be the biggest thing in the history of entertainment ever.'"

Like the Believers waiting for Bamsday, Zmuda and Kaufman fanatics anticipate Andy's return. "Every ten years we have a big event, thinking he might come back on the tenth or twentieth anniversary of his death. We're going to do it again on the thirtieth anniversary, and then that will be it. Every year, I take out ads in newspapers all over the world, saying, 'Andy, if you're out there, we're doing this show in your honor.'" Unfortunately, the thirtieth anniversary in 2015 passed, and still, no Andy. Zmuda has been advancing this faked death theory in his book *Andy Kaufman Revealed!* on TV and as a guest on radio shows. The theory got a boost in the zeitgeist recently when a young actress went onstage at the annual Andy Kaufman Awards at Manhattan's Gotham Comedy Club, claiming she was the comedian's daughter and that she spoke with him regularly. A few days later, Michael Kaufman, Andy's brother, revealed that he had sanctioned the prank. Nonetheless, the stunt catapulted Kaufman's name beyond the realm of fan boys and conspiracy theorists and onto the six o'clock news.

=====

NOT EVERYONE AGREES THAT a good old-fashioned death hoax is a wise career move. On February 14, 2013, ShaBe Allah, a staff writer at *The Source* magazine, broke the story that nineties rapper Tim Dog had died. Allah had received a phone call from a personal friend who happened to be an associate of the rapper, saying that Mr. Dog had passed. The *New York Times* and the *New York Daily News* followed, reporting the story, and then MSNBC called Allah requesting additional verification. So he began investigating. "I called the hospital in Georgia where he was supposed to have died," he said, "and there's no record of him being there, no death certificate, no burial records. If he did fake his death, he did a real good job. He's a tall black guy with gold chains from the Bronx. He'd be hard to miss in Georgia."

Allah, though, disagrees with the idea that a death hoax could make Tim Dog more popular. "If he isn't physically dead, then he's definitely mentally dead, because nobody is thinking about Tim Dog either way. Out of sight, out of mind." And like the Believers' detractors in the Jackson fan community, Allah, too, feels indignant about faked death enthusiasts and co-conspirators: "The type of person who would help perpetuate the idea that Tim Dog is alive is the worst type of human there could be. Life is so precious. I've seen people lose their lives in the blink of an eye, so to say someone is really alive is nothing to play with." Dog's death certificate surfaced a year and a half later, though some still have their doubts. Pearl disagrees with Allah's perspective, saying, "It's freedom of speech! I can do what I want as long as I'm not destroying anyone's reputation. A death hoax is beneficial only to Michael. It's better to be alive than dead any day of the week!"

None of the Believers I spoke with seemed especially crazy; rather, all were gainfully employed, properly dressed, and even eerily normal. Within the fan community, Jackson's death is like a great work of art: you can analyze it from many distinct angles, and it is complex enough to support multiple interpretations. And while it's easy to dismiss them as fanatics who can't let go, there is something quite noble about their worldviews. It's easy to overlook the determination that such a belief requires. In that sense, they are a resistance movement. Like faking your own death, believing in a death hoax is a way to rewrite the script vicariously. Why rehash the negative (he's gone), when you can have faith in the positive (he lives!)? Maybe letting your imagination unspool is a normal—even healthy—way of coping with and making sense of our nonsensical world. Combing cyberspace for clues and decoding secret messages transform dismal reality into an adventure. No longer grief stricken, the true Believer is now enlightened.

═══

LATE ONE SATURDAY NIGHT, I received a voice mail. "Hi, how are you doing?" a breathy voice asked. "I'm calling to check up on you and see how you are doing because I heard you are writing a book, and I wanted to contact you. So I hope to hear from you very soon. Take care, and God bless you." Though he didn't identify himself, I knew instantly that this was the legendary Peter Pan, or the undead Michael Jackson.

When Pearl had revealed that she spoke with him regularly, my first question was not "Are you out of your mind?" but "Do you think he'd call me?" And now he was delivering. The voice on the other end was a poor facsimile of Jackson's. A little too much falsetto, and some awkward phrasings that made him sound more like a recent immigrant to America than a native of Gary, Indiana. But maybe one acquires an unusual dialect when hiding out on Marlon Brando's private island?

Despite all that, I admit I got chills. Not because I thought I was hearing the most famous undead star of all time panting into my phone, but because there is someone in the San Fernando Valley attempting to convince me that He Lives.

The next afternoon, the same 661 area code popped up on my phone screen. My then-boyfriend, Elijah, and I were babysitting his nephew in Brooklyn, and we were getting ready to go to the park. I rushed to answer my phone.

"Hi," the voice on the other end of the line said coyly.

"Hi. Who is this?" I asked.

"This is Peter."

Elijah was making crazy faces at me, slicing his hand across his neck in an attempt to make me cut the conversation. Later he lectured me for talking to a potential serial killer hunting down his next victim. Elijah was always the more sensible (or paranoid) one, on the lookout for looming dangers: sinkholes in the sidewalk, toxic mold spores sprouting in the shower, fatal salmonella poisoning we could contract from undercooking dinner. Talking on the phone to someone who might or might not be Michael Jackson signaled stranger danger of the highest order.

But I had a pleasant chat with Peter Pan. We discussed movies we like and books we'd read lately. Peter said he reads a lot and prefers books on positive thinking, such as *The Master Key System*, a self-help book from 1912, which was originally a twenty-four-week correspondence course. He had recently watched the 1979 TV miniseries *Backstairs at the White House* and thoroughly enjoyed it. He's been working on "a music project to be released." As our conversation progressed, I found myself more and more engaged. He was so charming! "It's been an honor meeting you, Liz," he said as we got off the phone. No one has said that sentence to me before or since. I felt dizzy. A part of me wanted to believe that I was talking to Michael Jackson and that he had taken a break from producing his next hit to chat with me, a nobody.

I finally understood what Pearl and Olga and the Believers must feel when they are Michaeling.

But I wanted to do a more formal interview, to get to the bottom of some of the rumors circulating even in the Believers community itself: that Peter Pan is, in fact, Pearl. This Peter, or whoever s/he is, will contact Believers through Facebook or Twitter to alert them to a TinyChat—a kind of schizophrenic online group therapy session—where he will be present. Even diehards have their questions. I sat in on one of these forums and witnessed some Believer skepticism:

4love: lol no you're not Peter
ringell_jackson: YEAH PETER IS HERE NOW
peter_panpyt: i as real as it gets

newuser6098: Pearl is up her own Ass

Peter is a Poser

you are all mental

is that right

to trick others

4love: ppl believe what they need to believe

This is where it gets really meta: Michael Jackson uses Peter Pan as a proxy, who many believe is a fake. But in the Tiny-Chat, fans were questioning whether peter_panpyt was the real fake Michael Jackson, or a fake fake Michael Jackson. And then there was the metaphysical question of whether Pearl was indeed up her own Ass, a derriere so influential that it received proper-noun capitalization.

I asked Peter if he would go on the record with me. He called me several times in the middle of the night when I did not pick up, and once in the middle of the night when I did pick up, because I was drunk, in a cab, on the way home from a bar.

When I finally got the vaunted Mr. Pan on the phone with my recorder, he again called me from a 661 area code. Pearl has the same area code. But what Pearl said about his inaccessibility is true: when I tried to call the number back, I got a message saying the call could not be completed. I asked him about the similarity in area codes, and therefore proximity, between him and Pearl.

"Ummmmmm . . . it's a coincidence. I have a lot of numbers," he said. When I asked where he was calling from, he said, "an 'unclosed' location."

He peppered Michael Jackson clues throughout our conversation without ever saying "I am Michael Jackson" or even "I am an unusual person pretending to be Michael Jackson." Rather, he used thinly veiled references: "I wake up late because I'm a night person; I can never sleep at night." Jackson was known to be nocturnal. "God blessed me with a great family," he said, which could read as a prosaic platitude or a nod to the greatest showbiz family of all time. Peter seemed to spend a great deal of time online, posting rare Jackson photos to his Facebook page. Our conversation was punctuated every few seconds by a high-pitched dinging, which was the sound of his chat alert on Facebook. (I sheepishly admit that I was a teensy bit crestfallen that the legendary Peter Pan was multitasking during our exclusive interview.) I asked him why he stuck his neck out so much, communicating with fans through different social media sites, if he was simultaneously trying to keep a low profile.

"I've always been around on the internet," he explained, "but I've always been very quiet. I guess anybody who starts getting inquisitive about me asks, 'Hey, where did you get that picture from?' They ask me why I sound so much like a certain person. I say, 'Because I'm Peter Pan, that's all I can tell you.'" He was coy like this. William Wagener had mentioned that he and Peter had communicated in the past. I asked Peter about these interactions.

"Yeah, we've spoken on the phone a few times," Peter said. "I had heard a lot about him, so I had contacted him, and we became pretty good friends. He's a very sharp person, very intellectual. He likes to talk about court cases and injustice. I can relate to the injustice he talks about. I had gone through an injustice in my life, so I can relate to other people's injustice."

"What injustice have you experienced in your life?" I asked, ready for him to delve into the '05 trial.

"Well, it's a very touchy subject," he said, in a classic evasion. "I don't like to talk about it. It pains me."

I had asked Wagener his thoughts on Peter. "Oh, I know Peter Pan," he'd said. "Of course it's not Michael," he said sharply.

Peter and Pearl's intimate relationship disturbs would-be Believers. They might find Pearl as a gateway to the subculture but then get turned off by what they see as carpetbagging on his death. Since the pair are "close, close, close friends," as Pearl put it, I asked Peter what was up with the accusation that she profits from the death hoax.

"The people who say that are speculating. They don't know Pearl. Pearl is a sweet person. She doesn't make any money. She has a normal nine-to-five job. That's how she makes her money. She loves sharing information she comes across; that's one of her passions. People have a negative connotation about her, and I don't know why," he said.

Then I asked him straight up if Michael Jackson had faked his death.

"Wow!" he exclaimed with mock surprise, like he didn't know this was where we would end up. It was like Taylor Swift's "Who, me?!" face as she collects her umpteenth Grammy. And then he hedged again: "That's a very, very touchy subject. What do I say about that? I know there are people going around saying they're Believers. To believe in something is without reason or fact. These people are knowers, because they have facts, they have proof. That's something that's different than believing."

It really didn't matter if Peter Pan was Michael Jackson or not. When I was talking to him on the phone, for a moment I was totally outside myself, in something bigger than myself, my cranium dislodged temporarily from my own rectum. I was getting a phone call from the King of Pop. Or someone who cared enough to pretend to be. To me, I mattered. I understand why Taaj Malik and other Michael Jackson fans find what the Believers say to be hurtful. But to pick on them is to point out the blatantly obvious. When people take the time to comment on Pearl's mispronunciation of words (she often says Jackson is hiding out on "Marlon Brandon's" private island), the ridiculous haunted-house music she plays in every YouTube video, and the fact that she references the *Weekly World News* as a source, they are taking the death hoax both too literally and too superficially. It would be like going shopping with Tammy Faye Bakker and mocking her gaudiness. It's philistinism masquerading as connoisseurship. It's taking a cheap and dreadfully obvious shot. Believers harbor bizarre theories. But that's what makes them great. It takes a lot more courage to believe doggedly in something so outlandish and so weird. The believing itself is the point more than the outcome. It's faith.

When Pearl dropped me off after our day of Michaeling and our star-studded dinner at the Beverly Hills Hotel, she turned to me and said, "Please be kind. It took me a long time to get here. If I believe this stuff, I have a reason." After listening to every piece of evidence, trivia, and gossip, I wasn't exactly sold that Michael faked his death. I was a little shy about revealing this to Pearl. She'd generously invested a vacation day from work in patiently walking me through it all, in reconfiguring the timeline, in showing me the scenes of the crime. I didn't want to let her down or have her think it was because she hadn't done her due diligence. I don't Believe. But I love that she does, and it felt exhilarating to be around someone who was so sure about something. Earnest conviction is in short supply, and Pearl possesses it. If this is the way she has decided to spend her days and energy, it doesn't seem so bad to me.

I CAUGHT UP WITH her a year later. I wanted to know if she still maintained faith in the death hoax, now more than five years after the death announcement. "Oh, it's still going strong!" she told me over the phone in her characteristically chipper voice. She reminded me that I had only begun to scratch the surface of the proof and evidence that Michael faked his death. "There were a lot of clues on the last [posthumous] album, and I'm up to almost two and a half million views on my YouTube channel!" I asked her if his failure to return to his fans has frustrated Believers. "Some people have fallen off already, but there are always new people!"

Then I asked her if she was still in touch with Peter.

"Oh, the drama of all that!" she said with a sigh.

Turns out that Peter Pan had been identified as one Bobby Anderson from South Carolina. Anderson is a rotund African American man in his early thirties, and since his outing, he has become the subject of much scorn and ridicule for manipulating fans. He sounds like a guy with too much time on his hands.

Pearl, though, had a different theory:

"Michael can do whatever he wants to do! You think if he can fake his death, then he can't fake a Bobby Anderson? Or could Bobby Anderson be hired by the estate to fool people? Is he part of the Jackson family? Is he a setup? He still does wonderful things."

Rather than contradicting her ideas or validating her detractors, Pearl sees him as an operative in the greatest prank the King of Pop ever pulled. And if I squint, I see her point. Once you've invested in seeing the ropes and pulleys of such a fantastic behind-the-scenes operation, why would you suddenly discount the source? Peter Pan doesn't blot out the accumulation of facts that make up the mosaic proof of the death hoax. Though I was bummed momentarily that I wasn't actually talking to *the* Michael Jackson those few times, I don't find it sad.

I asked Pearl how she felt about her mission now, in light of this recent revelation.

"I don't want to let the fans down," she said. "I want to be there when he comes back. I want to be there when the fat lady sings."

5

COLLATERAL DAMAGE

L isa Boosin realized early on that her life did not come
equipped with a safety net, so she made her choices ac-
cordingly. Both her parents died by the time she reached
age nine. The grandparents who raised her passed when she
was in her early twenties, bequeathing her "orphan status," as
she put it—a very raw way to be in the world.

She didn't know much about her mom and dad. They
were hippies, with all the trappings of late-1960s libidinal
glamour, but more caught up in the seedy underbelly of the
scene than promoting world peace. Her father, Michael, was
the self-proclaimed "King of the Sunset Strip," and could be
caught prowling the boulevard in his iridescent baby-blue
Corvette, which he'd dubbed "the Candy 'Vette." Everybody
knew him because he knew how to get things—namely hal-
lucinogenics and barbiturates—and because he maintained

stalls at Hollywood's sprawling bazaar the Psychedelic Supermarket. Michael kept the shelves stocked with macramé belts, leather pants, fringe vests, bongs, pipes, rolling papers, rolling machines, underground comics, counterculture newspapers, incense, and essential oils. Full of the kind of directionless charisma that would today befit a reality-TV star, he enjoyed his fifteen minutes of fame when Andy Warhol cast him in a minor role as "the Big Kahuna" in the ad-libbed 1968 film *San Diego Surf*. Michael was discovered for his part in the nearly unwatchable movie when one of Andy's assistants crashed at his raucous party pad, known as "the Castle," on Melrose Avenue, and met the self-styled celebrity cruising the Strip in his Candy 'Vette, picking up various women.

One of those women was Carolyn Georg, a skinny, blond eighteen-year-old from the Valley. She fell deeply in love with King Michael, who was twenty-eight at the time. Before meeting him, she'd dabbled in pot, but was soon fully immersed in heroin. It was a brief courtship, and Carolyn was soon pregnant with a baby girl and nursing a heavy drug habit. Lisa Raine was born in Burbank in 1971, and her parents married a year later. They moved in with Carolyn's mother and father in the Valley to be closer to Michael's drug connections, and the contents of the Psychedelic Supermarket went into storage in their garage. Carolyn was in and out of rehab, Michael in and out of jail, so Lisa's grandparents took care of her. Before her second birthday, Michael overdosed on heroin. Seven years later, Carolyn died in the shower from a drug withdrawal seizure.

Lisa got to know her parents through the boxes in the garage. From the age of five, she would riffle through *Penthouse Forums* and photos of the young couple posed proudly before Michael's fleet of cars. She once found her mom's jewelry-making kit and discovered, at the bottom, what she thought were stickers. She gave her Barbies tattoos with the colorful designs. Only years later did she realize that she was decorating her dolls with tabs of acid. Most of the junk got thrown away eventually, but a photo of her father's famous Corvette always captivated Lisa.

Several decades later, Lisa was fixing up her first real home in LA. She had carried the photo of the Candy 'Vette with her through many moves, but now had it framed and displayed on a bookshelf. A friend came over and asked her about it. She told the friend what she knew: her father was good with cars, and he had died when she was young. She'd never really known him, so she didn't miss him much. But something in that conversation piqued her curiosity. Later that night, she searched "Michael Boosin Corvette." An interview came up on a fan site dedicated to Warhol stars. There Michael described his reign on the Sunset Strip and his harem of admirers, and how impressed Andy was with his groovy lifestyle. "One way or another," Michael told the interviewer, "it got decided that Andy would use me and that Corvette."

The information was nothing new to Lisa. But the date of the article stopped her:

Her father had given that interview in 2007.

══

"THIS PLACE IS TOTALLY changed," Lisa Boosin told me early one morning in May, driving up the same stretch of Sunset Strip where her father once held court. "Now the Strip caters to the children of *Jersey Shore*." What was once her parents' groovy playground is today more Orange County tweaker than freewheeling rock 'n' roll. The streets gleam with chrome surfaces and neon signs, yogurt shops and tourist-trap restaurants where one can mount a mechanical bull. Whoever has inherited the king's throne likely drives a Hummer and suffers from 'roid rage. His queen definitely has fake tits.

It was just past eight in the morning, and Lisa had retrieved me in her black Mini Cooper from an apartment I had rented in Hollywood from a Hungarian chef named Zoltan. (Later that same night, I came very close to torching said home in a tragic towel-and-halogen-lamp mishap that would result in a stinky apartment, a stern talking-to from the building manager, and Zoltan's threatened eviction. I'm still sorry, Zoltan.)

Lisa and I were en route to hike in Griffith Park for her second workout of the day. Before sunrise, she had plunged into an aqua aerobics class attended mostly by senior citizens, one of the only exercises available to her after a persistent back problem that she'd exacerbated by running long distances. Lisa is a tall and lean gazelle of a woman in her early forties, with freckles dotting her otherwise alabaster complexion, and she has wavy brown hair and a charming lisp. A native Angeleno, she lives in the enviable Los Feliz neighborhood with her two cats, Lisa Jr. and Mary Mary. Her longtime boyfriend is an art director for an ad agency.

She describes her eccentric parents as "fauxhemians—they were hippies but not into peace and love. They were very much into the style." And like many of that generation, they got caught up in the unsavory aspects of the scene, elements the Psychedelic Supermarket made readily available. She remembers her mother whipping through her grandparents' home once in a while, ravaged by drugs. One of Lisa's earliest memories of her mother is of a Christmas when she was four years old. Santa had delivered a Barbie motor home, and the girl was thrilled. But then her mother, who was on methadone in an attempt to kick heroin, fell into a seizure and collapsed on top of Barbie's RV, wrecking it.

Lisa was so young when her dad died that the paternal deficit didn't bother her much. It wasn't until a friend's older sister began calling her a bastard that she wondered what the epithet meant. Her grandparents showed her a dossier of documents on her father, including his notarized death certificate. "I remember the ridges," Lisa said. Her grandparents told her that her dad had snitched on several associates as part of a plea deal. Is it possible that he was placed in witness protection? Nobody seems to know for sure. High-profile informants who enter the US Department of Justice's witness protection program, also known as the witness security program (WITSEC), receive a new identity, complete with diplomas, birth certificate, and Social Security number. But the bureau doesn't typically bother fictionally killing the person who once was. Once someone is suspected of snitching, orchestrating a fatal accident isn't necessary because nobody would believe it.

Michael had gone back to his home state of New York to let things cool off in California, when he purportedly died in 1972 or 1973. "That was as much information as my grandparents offered," Lisa said. "When you're a little kid and an adult tells you something like that, it doesn't occur to you to ask what really happened."

I had to trot behind Lisa to keep up with her loping gait. The sun was just peeking over Mount Lee and the Hollywood Hills, but I was already drenched in sweat.

"Gotta stop smoking!" I heaved, jogging to catch up on the incline as nubile women in stretch pants with small dogs glided past me. "No, this is a really hard hill!" she yelled over her shoulder, graciously excusing the pallid, wheezing thing behind her.

Today Lisa works in advertising and marketing, and has won an impressive cache of professional awards. She loves fashion, especially bargain hunting, outlets, and sample sales, and she plows through the racks with the efficiency and eye of a seasoned connoisseur. She also writes, beautifully, which is how I found her, via an essay about her father's faked death. She is such a gifted writer, in fact, that I'd been encouraging her to write her own memoir since we first spoke, because her father's faking his own death is actually one of the more benign aspects of her life. Like her mother, she has struggled with various addictions: drugs, anorexia, cutting, extreme exercise. She was in and out of rehab as a teenager. Her grandmother was a highly sought-after astrologist who once read Frank Zappa's chart, and her grandfather was a material engineer for an aerospace company. As a child, she spent a good chunk of the year living in Las Vegas hotels, where her grandparents would decamp to gamble professionally. Armed with a roll of quarters, she'd spend days unsupervised at the video arcades. She still kicks ass at Galaga.

Her grandparents were determined that Lisa graduate from college, and she did, bouncing around junior colleges and universities all over Southern California. She'd always wanted to be a writer, but from a very early age, Lisa sensed that the bottom could drop out of her life at any moment. Pursuing such an unprofitable career was too risky a venture. "I got the idea that anything can change for the worse very quickly," she said, charging up the hill, "and I need to be able to take care of myself. I think that I've gotten really lucky because I know that, not having anyone to call upon, I just have to keep going."

When she stumbled upon the Warhol stars website, Lisa thought the author had simply cited the date of the interview incorrectly. "Like when you're doing a bibliography in college, and you have to indicate the date you accessed it," she explained. She immediately fired off an email to the guy who ran the site but didn't disclose her identity, saying only that she had a keen interest in King Michael. He responded minutes later, requesting more information. She revealed that she was his daughter, explaining, "My motives are decent, but this is something I've been dealing with my whole life." She really just wanted to know more about her dad.

He said that he knew Michael in the 1980s and 1990s, but that he didn't know exactly what had happened in Michael's earlier life. Michael had never mentioned Lisa directly, though he did indicate that he'd made some very bad decisions and done some stuff he wasn't proud of. The administrator reckoned that if he had disappeared, it was for his daughter's own protection. Michael likely didn't mean any harm, he said. He probably just thought it would be better for everyone if he made himself scarce.

Somewhere along the way, Michael Boosin had given himself the ironic new name Michael Saint. The website administrator passed along the most recent contact information he had for the former Big Kahuna. Lisa held on to the information for a while. She was sitting on an emotional grenade. She realized that if she reached out to him and he made no effort to get back to her, she would feel twice orphaned. "At that point in my life," she said, "I didn't think I'd be able to deal with it."

Some cursory research revealed that Michael Saint had worked at Expo 86 in Vancouver but that was about the extent of the information she could find on his biography. He had a thirty-odd-year gap in his history—an ellipsis that essentially spanned Lisa's entire life. When she finally called the phone number she had for him, it was out of service. No new information in the white pages turned up. The domain of his email address had been taken down. She didn't pursue it further. It had been a hard year when she found the 2007 interview with her father: she'd lost her job, gone through a breakup, and found herself in the midst of a depressive episode. "Having so much to deal with every day, the family stuff didn't come on my radar," she explained.

Her identity as an orphan had been a certain source of pride for Lisa since she lost her grandparents at the age of twenty-one. The ferocious independence of being untethered in the world was her compass needle pointing north, and it informed her decisions. "Everyone's parents divorce, and we all experience loss. But I was a unicorn because I just didn't have parents," she said. Nor did she have siblings or cousins. As a result, she developed a scrappy self-reliance and kept her emotional reserves well stocked. She is outgoing and friendly, but you get the feeling that it takes a lot for her to let people all the way in.

She was thirty-seven when she found out her dad had faked his death and could possibly still be alive. Learning that she had no blood relation but her father threw her entire conception of herself and her life story into jeopardy. She explained the distinction: "I think we all internalize the death of our loved ones. We ask, 'Why wasn't I special enough for them to stick around?' But finding out that your father faked his death, just so he could go away? That's as much of a personal affront as there is."

I asked her what that felt like.

"It was like having every insult at the world you've ever thought hurled at you," she said. "I just felt like a tremendous loser. I was very angry at him. One of the fundamental pieces of my identity had just been tweaked. Hard."

Lisa understands that it comes off as strange to outsiders that she did not pursue the mystery of her father with more gusto. But it was a matter of pure pragmatism. "If he was alive," she said, "why wouldn't he try to find me?" She'd learned to avoid the backward glance in order to keep forging forward. "Things had been such a struggle to get through that digging seemed like a luxury I couldn't afford. The thought that my father was out there, alive, and that I had to put any effort into looking for him? That just wasn't something I wanted a part of."

Then, three years after discovering the interview, she got a message on Facebook from a woman who was also seeking Michael. This woman had dated him around the same time as Lisa's mother. Lisa Googled her and saw that she had posted a similar want ad on the website Hollywood a Go Go.

Lisa was hesitant, but she decided to talk to the ex-girlfriend in order to learn more about her parents. She did a little more King Michael research to prepare.

That was when she found his real obituary, from 2008.

He had died at the age of sixty-six in Florida, just a few months before Lisa stumbled upon the Warhol stars site. She missed meeting her father by just a few weeks.

The cliché is that life is all about timing. Usually that seems to imply that the timing is a net positive—how in the face of improbable odds, even as the universe conspires against us, we converge to make some kind of contact. Synchronicity and cir-cumstance somehow put us in the right place at the right time. But what about the inverse? What about the missed connec-tions? If you are the sort who extrapolates meaning from these kinds of coincidences, perhaps Lisa was protected from meeting her father, who sounds like he went out of his way to avoid defiling her with his presence. But another way to look at it is simply: What the fuck? What kind of cruel joke was this, and who was laughing?

Lisa and I eventually made it up to the top of Griffith Park and discovered that the space observatory wasn't open yet. (She had loved watching old episodes of *Star Trek* with her grandfather, and remembered how truly exciting space exploration seemed when she was a kid.) We began our descent back down the mountain, with the California sun baking the pavement. With gravity working in my favor, I could finally walk next to her. Having learned about her father's existence and how it upset the narrative of her own biography and standing in the world, I asked her if she wished she'd never found out and had gone along assuming that her father was still dead. As far as Lisa knows, her grandparents took the news of his overdose at face value.

"I don't know," she said. "That would've been cleaner. I had given up a long time ago on the idea that one can choose what happens in one's own life. But there was always a part of me deep down inside that knew he wasn't dead."

Lisa seemed in such deliberate and determined control of her own life. She described being at her office job and looking around at her highly educated colleagues who all hailed from affluent backgrounds. "It just trips me out that I am not poor white trailer trash somewhere! That's due largely in part to the interventions and love from my grandparents. But given my predilections for addiction . . . how the fuck am I not living in a trailer park?!" she marveled. Lisa has managed to juke the stats on her own life, to rewrite a destiny that seemed preordained. I couldn't help but catch a whiff of her father and his self-styling as King Michael and then as Michael Saint—she, too, reinvented herself and refused the role she was supposed to play in the script of her life. She hustled. She willed herself into a different shape. But in spite of all the pain and suffering her father had caused, I was still straining to see the magic and the miracle of pseudocide. I asked her if she saw anything admirable in his faked death.

"No," she said without hesitation. "He did it for purely selfish reasons. His reasons were little, not big. If you lived next to a nuclear test reactor site and faked your death to draw attention to the dangers? That would be a noble reason. There are certainly more honorable ways he could've gone out."

"Like what?" I asked.

"Divorce? Just plain old divorce. Or straight-up honesty. It was a very shortsighted thing he did for his own gain," she said.

We got back into the Mini Cooper and drove to her apartment, an airy, light-filled 1920s-style bungalow. She opened up a box of photos. We sat at her glass-topped table, with the two cats pushing over water bottles and vying for her attention. She pulled out scallop-edged and curling photographs of her parents in their fauxhemian fashions. Michael stands proudly next to his curvaceous cars. In one photo, he is wearing what looks like a space racing suit, and Carolyn leans against the Candy 'Vette, wearing a yellow gingham shirt tucked into navy-blue bell-bottoms. Her flaxen hair is pin straight and parted down the middle. They look like they are on the brink of something big. Lisa pulled down from her bookcase the infamous photo of the Candy 'Vette—the artifact that undid her notion of self for a while, the thing that further complicated an already chaotic life.

Cars always get people caught, Frank and Steve had told me. Bennie Wint got busted for his broken license plate light after being declared dead twenty years earlier. The Candy 'Vette was clearly such a point of pride for Michael Boosin. How could he have known that his car would resurrect him? But perhaps he did know. Perhaps he knew, and that is why he boasted about it in that interview. It was the most distinctive thing about him. Maybe he used it as a towline to pull him back to his daughter from the point beyond the horizon where he disappeared. That's what I'd like to think, but I don't offer this interpretation to Lisa.

"My childhood was not completely idyllic, but it was great," she said, choking up while looking at a picture of her grandmother and grandfather. "My grandparents were kind of fucked up, but they did their best. I have no idea what I'd be if it weren't for them. Since they were from another era, they placed a lot of emphasis on manners and etiquette and integrity. I often feel out of step with a lot of people. Fundamentally, I think I'm a good person. I take integrity seriously." She wiped away her tears, put away the box, and then changed into a flowing red chiffon dress. We set out on an afternoon that took us to a sample sale, a fish taco stand, and a Japanese market. She had taken the day off from work, and she was going to get the most out of it.

=====

PRIOR TO MEETING LISA, the mess that a death faker leaves in his wake had been largely theoretical to me. From talking to John Darwin, I learned that his family dynamic had been altered forever. The Believers felt left behind but so hopeful that their faith in Jackson's return would one day be rewarded. They transformed their (temporary?) loss into something that gave their lives meaning. But Lisa, sadly, felt no such hope. She was the first person I had met who could speak to what it felt like to be on the other side of such an act. Since no one actually dies when one commits pseudocide, it seems like a victimless crime. And in the minds of those who'd gone through with it, the seamless nature of the escape is one of its big selling points and a major rationalization to do it. But the way Lisa described learning that her dad had been alive for most of her life? Like absorbing the worst insult? This was a crime, and there were indeed victims, and survivors.

Though Lisa remains stoically rational about the experience, and though her discovery seems so singular, she was not the only person I encountered who had endured such an inconceivable revelation. Since pseudocide occurs more frequently than you might guess at first, so too do many people who become collateral damage in such schemes. But while being somehow connected to pseudocide was a trauma for everyone I spoke with, the shape of the disturbance varied greatly.

═══

JAKE ISRAEL HAD JUST finished his freshman year at the University of Maryland when we met on a thick summer afternoon in White Plains, New York. He was sweet and soft-spoken, with screaming red hair, and was working a summer job as a server at a country club. He drove me in his SUV to "the strip": a short row of overpriced upscale pubs that can get rowdy on the weekend.

He and his father, Sam Israel, had always been close. Jake was only in junior high in 2009 when Sam was indicted on fraud charges and served with twenty-two years in federal prison. He remembers his father telling him he couldn't do the time and that he was going to disappear for a while.

"I don't advise it," thirteen-year-old Jake told his father, "but do what you have to do."

In an email to me from Butner Federal Prison, his father described that exchange as heart wrenching. Sam had taken Jake along with him to Long Island to buy the getaway RV. He told his son that he couldn't stand to spend "the rest of our lives looking through glass at each other." Because the FBI agent mentioned Costa Rica, Sam figured he'd have to go away for only two or three years until things cooled off, and then return with impunity. Jake started crying, but Sam assured him that two years was better than twenty-two. Jake told me that he knew his father was in trouble, and once Sam clued him in to what was going on, he understood.

Of course, this idea of faking death to lie low and wait out an ugly mess was by now familiar. These mental gymnastics—convincing yourself that profound debt or insurance fraud will be forgiven and forgotten after just a few years—speak to just how strongly the instinct of self-preservation is imprinted upon us. To fake your death is, of course, to save yourself; but the leaps of logic that Sam Israel and John Darwin made imply how terrifying the circumstances were, or maybe just how badly they wanted to evade the consequences.

"I didn't want to freak him out with the bridge thing," Sam wrote me. "I told him that whatever he heard, nobody could hurt or kill Daddy. I swore to him that nothing would happen to me but that it had to be our secret." Laying this on his young son wasn't easy. "I was crying, but I told him there was no other way. I wanted him to watch after his sister and mother until my return." It does seem like an awful lot of knowledge and responsibility for a thirteen-year-old to shoulder. But Sam saw it as a necessity, and even as a kindness: "I could not let him think I was dead. That would be too fucked up," he wrote.

The day the news broke that a disgraced Wall Street

financier had plummeted from the Bear Mountain Bridge, Jake was on vacation at the Jersey Shore with his mother and sister. Sam had informed only his thirteen-year-old son of the plan, and not his ex-wife, thus handing him the double burden of keeping the secret from his family, not to mention the police. He came back to the house they were renting to find his family in hysterics with the TV blaring. They told him his father might have jumped.

Jake reenacted his amateur dramatics for me in deadpan monotone.

"I was like 'Oh no!' " Today he can laugh about it. "I tried to play along, but I was too young." His family asked how he could be so stoic in the face of this news. "I'm just in shock?" he offered.

"I tried to keep it going," he continued, "but it was alarming, seeing my mother and sister so upset. I feel like I gave it away. But I was only thirteen at the time."

I asked Jake if he was angry with his father for putting him in such an awkward position, for freighting him with such knowledge—and conceivably making him an accessory—at such a young age. "I would've been more angry if he hadn't told me," he said, laughing. I asked him what the experience has taught him. "It made me realize how important family is," he said. He added quickly, "And don't break the law!"

———

LISA WAS INNOCENT OF any knowledge about her father's pseudocide; Jake had been let in on the plan. But some progeny have actually colluded with their parents to commit death fraud. And from what I can tell, this kind of co-conspirator takes the hardest hit.

On July 28, 2012, Raymond Roth and his twenty-two-year-old son, Jonathan, drove in separate cars to Jones Beach on their native Long Island. The father laid out his wallet, clothes, and shoes on the beach, away from the lifeguard-protected swimming area. He then got back into his car and headed south to his time-share in Orlando, Florida. Jonathan sat on the beach for almost an hour, getting into character.

He saw a few guys casting lines into the sea and told them they couldn't fish there. His father had been swimming in the area. Just as he'd anticipated, the fishermen said they hadn't seen any swimmers. Jonathan went into a panic. He called his stepmother, Evana, who was in the midst of a bitter divorce with Raymond. She then called Jonathan's uncle, who is a cop in Long Beach, New York. He asked why Jonathan didn't think to alert the lifeguards. Within an hour, the beach was crawling with cops and Coast Guard rescuers, while helicopters buzzed in the otherwise pristine sky.

The week before, forty-seven-year-old Raymond had named Jonathan the beneficiary of his life insurance. But the scheme was stillborn. The duo never got to collect, because over the weekend, while Evana was planning her husband's funeral and apparently harboring suspicions, she also enlisted a hacker to break into Raymond's email. She discovered messages between her soon-to-be-ex and her stepson outlining their plan to stage Raymond's drowning and collect a policy worth $410,000. Evana had no knowledge of the plan, and was gobsmacked to see it in black and white. She told reporters that he had recently been fired from his job as a telecommunications manager for threatening to shoot two supervisors, and that he'd been emotionally abusive to her for years. (I reached out to Evana several times for more detail, but she did not respond.) Raymond Roth had been savvy enough to erase the incriminating correspondence from his in-box; he'd just neglected to do the same for his out-box. Five days after he was supposed to have drowned, he was pulled over for speeding in South Carolina.

Jonathan Roth told me his story from behind a short partition in an echoey room that otherwise resembled a school cafeteria. He'd been in the Nassau County Correctional Facility for three months. He wasn't expected to get any jail time for colluding with his father, but he had skipped bail several weeks earlier, a year after the original crime. His capture by Empire Bail Bonds, which used a "honeypot" trap to lure in the younger Roth, made the *New York Post* with the headline "Sexy Bounty Hunter Seduces Bail Bozo." The CEO of the bail bonds company, Michelle Esquenazi, explained the decoy: "We sent a hot piece of pussy to his door." Jonathan was twenty when I met him, but he seemed much younger in some ways. His manner was goofy, and he broke into a wide smile with little provocation. "I couldn't care less that I'm in jail!" he declared. He had trouble maintaining eye contact. He had a broad nose and a chinstrap beard and the swagger of a Long Island street tough, plus the gaping-voweled accent to accompany it. He reminded me a lot of the Worcester boys I grew up with, in their Celtics jerseys and crisp white sneakers. His stated interests include "weed and huskies." "You're not the only person who wants to talk to me," he said quietly, leaning in toward the barrier. "Everyone wants to talk to me."

Earlier in the day, when I queued up with a few dozen women outside the visitors' trailer, I felt a slight paranoia about the nature of my mission. I was visiting Jonathan as a "friend," since gaining press access had proven virtually impossible. This wasn't my first time visiting a friend in jail, but it was my maiden attempt at a surreptitious interview. The other visitors shifted from foot to foot to keep warm and compared notes on visiting policies in the local jails. Rikers Island, New York City's primary prison complex, occupying a tiny land mass in the East River between the Bronx and Queens, is the worst. If you wear leggings, the guards make you wear a knee-length baggy T-shirt to cover your curves. Here at Nassau, you'd better not have even underwire in your bra or a belly-button ring because the metal detectors will screech. I learned, dubiously, that herpes can be transmitted via car seat upholstery. This theory was advanced by one woman who had been driving with another visitor, but referred the passenger to the bus upon learning of her diagnosis. The tinny sounds of several different Candy Crush games filled the air.

"You here to see your boyfriend?" a tiny woman with a long braid down her back asked me.

"Uh, a friend?" I said, my eyes darting around to see if any corrections officers were eavesdropping. As if they cared.

"I know, right? It's complicated. But like I always tell my man, nobody made you do it. You put yourself in here."

But Jonathan does maintain that somebody did indeed make him do it. He said he was abused by his father, who beat him using belts. Salvation came on his eighteenth birthday, when he enlisted in the Marines. His principal motivation was getting out of the house. "My recruiter had a big cake for me," he recalled. (His father's lawyer denied that any abuse occurred.)

Jonathan served for two and a half years, working mostly in a warehouse. "I was in charge of six million dollars of equipment! At eighteen years old!" he said with pride. He recalled that stint as the happiest time in his life. He made a good friend. But he and his friend were both discharged less than honorably when they were caught smoking weed. Jonathan moved back home to Long Island, where he was saving up money to get his own place. He was working at Jiffy Lube, making good money under the table, when he met a woman he called "the love of my life." Jonathan was dating Kristi when his father got fired. Now Raymond was out of a job, and the divorce with Evana was growing nastier by the day. Raymond saw that he wasn't going to get as much as he thought he deserved from the sale of their house in Massapequa.

According to Jonathan, Raymond still held him in the palm of his hand. He bullied his son into going in on the insurance fraud scheme. They bounced around the idea for a week and were planning on staging the drowning a while later. But after a nuclear fight with Evana one night, Raymond told Jonathan they couldn't wait any longer. They would have to do it the following Saturday morning.

After reporting his father missing at Jones Beach, Jonathan went to Kristi's family home in New Jersey. She wasn't privy to the plan, but she could tell something was up. That night Jonathan says he got a call from his father threatening to kill him and Kristi if he spilled the beans. At some point, Kristi realized that Jonathan was lying to her and dumped him. She later took out an order of protection against him. He violated it when he called her 150 times in a twenty-four-hour period. (I also reached out to Kristi several times, but she did not respond. Most of the women who had been in some way connected to male death fakers did not get back to me. While I would love to have heard their stories, their silence reinforced my sense that women are superior at pseudocide. They know how to commit to making themselves scarce.)

Jonathan takes a certain pride in his prowess with deceit.

He said he has reformed here at Nassau, but in the past, he said, "I could look in your eyes and lie to you, no problem. Lying came second nature to me." His father was also awaiting trial in Nassau County Correctional but was housed in a separate facility. As codefendants, they couldn't have contact. The only time they saw each other was in the jail's church once a week. In March 2013 Raymond was out and awaiting sentencing, having pled guilty to conspiracy charges. But he was arrested again just hours later for impersonating a police officer and trying to lure a woman into his van in Freeport, Long Island. I wrote to Raymond, but he declined to be interviewed, saying in his letter, "Your fascination with my story is terribly misguided. You have become a victim of the quick headline that plagues today's media."

Jonathan told me his family has abandoned him since he conspired with his father. And he couldn't get his attorney to return his phone calls. The attorney had taken him on pro bono because of the high-profile nature of the case, Jonathan reckoned. Now that the media attention had died down, he seemed to matter little to his attorney. Jonathan was hoping to get out of jail soon. When he does, he said he wants to take a bus to Columbus, Ohio, where his old Marines pal could get him a job working with him at a Bob Evans restaurant.

The last time I visited Jonathan was just before Christmas. The temperature was frigid, and I waited beyond the shadow of the visitors' trailer to heat up in the sun a little with the wives, girlfriends, and mothers protecting their spots in line from newcomers. The guards were in a good mood for some reason.

Jonathan had recently shaved his head. He looked gaunt. I asked him how he was feeling and if he'd had any contact with his family. He said he hadn't. I asked him what would happen on Christmas. "It's just another day in here for me!" he said cheerfully. "You can either laugh about it or cry about it," he added with the same goofy grin. "I refuse to cry about it. I refuse to be broken by it." He said he's remorseful—who wouldn't be? He lost his girlfriend and family, and didn't even collect an insurance windfall. The highlight of the whole caper was his appearance (prior to going to jail) on an episode of *Dr. Phil*, when he and Kristi were flown out to "Cali" and put up on the program's dime. But he has hope for the future. When he gets out, he plans on earning a degree in computer programming because it would lead to a good job, but he'd really like to study marine biology. His demeanor was upbeat, but his eyes were full of so much loss.

I'd been so intrigued by the idea of starting over. Now I had seen the other, heatbreaking side, through the grown children of fathers who had faked their deaths. Lisa, Jake, and Jonathan experienced their fathers' faked deaths differently: Lisa endured the double deprivation of being abandoned twice; Jake was charged at a very young age with the secret knowledge of Sam's plan; Jonathan actively helped Raymond stage his death. Yet despite these gradations, they were all subject to the whims of men on the make, either the afterthoughts or the pawns in their schemes. Though the fathers' rationales were different, and each relationship distinct, they all left their children in astounding, operatic fashion. But each son or daughter responded in radically different ways. Lisa seems the strongest and most well adjusted, despite the fact that she arguably suffered the most damage from her father's faked death, in that he was not around at all. But perhaps that is what preserved her. Jake and Sam still keep in close touch and have a loving relationship, and Jake clearly looks up to his father. Jonathan, the one who played an active role in the pseudocide, seemed the most broken by it. Maybe because he was in the very process of paying for the act. Or maybe his experience was testament to the destructive nature of the act itself.

The glorious pressure valve didn't seem so enticing anymore. Walking back to wait for a cab in the parking lot of the jail, where Christmas lights had been strung over the razor-wire fencing, I thought about what Raymond Roth, later convicted and sentenced to twenty-seven months to seven years in prison, had written me. Maybe my entire fascination *had* been terribly misguided. Here were the human faces, irreplaceable by fantasy. After meeting Jonathan, the whole enterprise of faking one's death seemed pointless—just a tremendous waste. As soon as I slammed shut the door of the musty Lincoln that was to take me back to the train station, I started to cry. I recognized the ridiculous irony that I was the one weeping as I was being shuttled out of the big house with my freedom intact. But I couldn't help it. I stared out the window at the frozen municipal golf course and skeletal trees lining Salisbury Park Drive and let tears stream down behind my Wayfarers. The driver sucked on a Kool and blew the smoke out the cracked window with the heat on full blast.

By the time he dropped me off at the train station, I had already blown my nose and dabbed at the half moons of mascara under my eyes. Here was a man to pay and to overtip. Here was a hangover to nurse, notes to write up, a vending machine lunch to eat while staring out the window at the low December sun glazing cars and billboards on the highway. Here was a train to take me home, and then another train to my mom's for Christmas the next day. Here were bills to pay and apologies to extend, and the little dog shivering in my empty apartment, summoning me home. Here was loneliness, and worry, and dinner plans, and dirty laundry. Here was life. The weight of these banalities and their redundancy had felt so oppressive before. As I drove away from the jail, though, these daily chores felt right. The trifles of living felt more like a bolster than a burden. I no longer wanted to turn away.

But when an opportunity to peek inside the death fraud industry presented itself, I simply couldn't resist.

6

FAKING MY DEATH WITH MR. CLEAN AND MR. BEAN

On the afternoon of July 18, 2013, a street sweeper had finished lunch and was returning to work when he witnessed a car crash near the corner of Libertad Avenue and Roxas Boulevard in Pasay City, Manila. He reported to Officer Bautista that he saw a red Toyota Innova collide with a gray Mitsubishi Montero Sport. Both vehicles were traveling at high speeds when the Innova suddenly went against the flow of traffic. A store owner, a gasoline attendant, and a traffic attendant also witnessed the collision and corroborated the street sweeper's testimony.

Both vehicles suffered severe damages, and the drivers were rushed to the nearby San Juan de Dios Hospital. The driver of the Montero was a Caucasian American female, Elizabeth L. Greenwood.

She was pronounced dead on arrival.

EVERYTHING THAT HAD COME before—badgering Frank and Steve, reliving the hoax with John, wading through Believers logic, listening to Jonathan Roth's story across a jail partition— all of it led to this terminal moment. But the moment felt interminable. Time passes slowly when you're waiting on your own death certificate.

It seemed as if forces beyond my control had been conspiring to place me here. Only two weeks before, I received an email out of the thin blue ether from a college friend who was working for a magazine in Manila inviting me to the Philippines for an all-expenses-paid trip as a "blogger." I didn't believe it. I'd had my eye set on this South Pacific archipelago for ages, since first reading about those fabled black market morgues and death kits, but I'd had no idea how I would cobble together the plane fare to cross the globe and cultivate the contacts to assist in my literal entrée into the underworld of death fraud. Plus, after becoming so intimate with the nastier side of pseudocide, especially the shattered lives left in death fakers' wakes, I wasn't exactly gunning for an exodus any longer. But the chance to tout the glories of this country and to tack on just two little extra days in the capital to see how one were to fake one's death in this epicenter of pseudocide, if one were so inclined? Subsidized and underwritten? I'd always wanted somebody to make me an offer I couldn't refuse.

I found the Philippines to be heavenly. It was the first time in my so-called career that I was treated like more than a human hemorrhoid. My hosts rolled out the red carpet. And thereby created a monster.

On my weeklong tour, I lazed on white-sand beaches, which

FAKING MY DEATH WITH MR. CLEAN AND MR. BEAN   203

bore a striking resemblance to the sunny, anonymous setting of my après-pseudocide destination. I received transcendent massages and consumed animals new to me, many with faces still intact. I met the tarsier, a tiny primate native to the island of Bohol with eyes the size of grapefruits, which can commit suicide by holding its breath. I was introduced to a new form of roving entertainment wherein elderly Filipinas sing karaoke to the captive audience of a tour bus in transit to the next delight. I feigned sleep while "Memory" from the *Cats* soundtrack was sung off-key and at earsplitting volume. Within twenty-four hours of deplaning, I met the president of the country. I encountered a bountiful buffet (my personal nirvana) at every turn. The first day, I deferentially cleared my own dishes at the resort. By the last day, I found myself wishing the cabana boy would return to massage aloe into my sun-scorched shoulders yet again, and was disappointed when the baked goods in my welcome basket included only one swan-shaped coconut confection. I fell in love with the Philippines. The Philippines is God's country. I wrote about it thusly. I prostituted myself as a writer, and it was worth it. I've done a lot more for a lot less.

But as I sat waiting on the document that would pronounce me dead in a fatal car crash, I wondered if even this would be so free and easy. How would it feel if my new friends (and accomplices) Snooky and Bong were to be the last people I saw before I got busted for fraud, handcuffed, and detained in a Southeast Asian women's correctional facility? I constructed a convincing explanation to feed the cops when they discovered my authentic death certificate on my very alive person. The promise of death (on paper, at least) is what I'd been praying for. The entire deranged journey, which began with Googling "fake your own death," had brought me to Manila, and now

I was scared, stuck with the classic comeuppance of getting what I'd wished for.

======

I MEET MIKE DOMINGO the night before in the cavernous lobby of the Holiday Inn Makati, the heart of the globalization-slick business center of Manila. He is a fifty-one-year-old Pinkerton-trained investigator who has specialized in fraud—from phony insurance claims to counterfeiting operations—for twenty-six years. He has helped Steve Rambam on a number of Filipino death fraud cases. There is an amphibious quality to Mike. Tiny moles speckle the sunken hollows of his cheeks, and the whites of his eyes are cloudy, a bright blue outlining his dark irises. He speaks slowly, deliberately, and in a deep, soft tone that makes you lean in to hear what he's saying. He looks menacing until he smiles.

"Tomorrow morning you will meet Snooky and Bong. They will pick you up and take you wherever you want to go," Mike whispers, while I crane all my gangly hulk into his personal space.

Snooky and Bong? Okay. Tomorrow I am to get in a car with Snooky and Bong, and they will tour me around the death-faking hot spots of the capital city. It sounds like the premise of a straight-to-DVD movie: *Hostel* meets *Taken*, with a touch of *Kindergarten Cop*. Or the stuff of Nancy Grace's dreams.

But I am relieved. I am on a tight timetable—less than thirty-six hours—in the mecca of pseudocide. I think back to Hector Mendoza, who passed off the dead body of the neighborhood drunk as his own. Snooky and Bong sound like saviors to me.

More than serving as a helpful conduit to my local fixers

with the charming names, Mike has worked a great many death fraud cases in his day and can demystify the macabre rumors. Both Richard Marquez and Steven Rambam cited the Philippines as one of the more theatrical stages for full-monty death fraud. Could this really be, even today? Even with homeland security always finding new ways to stamp out phony documents and, of course, the buying and selling of human remains? The Philippine economy has boomed in recent years, so I had wondered if this sector of the informal market was still thriving.

I am dying—pun absolutely intended—to ask Mike, along with the more exigent questions of "Where are the bodies?" "Any blondes in stock?" and "How much?"

Undoubtedly, inquiring about purchasing Mike's deceased countrymen could be construed as culturally insensitive. Asking him from the jump would be like a foreigner entering America and at customs requesting directions to the Calabasas mansion of Kim Kardashian. She might be a dismal fact, but she's not the patriotic face we wish to advance. Not wanting to offend my host in his own country, or even in this ostentatious hotel lobby, I proceed gingerly, sipping nervously at my over-priced bottle of water, and ask him about some of the fishy life insurance cases he has investigated.

"A family filed a claim for a female, a Filipina American, who was insured in the United States," Mike says, looking out the plate-glass hotel window to the gray drizzle swallowing up the half-finished skyline outside.

"They claimed that the female was out strolling along the promenade of Manila Bay when she fell through the breakwater structure and dropped in. The fishermen around scooped out the body and brought it to the police, and gave their statements.

The insurance company wanted to verify the authenticity of the documents the family submitted. The first thing an investigator will do is verify the authenticity of the death certificate." Just like Rambam said: death fraud is carried out mainly with documents. Mike continues: "So the investigator visits the funeral parlor and asks for records. In this case, the body was cremated. I went to the crematorium," he says, still gazing at the thick tropical fog outside.

Through his investigation and comparing photos of the deceased, Mike learned that the body presented to the police, the funeral parlor, and the crematorium was not the woman in question. "It turned out later that what this woman did was buy an unclaimed body at a funeral parlor," he tells me. "Back then"— fifteen years ago—"you could have acquired a cadaver for only twenty thousand to thirty thousand pesos." That's roughly $430 to $640. "She found a fresh body to match her claim, dressed it up in her clothes, and threw it off the promenade into the bay," he says, chortling at the absurdity of the story.

This woman purchased and costumed a dead body and carted it around Manila. My mannered deference suddenly feels quaint.

"So what happened? Did she go to jail?" I ask, absorbing the image of a lady chucking a body in her likeness off the side of the road.

"Very few of the insurance claims we handle go into prosecution. The objective is to deny their claims. When we investigate cases, we charge up to a thousand dollars per day. The companies don't want to spend any more money on this person," he explains.

Mike echoes the shocking consensus I had been hearing all along, from fieldwork specialists to the Coalition Against

Insurance Fraud: in the vast majority of insurance frauds that come under investigation, the only punishment is the company denying the claim. Most insurers will not seek retribution or press charges. If you are bold enough to manipulate your mortality, there is really no legal disincentive to trying your luck at collecting a chunk of change for your untimely demise. This seems really surprising, given how much American businesses like to make examples of no-goodniks. No jail time? Not even a fine? I'm glad to hear this, considering what tomorrow's itinerary entails.

"Just send me an email with all of the places you want to hit and people you want to interview," Mike instructs. "Then I will forward it to Snooky and Bong, and they will support you, whatever you want to do."

I run up to my comfortingly unremarkable hotel room and fire off a wish list:

—Morgues where people can purchase/have purchased bodies
—Shady crematoriums
—Funeral parlors where fraudulent funerals/wakes have occurred
—People who can procure fraudulent documents, e.g., fake death certificates, passports, witness statements, etc.

Mike responds right away: "Sounds good. Snooky and Bong will pick you up in front of the hotel at ten in the morning." I am off to see the wizards.

Imagining the individuals attached to the names Snooky and Bong is not without specific cultural resonance. The former evokes the *Jersey Shore* siren, and the latter conjures the bulbous glass filtration system indigenous to dorm rooms the world over. So when two perfectly normal-looking middle-aged men approach me in front of the Glorietta Mall adjacent to the Holiday Inn the next morning, I am actually taken aback by how unassuming they seem. Bong is slight, with pockmarked skin and a swooping black dye job. He is wearing a short-sleeved white button-down shirt and black slacks, and looks exactly like the bank manager he once was. Snooky is slightly younger, a cop's cop: he has a shaved head and wears an open button-down shirt over a T-shirt and jeans. He walks with the swagger of a Texas sheriff and smiles incessantly.

Bong shakes his head wearily.

"We saw your list last night, and we said, 'Oh my God!' " he says, laughing in a way that makes me nervous.

"Do you have your own contacts?" Snooky asks me. My own contacts? Wasn't the whole point that these two *are* my contacts?

"Uh, no. I think Mike said that you guys would set me up."

"Mike told us that you had your own contacts and that we would just drive you around," Bong says. "*Fuuuuuucccckkk*," I think. How, and whence, this communication breakdown? I just went from twenty-first-century Joan Didion to incompetent blogger reject.

At that moment, Mike, the duplicitous amphibian, rounds the corner. Mike, enabler of death fraud delusions. Mike, you got some 'splainin' to do.

Snooky and Bong perk up when they see their superior. Mike walks over and punches them each in the stomach.

"Hey, boss!" they groan.

"Good morning," he whispers menacingly, soft and deep. "I have a breakfast meeting. We are setting up an entrapment of a woman." Good God. Am I the entrapped woman? Mike slinks off, and Snooky, Bong, and I face one another with consternation.

"It would take a few weeks to set up everything you want to do," Bong says. "But I came up with a plan B: Do you want your own death certificate?"

While I want to experience death fraud firsthand, I never thought I'd get a chance to see my own name in cold, hard type. Never before had such a question been lobbed in my direction. And when the universe arranges itself for such queries to be posed, one can answer only in the affirmative.

"Duh, Bong, yes!"

"Okay, I'll call my guy, and we will see what we can do."

In the meantime, we return to the lobby of the Holiday Inn, which is trying to distract us from the fact that it is a midbudget hotel by splashing lurid geometric patterns across every available surface to cover up the chintzy hardware. I appreciate this strategy of diversion because I employ the same tactic with my wardrobe of Forever 21 cocktail dresses. Now that I'm past the age of thirty-one, the frocks might scan as more poignant than playful, but usually I can pass off the polyblend monstrosities. Unless the setting is formal, that is. You can divert attention with spangles and peplum for only so long until you reveal your lack of resources, and then everyone is embarrassed.

Anyway, Snooky, Bong, and I find a quiet corner in the lounge, surrounded by Chinese businessmen with laptops, the chipper staff hovering nearby.

Bong has investigated over fifty cases of death fraud in his fifteen-year career, and as Mike said last night, the first place he starts is with the death certificate. The theatrics of lobbing a body off a bridge are superfluous. And sourcing bodies, though delightfully lugubrious, is often unnecessary. The Philippines is fertile ground for death fraud because of the widespread corruption of developing countries. In fact, the "corruption" is so commonplace that the word isn't an accurate term. It's just another way of doing business.

Take, for example, the guy who is helping to secure my death certificate. A friend of Bong's, he goes under the code name Smith and works for the National Bureau of Investigation (NBI), the Philippine equivalent of the FBI. This arm of the law goes after people who commit fraud, and yet the person helping me to commit fraud is the person in charge of stamping it out. One thinks of the *Ouroboros*, the ancient symbol of a serpent eating its own tail. With Smith working both ends, he will never be in short supply of fraud to investigate, and he will always be doubly employed.

Before Bong gets on the phone to organize the certificate, he asks, "Hey, do you want to graduate from medical school today too?" In addition to supplying death certificates (which is a "very rare" request), the counterfeiter mostly makes diplomas and transcripts required for many good jobs. (This is a ubiquitous practice the world over. In 2012 a Mexican university president was found to have a fake degree. A retired University of Rhode Island adjunct professor convicted of embezzling state research funds in 2014 had landed his job with a phony diploma.) Both Snooky and Bong use fake IDs from Smith's forger when they go undercover, and the counterfeiter's work is so good that Bong blackens the upper left corner of his false ID so he doesn't confuse it with the authentic one. "Always use the same first name!" Snooky says. "It's instinct to respond to your first name." Just as John Jones, née John Darwin, advised me in England.

Most people in the Philippines with fake licenses don't get them to assume a different identity or for malevolent purposes, but just to save time. Fraudulent driver's licenses and passports are a prosaic part of life. The few tedious hours you might pass at your local DMV in the United States are cake compared with the endless coiling line at the Manila counterpart: "If you arrive at eight o'clock when they open the window, you might be two-hundred-fifty-eighth in line," Bong says. "Then they close at three in the afternoon. So you go back the following morning. You will be in line at six. Then you will be in the first one hundred. Then it will take all day, under the hot sun or drizzling rain." If you want to get a fake ID card or death certificate, they are quite easy to obtain and won't arouse suspicion.

So who are the people who come to the Philippines to take advantage of the amenable fraud climate? I ask Bong to walk me through a typical case.

"Most people who commit death fraud in the Philippines are Filipino but citizens of the United States," he says. "If they are not Filipino by birth, they will have some connection to the country, like they were stationed here in the army. They come back here and meet their untimely death. One such person is Eduardo Medina. He had lived in Detroit for years, but came back to visit his country and went swimming at the beach in the northernmost part of the country. This beach is known for rough waves. That's why they picked that area: it's the perfect cover-up. According to his companion, he was so drunk that he was swept away in the tides. So there's no cadaver. After a few days, a body will usually wash up. But in this case, there's none. I don't know why he would choose to swim at that beach. He is from central Luzon. Why would he travel four hundred kilometers to go swimming? Then we found out that he has another family in the Philippines that his wife and children back in Detroit don't know about."

This case sounds familiar, like Wint or the Canadian scuba instructor.

"In the new family, his wife is young," Bong says. Shocker. "I sense collusion between the first wife and the missing husband."

"Really? Why would the first wife help him fake his death?" I ask.

"We found out he wasn't doing well in America. His wife is a doctor, and he had a jewelry business that was failing. So they probably thought that they could collect eventually, even though they'd have to wait five years, without a cadaver."

"So she didn't know about the other family?"

"No, she probably just wanted to get rid of the husband and collect money while she's at it."

"Why not just get divorced?" I ask. I think about Lisa Boosin's wish for her father. This seems like a really crazy and complicated way to leave your family.

"Probably because he's afraid of his wife!" Snooky guffaws, and Bong joins in laughing. This casual misogyny, this "Take my wife!" Borscht Belt repartee, is a big part of Snooky's and Bong's banter. I am an ardent feminist. But their gag lines are so predictable, and the middle-aged-guy outlook so Central Casting, that their jokes feel more cute than offensive. Snooky's designated ringtone for his wife is the theme song from the TV show *Combat!*, because she is the sergeant. I laugh right along with them. The two-timing jewelry maker wants to leave the wife! But he's afraid of her! So he fakes his death! Of course!

But does it work the other way? Do women try to ditch their fat, balding, charmless husbands for younger models? Do they become Cavalli-swathed cougars with their newly minted insurance windfall?

"Out of the fifty investigations you've done, how many have been men and how many have been women?" I ask.

"There was only one female," Bong says.

"So why more men than women?" This question has been nagging at me all along, especially after meeting John Darwin. He shirked his paternal and financial obligations because he felt entitled to something better. Does it have something to do with masculinity in the twenty-first century? With men's adeptness at compartmentalizing or rationalizing their misdeeds? Their ability to forget about their familial responsibilities?

"They want to live with another girl! *Ha!*" Snooky says, cracking up, and Bong bangs the table. According to guys who have investigated loads of these cases, "living with another girl" (along with a handsome insurance payout) is the primary motive. So much for my pseudosociological theorizing. Snooky continues: "Usually male criminal minds have more guts to run to another country. A single lady would find trouble, attract the wrong attention. We've got a lot of army bases here, and retirees from the service. It's normal to see an old white guy in the provinces with a family. But for a female American white girl and a local male guy? I haven't seen that—unfortunately! *Hahahahaha!*"

So the Philippines is a good place to die if you fit a certain profile. I apparently don't cut it.

Back to Medina, the "drowned" swimmer from Luzon. How did Bong investigate?

"The police report looked legit, and it said he was with two male companions. Medina was drunk, but the other two weren't. How long would it take for those two guys to notice he was gone? So definitely the other two are co-conspirators. It turns out one of the guys is Medina's godson."

"So did he cooperate with you? Or did he try to cover up for his godfather?"

"When I arrived to interview him, I introduced myself. 'Hi, I'm Mr. Bong from Manila. I'm here to investigate the death of Eduardo Medina. I believe you are his godson.' You can see from the surprise on his face, 'How did you know?!' They are not prepared. They're only focused on the local problem."

No one expects Mr. Bong's inquisition. This reminds me of something Mike said last night about how there's actually a lot of money in death fraud claims for the investigator himself, because once accessories get tipped off that someone like Bong is nosing around, they will bribe him to write a clean report. My guys, however, would never do such a thing. I think.

Bong continues: "The godson is a bus driver, and I interviewed him in front of the terminal. I asked, 'Why did you and your godfather go swimming so far north?' He said, 'His wife is from there.' But I knew his wife wasn't from there. Something suspicious is boiling. I asked him, 'What's the name of your godfather's wife?' 'Elsie,' he said. Again, I know this isn't her name. 'What does she do?' 'She sells cell phone accessories.' Then I turn around, and across the street is a cell phone accessories store called Elsie's Cell Phones. He made it up on the fly! *Ha!*"

We are all cackling at the ingenuity. I'm waiting for the dramatic coda—which, before delving into the world of death fraud, I would have assumed involved people going to jail, maybe even including the godson as an accessory (to a crime, not a cell phone).

"As an investigator, I had a gut feeling that something was

wrong," Bong says. Gut feelings seem to be a guiding principle in death fraud investigations. Steve Rambam said that most insurance fraud investigations begin in the office, when a claims adjustor intuits something is not right.

Bong continues, "So I filed my report to the insurance company, and they decide. My boss called me up and said, 'Job well done, but the company doesn't want to pursue the case.' So they will get paid in five years, even if a body doesn't appear."

It seems crazy: it appears that Medina committed death fraud without even using a body or procuring a fraudulent death certificate like the one I'm waiting on. If he can just sit tight for the next few years, he will collect hundreds of thousands of dollars. This scenario definitely sounds preferable to (and more profitable) than simply disappearing. His case underscores how easy it is for fraudsters to collect a payout because of the tight spot the company is in: it can't prove that Medina is dead without a body, nor can it prove that he is alive, short of smoking him out. And crazier still, these types of faked death cases rarely make the news in the Philippines. Unlike in the United States and the United Kingdom, where death fakers such as Raymond Roth or John Darwin become tabloid fodder, local Filipino guys who go missing under mysterious circumstances do not attract the same media attention.

"So the Philippines is a great place to die!" I conclude.

"It is!" Snooky says. Bong nods, and bangs his fist on the table. "But it really is. It's English speaking. We are used to foreigners because we've been colonized so many times."

Bong's flip phone skitters across the tablecloth as it buzzes. It's the fixer who is arranging my death certificate. He steps away from the table for a minute. In the interim, Snooky regales me with some colorful tales of working private security with Bong, their other job together. They have been bodyguards for David Beckham, Bill and Melinda Gates, and, most recently, the opposition leader in Malaysia during a six-month campaign—a superdangerous job, because they had to deflect numerous attempts on the candidate's life. And, trickier still, because you must be licensed to carry guns, knives, and even ammunition in the Muslim country. Their only mode of defense was a ballpoint pen. Snooky gives me a quick demo on how to take out an adversary with a Bic: "Make a slashing *X* in front of you, to create kind of like a shield! Then—*guh!*" He makes a stabbing motion, a little too close to my person. "Go for the eyes!" Bong returns to the table and adds a caveat to Snooky's lesson: "You should also know how to run fast!"

The forger, it turns out, is not impressed with our expedited request, Bong explains.

" 'What do you think I am, Superman?!' he said. You have skipped the line! Very important person, VIP! *Hahahaha!* He wants to know: How would you like to die?"

"What are my options?"

"A car accident is good. The traffic here is awful." Well, with my driving, people would believe it. Contrary to the Volkswagen ad, on the road of life there are not passengers and drivers. Rather, there are drivers and those who should be driven. I am terrified of driving—and, more specifically, of dying in a gruesome car accident—because I was in a gnarly one as a teenager. Today, going over fifty miles per hour on a highway gives me heart-constricting anxiety, even when I'm not behind the wheel.

For the first time in all our joking about killing me and creating my own death on paper, I feel a little queasy. Of course, the way I most fear myself dying is the way I am now tempting fate to fake! I'm not so sure I like this anymore.

Locking down my own death certificate looks like it will be surprisingly easy. But what about those dead bodies? Snooky and Bong place some calls to their cop friends, since, sadly, I do not boast the kind of contacts Mike claimed I did. Now we're playing the waiting game, and time is ticking down. I'm scheduled to leave the country in less than eighteen hours.

"In the olden days, people didn't even buy a cadaver from the morgue," Bong says. "They would put a live person inside the coffin and collect contributions for a fake wake. Sometimes they would tell mourners, 'You can only have a little peek because he died of a contagious disease, so the casket is closed!' *Ha!*"

"In Manila, you are allowed to have gambling if you have a wake," Snooky says. Gambling, while ordinarily illegal in the devoutly Catholic country, finds a convenient loophole in the case of a death. If a family hosts a numbers game or mah-jongg at a wake—but only at a wake—police will turn a blind eye. "So what they do now," Snooky explains, "is loan a dead body. If a family member dies, they will loan the body all around the community, and everyone gets a percentage."

"Where else have you seen a wake that lasts two weeks?" Bong asks breathlessly.

"I'm pretty sure the police are also getting paid," Snooky says. "A cut of the winnings, usually fifteen percent to twenty percent, goes to the family to provide for burial expenses."

In this scenario, the sin of gambling acts as charity. And organizers go to great lengths to earn a degree of verisimilitude so as not to arouse suspicion from local law enforcement.

"They even rent crying girls!" Bong says. Just as you can with Irish keeners, you can pay local slum dwellers a few pesos to get into character and weep over the coffin.

Since running a weeks-long gambling game can be lucrative, but is rare when you have to wait for someone to actually die, local entrepreneurs find a more creative way to raise money: they purchase unclaimed bodies at an unofficial morgue and host fake wakes. In the Philippines, supplying dearly departed family members for gambling games is the primary purpose of black market morgues—not death fraud for insurance purposes, not to leave behind your family, not to reinvent yourself.

This revelation is the most shocking thus far: while I was initially afraid of broaching the topic of illegal morgues and bodies for sale, it turns out that exchanging money for dead human flesh is a relatively common practice in the Philippines, even something of a cottage industry. I wonder why the Department of Tourism isn't peddling this unique and authentic experience to foreign visitors. The country's relationship with death is complex and contradictory. The law of the land is based on Catholic dogma, and gambling doesn't jibe. But when it comes to creating the appearance of death, manipulating mortality and pulling out all the stops with a show funeral just to gamble, which is the bigger sin? It seems strange that pantomiming a funeral would be kosher, but a card game would not. I suppose it comes down to poverty: if you have a chance to make a few bucks, you can probably rationalize throwing dice over a dead body.

But it's not just poverty that accounts for the existence of such a market. Lack of adequate governmental resources for proper body disposal is another reason so much death fraud occurs not just in the Philippines but also in other developing nations generally.

The United States, for example, boasts a stunningly comprehensive system for retrieving, storing, and locating the relatives of unclaimed bodies. In the United States, if the stink from a bloated corpse in an hourly motel so offends a neighbor that she calls the cops, the coroner collects the remains and will store them on ice for three to four months. The Public Administrator's Office attempts to locate next of kin, combing through any personal effects and financial records and reaching out to former employers and neighbors. These administrators act essentially as detectives, tracking down any family who can serve to identify the body. If no one can be located to claim the body after four months, the body will be cremated. Caitlin Doughty, the writer who worked in crematories in Los Angeles, explains: "Sometimes the coroner keeps the jawbone, because once someone is cremated, there's no identifying them." This happens more frequently than you would think. In Los Angeles alone, as a result of the city's large homeless population, the coroner cremates around 1,500 unclaimed bodies each year. The city holds on to the cremains for at least another two years, and often longer. Each December, a cohort of cremains that has passed its expiration for being claimed gets deposited into a mass grave behind the Boyle Heights crematory. Workers in Hazmat suits and masks empty metal boxes and dump ashes into a hole in the ground. The air becomes a thick white cloud of human remains for several hours, until the dust settles. In 2014 the county buried 1,489 unclaimed people it had been storing since 2011. Clerics and community leaders attend the ceremony to see these mysterious mortals off to the next world.

Such an organized infrastructure in the United States makes it difficult to cut through bureaucratic red tape, and the palms of desk workers are not greased easily. But Doughty says that, like their Philippine counterparts, coroners' offices are still overextended and eager to unload inventory: "If the body has been there for a while, and you show up, like, 'I'm his third cousin, I want to see him well taken care of!' they would probably just release it. The idea is that you would take it away and pay for it. The typical fee is three hundred to four hundred dollars for the coroner's office, and that includes the autopsy. If you want a basic cremation in LA County, it's about seven hundred to eight hundred dollars. You're looking at about a thousand dollars total to get the body out of there." Buying bodies for insurance purposes, or bogus wakes, is not the principal corruption Doughty encountered in the funeral business. "There really aren't black market morgues, but there are definitely more shady funeral parlors," she explains. "The organ trade is on the nursing home and hospital side of things, before the bodies get to the funeral parlor." Those funeral parlors tend to remove skin, tendons, and bones from corpses without family permission and sell them to hospitals for surgeries for thousands of dollars. Different economies, cultures, and health care systems yield different death crimes, it seems.

Bong texts Smith to get an ETA on my death certificate.

"We're still killing her!" Smith texts back.

In the meantime, Bong makes a few phone calls. He learns that there has been a recent crackdown on black market morgues and even on the regulated, police-affiliated morgues. Just that morning, two boys, ages three and four, were found dead inside a Mercedes with heavily tinted windows in Taguig City in Metro Manila. The boys had been missing for four months. They were brought to a private morgue first. Seeing an opportunity to squeeze some money out of grieving parents, the morgue charged 70,000 pesos (about $1,500) to release the remains to the family, citing a "storage fee." This isn't the first time that Manila morgues have been criticized for such unseemly practices. One morgue in the Quezon City district was found illegally harboring the bodies of eighteen to twenty children and selling them to the local medical schools.

The case of the two suffocated boys made national news headlines and left people duly enraged. Bong describes the shoddy quality of the local morgues when the government in Quezon City checked them out in the last round of crackdowns: "Sometimes the cadavers are just stacked in old bathtubs and drums." And these bodies go cheaply because the morgue is happy to get rid of them.

When I returned to New York, Steve Rambam further contextualized the shady mortuary business: "The government morgues are attached to the police agencies, like the NBI. So if someone gets shot, forensics will examine the body, then it goes to the morgue. If the body is a criminal, no one wants to claim it, especially in the provinces. So it will be left behind. What is a little morgue out in the middle of nowhere going to do with them? Chop them up and bury them in shallow ground? They need a special cooling system. That's why I'm telling you it won't cost much, because they want to get rid of them."

So who are the enterprising brains behind these institutions? Usually it's a family business that's been handed down for generations, people with contacts in law enforcement. They will give local police a cut. Proprietors get not only protection from the police for bribes but also a steady stream of capital when police bring in bodies from crime scenes. And then, as with the current crackdown, police know exactly where to make their cursory busts. Again, the snake eats its tail.

According to Bong's contact, three of the most infamous private morgues in Manila have been shuttered temporarily in the last few days due to the kids-trapped-in-the-car incident. "But in the provinces, you can still get a body, no problem," Snooky reassures me. The next day, Bong will be appearing on a morning news program as a security expert to give advice on what to do if a kid is locked inside a vehicle. What tips will he dispense? I ask. "Make sure they have plenty of food so they don't die, *ha!*" he responds.

Bong's television contact, incidentally, is his eldest son, who works for the news program based in Manila. Given the dangerous nature of Snooky's and Bong's work—bodyguarding, investigating fraud—both men lead quiet home lives, in stark contrast with their high-octane professions.

While we're waiting for the death certificate (Bong answers his cell phone and shouts in a mix of Tagalog and English, in which I can make out "Green*wood*! Green*wood*!" Apparently the forger had a question about my surname, which is important to get right), I gain some insight into their personal lives. Snooky is an adrenaline junkie. He has gone skydiving more than 260 times to date and rides motocross on the weekends. This is how he and Bong met twenty years ago, when Snooky joined a motorcycle club that Bong led. They have been partners ever since, although the nature of their relationship is often called into question. At the office, their big boss refers to them as "the two scoundrels," and their peers call them "the sissy partners." But the judges they train regularly in self-defense—in case someone on the wrong end of a verdict seeks vengeance—refer to the pair as "the Clean-Bean Connection," due to Snooky's Mr. Clean–like shaved head and Bong's likeness to British actor Rowan Atkinson's character Mr. Bean.

To what do they attribute the longevity of their relationship? "We don't fight about money, and we don't fight about women!" Snooky says. He pulls out his cell phone and shows me pictures of three adorable girls: one infant daughter and a set of nine-year-old twin girls whom he is grooming in his image. Both are ranked nationally in the Philippine martial art kali, and he has been training them to shoot guns since they were four years old. Now one is into artillery, and the other is into archery and knife throwing. "The Little Nikitas," Bong calls them. He, too, is a father, though his four children are grown up and out of the house. Bong started out working as a bank manager, then worked at the NBI investigating financial crimes, and then went into private security after his retirement.

Snooky and Bong are not their Christian names, though the nicknames' origins are just as wholesome. Bong is named after a Philippine cartoon from the 1960s that shared his real first name, Perlito, and Snooky had a lot of hiccups as a kid. "The Tagalog word for hiccups is *sinok*, so that turned into Snooky," he explains. "It's a girl's name, actually. It was good during high school and college because it sounded harmless—"

"The irony!" Bong interjects.

"The irony!" Snooky agrees.

Mr. Clean and Mr. Bean do seem harmless to me, in spite of their cartoonish machismo and the concealed guns they carry. On this day in particular, Snooky is packing four guns, and Bong, three. Unlike in Malaysia, guns are quite legal here. Maybe the Philippines and all its aggressive friendliness has worked its magic on me, but I have felt very safe the entire time I've been in the country. Prior to flying in, everyone I knew—especially my best friend from college, who is Filipina American—warned me to be careful. "I know my people, Liz," she said with resignation. And that was without my having mentioned that the primary goal of this trip (beyond my advertorial assignment) was seeking dead bodies for purchase. Now I'm sitting across from two heavily armed guys who could kill me with a ballpoint pen, waiting to get in a car to drive across Metro Manila to pick up my own death certificate. Given what I've learned about corruption and how life is lived here, putting trust in law enforcement—or in these two guys who run interference between the police and the criminals—maybe isn't the wisest idea. But what can I do now, go barricade myself in my hotel room? At the same time, I wonder how Snooky and Bong perceive me, an American weirdo who really, really wants to know the finer points of pseudocide. Why should they take my word for it that I'm a "writer"? I often have trouble giving my job title with a straight face myself.

I ask them if what I'm doing—inquiring into illegal morgues, fake documents, and unclaimed bodies—is dangerous. They dispel my fears quickly. Nosing into death fraud is a breeze. It is reporting on the government that will get you killed.

"It's a dynasty here," Snooky says, referring to the government's iron-fisted control of the media. This became deadly clear in the Maguindanao massacre in 2009, where at least thirty-two journalists were slain in the small town of Amaptuan because the incumbent mayoral candidate dispatched his security team to kill everyone in the opposition party's convoy. Fifty-seven people were killed and buried in a mass grave. No one was ever convicted. The Committee to Protect Journalists called the massacre "the single deadliest event for the press since 1992," when the organization began keeping records of reporters killed in the field. Prior to the massacre, the committee had labeled the Philippines the second most dangerous country for reporters, lagging behind only Iraq. Snooky and Bong also teach a self-defense class for journalists. Some Clean-Bean alumni were reporting the day of the massacre, but made it out alive because they heeded Snooky's and Bong's advice to avoid big groups and split off. In spite of such horrors, they both insist that what we're doing today is safe. So long as we don't get involved with local politics, we are in the clear.

The anxieties I harbored prior to landing in the Philippines are turning out to be unfounded. I thought I was willfully putting myself into some kind of imminent danger, sniffing around purchasing corpses and ripping off American insurance companies. But it turns out that faking your own death, at least logistically speaking, is not as perilous as it might seem. Before touching down in the Philippines, I'd imagined that organizing the endeavor—sourcing my body, plying the right people, securing the necessary signatures—would make me something of a low-budget Jason Bourne. But my subterfuge is turning out to be as dangerous as Drew Barrymore going undercover as a high school student in *Never Been Kissed*. I am not trolling the docks, talking to men in long trench coats, or lying on my back on a dirty mattress in a stuffy flophouse with a listless ceiling fan stirring the muggy air while a Dickensian child hustler uses his wits to bring me a body. No, my death fraud is all going down as I sit in the air-conditioned lobby of a multinational chain hotel.

This distinctly unglamorous experience mirrors the revelation about the rampant use of false documents in the Philippines. People aren't seeking fake IDs so they can be somebody else. They need them for the purely pragmatic and understandable reason of avoiding throwing away several days' time and wages wading through a labyrinthine bureaucratic process. It's hardly swashbuckling, but it's much more relatable. Could it really be this easy? If you know the right people, you can get a trustworthy fixer to hook you up with whatever you need. And how do you find the right people? Pose as a journalist!

But I still have one last question, one I've been trying to answer since the beginning: "If your goal is just to get away from your life—not to collect insurance money—is it better to disappear or to fake your death?"

"The main ingredient is the family you leave behind, unless you are a single person," Snooky says. "Because if a wife or kid is looking for you, chances are they will find you."

"If you were investigating this type of missing persons case, where a person with no known enemies just vanished one day—how would you do it?" I ask.

"The first thing I would do is check immigration. Did you leave the country? If so, which country? You follow the paper trail, and the investigation starts."

"How easy is it to travel on a fake passport here?" I ask. Prior to working in private security, Snooky was at the US Embassy. Passports were his specialty.

"If the fake passport comes from a foreign country, then it's okay. A US passport would work. Unless you're wanted or on the blacklist, I think you'd be okay. They don't have that technology at the airports; they don't scan passports. Manila isn't the only international airport, though. You've got Cebu, Mindanao . . ."

I know what he's getting at. I flew out of Cebu a few days ago during my prissy press junket. The security was as meticulous as that at a minor league baseball game.

For those who feel a little uneasy trying to pass off an unclaimed provincial Filipino cadaver as your likeness, disappearing might be the way to go. As with Ahearn, Rambam, and everyone else said, it comes down to motivations. Why do you want to leave, and who is looking for you?

Bong's cell phone skitters across the table. He reads the text: "Your friend is dead."

It's time.

We step outside into a wall of hot, gray steam. We walk to the underground parking garage, where Bong has parked his new Mercedes SLK. I climb into the backseat and settle in for our journey to NBI headquarters, where we will pick up Smith and my you-know-what. Since I died in a car accident, I urge Bong to please drive carefully. The two guys in front both crack up, but I really mean it. It's four o'clock, and Manila rush hour is commencing. Even along the back road shortcuts that Bong takes, every intersection is a bottleneck. We pass fruit stands with women selling dusty bananas, lines of autorickshaws with the drivers napping in their cabs, beggars weaving through the gridlock asking for change. One such beggar approaches the passenger-side window, but Snooky taps his knuckles twice on the glass.

"That means you are part of the syndicate, so they go away," he explains.

"What do you mean?" I ask.

"The beggars are a part of the syndicate, and the syndicate runs the begging. They house them and feed them at night, and they go out begging during the day. They get a little bit of money, and protection. With room and board paid for, the beggars make more than the basic salary earner!"

Even the begging is organized, and even the begging is corrupt.

We pass the hulking concrete Manila Film Center, modeled after the ancient Parthenon and commissioned by then First Lady Imelda Marcos, the profligate, shoe-centric wife of dictator Ferdinand Marcos, for the first Manila International Film Festival in 1982. Urban legend says the place is haunted because of an accident that happened just prior to the structure's completion. A dozen workers plummeted to their deaths, but, not wanting to delay the film festival, the Steel Butterfly, as she was known, ordered that they pour concrete over the bodies and continue construction.

Soon we pull up in front of another dismal concrete monolith: NBI headquarters. Everything in the Pasay municipality looks like it was built during the Cold War. The neighborhood resembles the plaza and discothèque illustrations from my out-of-date junior high school Spanish textbook. A stocky man in a baseball hat with a chipped front tooth slides into the backseat next to me. This is Smith, who, despite his double-agent status, looks just as unassuming as Bong and Snooky. He is holding a long brown envelope.

"Give it to her!" Snooky yells to the backseat. Smith understands English but prefers to speak Tagalog.

He hands me the package. I undo the clasp and pull out a two-page document. The first page looks like a diploma, with red ribbons bound by gold foil seal and calligraphic flourishes. But my eyes are drawn immediately to the lower right corner, which reads:

NSO CERTIFIED

TRUE COPY OF DEATH CERTIFICATE

ISSUED TO ELIZABETH LOGAN GREENWOOD

"I'm dead!"

"Should we start crying?" asks Snooky.

"We need to hire the crying girls now! We can make some money from your wake, *hahahaha*!" Bong says.

I flip to the second page, a yellow sheet with the details of my life, and my death.

Elizabeth Logan Greenwood died on July 2 at San Juan de Dios General Hospital in Pasay City. Cause of death: car accident. According to the document before me, I am married, Catholic, and a businesswoman. I managed to tie the knot, convert religions, find a viable career, and die, all within a few hours.

Below my new life story is a grid of boxes with signatures and dates, from the chief of police, the mortician, the doctor, the civil registrar. I'm no investigator, but they look pretty legit to me.

The accompanying police report, on official Philippine National Police letterhead, describes the accident. While the Spanish and Tagalog names of the places where my accident went down are unfamiliar, a few phrases stick out as plain as a recurring nightmare:

Both vehicles suffered severe damages, the driver of the Innova was rushed to the nearby San Juan De Dios Hospital as well as Ms. Greenwood which later proclaimed (DOA) Dead on Arrival.

The relatives of Ms. Greenwood will be notified as soon as the representative of the US Embassy Manila finished their own inquiry on the matter.

All items and belongings of Ms. Greenwood will be forwarded to the US Embassy Manila for safe keeping purposes.

I think back to the questions Rambam and I had concocted for those considering pseudocide. If I'd known then what I know now, I definitely would have inserted a box in that decision tree about one's ability to look the eternal footman in his eye and snicker. Whether or not one is especially superstitious, seeing the end of one's life typed out on a police blotter gives one pause.

We are now weaving in and out of traffic, with Smith and me sharing the backseat.

"I have to be very careful driving now!" Bong says. "If we get pulled over, I will say I am rushing you to the hospital. *Ha!*"

"Hey, do you like seafood?" Snooky yells back to me.

We are on our way to a seafood restaurant for a very late lunch or a very early dinner. I suddenly realize I'm starving. Or am I dying of hunger? I am dying for seafood. *Ha!*

We pull onto a narrow pier, and the briny funk of the fish market wafts into the car, even with the windows rolled up. The sun is beginning its descent over Manila Bay, casting an orange light over the rows of restaurants. We are the first diners at Papa Don's. We sit at a round table for eight, though we are only four. We get a round of San Miguel beers, and Snooky orders what seems like one of every item on the menu: grilled lobster with lemon butter sauce; deep-fried squid, shrimp, and crab; seafood soup; tuna belly; pork belly; and steamed rice. When the food arrives, I make the requisite joke: now I've died and gone to heaven.

Bong sidles over and explains the finer points of my death certificate. The first page is from the Department of Foreign Affairs, because I am an American. While the certificate itself bears today's date—July 17—the accident actually took place on July 2. Why the time lapse?

"It takes a few weeks from the time of death to process the paperwork," Bong explains. "This is very authentic."

According to the paper, my cousin requested the certificate, and it also states that we live together. "Maybe he's also my husband?" I offer.

"You even have the funeral permit here!" Bong is very impressed with the forger's work, maybe even a little proud.

Now that I have my own death certificate, which yesterday wasn't even an item on my wish list, I have a pressing question.

"Is it illegal to have this?" I ask.

"According to who? *Ha!*" Bong responds, and all three of them crack up.

I have no idea what this means. All I know is that I have to get on a plane tomorrow and fly to Tokyo and then to New York. If my bag gets searched, as is wont to happen because I arouse suspicion at every turn, I want to know what I should say.

I won't find out today, though.

Instead, I chat with Smith about his extracurricular job, while Bong translates. It turns out that he takes only a small cut, and sometimes nothing at all. But why would a forger work with someone from the NBI, even given the level of corruption in Manila?

"I want someone in law enforcement watching my back," Smith says. Bong interjects: "It works both ways, because sometimes we need our fake IDs for investigations, or documents like today."

All of the papers are authentic, obtained by a mole inside the National Statistics Office who siphons off the documents slowly. Diplomas are the most requested item. He can do a passport with biometrics, but that takes more time and money. None of the documents he produces have come back to bite him yet. My death certificate would usually cost 5,000 pesos, or about $100. Except they are sweet enough to give it to me on the house.

I ask Smith how old he is. He's fifty-seven, and I can't believe it because he looks so young.

"Even my face is fake," he says, to more uproarious laughter.

We eat, and most of the food I am arranging and rearranging on my plate has googly fish eyes staring up at me. I know this place, though charming in its down-home authenticity, will not agree with my delicate gringo stomach. (It doesn't. I can't venture too far afield from the commode for two weeks after this.) I had planned on paying for the meal. After the generosity that Snooky, Bong, and company have shown me, it would have been my pleasure. But they don't let me pay. "We charged it to Mike's account!" Snooky says. The Department of Tourism might not approve of this illicit window into the Philippines, but what goodwill ambassadors these three guys are. My love for this country is cemented yet again.

We walk out of the restaurant, and the pier is now packed. A young father and mother walk into Papa Don's with their infant baby. Outside a boy is skinning fish into a bucket. Two men are laughing. The sky over the bay is streaked with purple and orange, and the smog from rush-hour traffic creates a colorful parachute over our heads. There would be so much to miss about this life.

I will say good-bye to Snooky and Bong. I will pack my bag, wrapping my death certificate carefully in plastic and placing it nonchalantly between a few glossy Department of Tourism promo magazines ("It's More Fun in the Philippines!") in my backpack. I will wake up in a few hours and take a taxi down a deserted highway to the airport. I will go to the ticket counter and customs, and get on the plane. I will travel with a declaration of my death in my backpack. I will go through security in Manila, Tokyo, and New York. On paper, I am already dead. But a part of me has never felt more alive.

EPILOGUE

ow, not bad," Steve Rambam says as he rotates the Department of Foreign Affairs Authentication Certificate two inches from his eyes. We are having dinner after my return from the Philippines. I want his expert opinion on how my certificate would hold up under scrutiny. We'd come full circle, in a way. He first put me onto the overseas death fraud industry, and now we can trade notes on our international intrigue. As usual, though, Steve is all business, skeptical of my unremitting romance with pseudocide.

"It's a good watermark," he concedes, holding the sheet up to catch the light at different angles. "This first page is about ninety-five percent of the way there." Then he flips over to the Office of the Civil Registrar General's Certificate of Death.

"Okay, this one sucks. They actually double printed it with an inkjet printer!" In a matter of seconds and with a quick glance, Steve unravels the forger's work. But hope is not lost. He explains how I would proceed if someone were to file and document my death on my behalf. First, my trusted co-conspirator would take it to the US Embassy in Manila, which would issue an embassy certification. And what if it found this document fishy? Would it investigate the papers right there?

"Probably not," Steve says. "That's one of the biggest holes in the process. If whatever you take to them appears to be an authentic local certification, they will validate it. They don't investigate anything."

With the embassy's endorsement, my death still would need to be registered domestically in the United States. I'd want to avoid a populous jurisdiction with more resources.

"What are your parents' names?" Steve asks.

"Merritt and Janette."

"These aren't even their names!" he exclaims. In the forger's haste, he'd failed to collect some requisite data. "But if you presented this in some Podunk county . . ." Steve trails off, not wanting to encourage me, I think. "I don't know. It depends on how closely it's investigated."

In the end, I didn't file. I'd never really planned to. So I can't say whether I would have been successful or not. A part of me likes to think I could have outwitted the experts and gotten away with being dead among the living. But I know I'd end up like so many of the people Frank and Steve have investigated who get caught because they can't sustain their new identity. I'd take up a disguise the way John Darwin advised. I'd dye my tresses jet black and whittle a svelte new figure, only to get caught on a Walgreens security camera fondling a box of hair bleach and a Reese's bar. We are who we are. Even though we fantasize about leaving ourselves behind, we don't know how to be anyone else. And the problems begin when we turn away from who we are in favor of some theoretically superior version. As Sam Israel wrote me in an email from prison, with fourteen years left on his sentence, explaining what had put him there: "I got away from myself."

I never filed, so in that sense, my death certificate experiment is incomplete. But the question remains: Is it possible to fake your own death in the twenty-first century? Despite my anonymous requests on those shabby websites doling out death-faking advice, no one ever came forward who had committed pseudocide and was still presumed dead. The people I interviewed had all been caught or turned themselves in. They provide scalable insight to the question. John and Sam got away with it, but only for a while. And even though I walked right up to the edge when I ordered documents in the Philippines that could have killed me, I don't know what it feels like to witness my own funeral. I don't know what it would mean to unburden myself of my debt, along with necessarily and simultaneously losing my family, my friends, and my identity.

But here's what I do know:

This quest was a catharsis. Handling my own death certificate and a police report that narrated the details of my fatal car crash put me far enough out on the precipice to realize that I didn't want to jump. But I felt the exhilaration nonetheless. It's like the moment when you catch your breath after nearly being run down by a taxi: a brush with death shocks you back to life. Somehow, holding a fictional story of an accident and the official stamps and seals that confirmed its existence passed my anxieties through a sieve and purified them on the other side. While I didn't commit pseudocide, I survived a pseudocide attempt. And the world looks forever different to me.

Like the Believers, I entertained possibilities that cracked open another reality. I saw the world as a scavenger hunt. Everyone I encountered told me that things are not what they seem. Death fraudsters and conspiracy theorists occupy similar strata. After all, if you know either through firsthand experience or evangelical insistence that the most essential component of mortality is not necessarily hard-and-fast fact, then all bets about anything else are off. When I let the accumulation of "facts and evidence" that Pearl described wash over me, I didn't necessarily buy it, but I felt energized. Their theories, applied beyond their own enthusiastic context, demonstrated that you could rewrite a story. I thought back to what Frank Ahearn mentioned about fielding emails from people who are thinking about disappearing for no reason other than disenchantment with their dull existences. They might have no real intention to disappear beyond daydreaming. But hitting Send on that message exorcises some sort of demon. It acts as a gentle reminder that our realities are far from fixed.

The impulse and instinct to begin again is as deeply imprinted on our psyches as it is to begin in the first place. We are creatures of equal parts aspiration and foible. Our very humanity provides the perfect conditions to set us up to fail, sometimes on a grand scale, and yet compels us to try again. Our egos want to wipe the slate clean. But our roots, our selves, can't be extinguished. The tragedy is not attempting to carry out our fantasies of rebirth; the tragedy is that it's so difficult to do.

When I first met Frank, he summarily dismissed some of the death fakers I later got to know as "morons and idiots." I had laughed along, shaking my head at the absurdity and shortsightedness of their plots. But after getting to know these individuals and their particular contexts beyond the brief newswire pieces detailing their crimes, I realized that everyone's story was far more complex. And getting to know them as people made it easier to put myself in their position—to understand the desperation that can drive one to this extreme.

But I appreciate that there is more to the story, and I fear that the people I have written about in here will say I got it wrong. That I couldn't possibly understand what it's like to be in their shoes. I've tried throughout to see the world, their lives, and sometimes their crimes from their vantage. I've tried to be fair, but I have my own perspective. Over the course of faking their own deaths, some of these individuals stretched, broke, or rounded off the truth. The stories I've told are true, but the people who told them have told lies in the course of their experience. I am more interested in the stories they tell themselves, and the ways in which they tell them.

What it comes down to is choices: how the assemblage of tiny decisions we make all day can, before you know it, accumulate into a mountain so high that jumping off with a hidden parachute appears to be the only way out. Life is a trip wire, with one turn ricocheting and activating the next. Albert Camus said that life is the sum of all our choices. But I see now how minuscule those choices can seem and how massive their outcomes can be. I had the unique privilege of hearing people work backward over their lives. If the credit card bill had gotten to John Darwin in time, he would've paid the minimum and never had to kayak into the sea. Sam Israel said that if he could do it over, he would never have gone out on his own to form the hedge fund that turned into a massive fraud. He would have stayed at his job on Wall Street, still making a comfortable living. You don't just wake up one morning having lost $450 million. Until you do. I doubt that John and Sam drafted trapdoors and hidden staircases in their original blueprints. But each decision determined the next. And, assuming a logic that often required a bit of cockeyed strain for me to follow, it usually made sense.

What have I learned from all this? I've learned that faking your death is less romantic than I thought it would be. The people I met traded in the dark and the bizarre, but they all still waded through the quotidian business of living. Pearl now works for a car dealership in Southern California. Steve takes care of his parents in Brooklyn. Snooky and Bong look after their kids.

I've learned it is still possible to fake your death in the twenty-first century, and, in some ways, it's easier now than ever. But digital products that claim to anonymize, such as burner phones and Tor, are fallible. Analog technologies—pen and paper, a pay phone (if you can find one)—are more secure than anything processed through a microchip. At the end of the 2014 documentary *Citizenfour*, about the National Security Agency's surveillance on Americans' every move, NSA whistleblower Edward Snowden and reporter Glenn Greenwald exchange messages on sheets of notepaper and then tear them up into pieces. As Steve Rambam said, privacy is dead. Get over it.

While faking your death holds an intrigue that simply disappearing doesn't, vaporizing without the guise of a fatal accident is more effective.

But I've learned that if you fake your death, don't come back. Not for your wife. Not for your girlfriend. Not for your kids.

If you fake your death, don't do it at sea. Go for a hike.

If you're interested in claiming a life insurance payout, don't get greedy. Keep the policy modest.

Don't bother with a stand-in body and an elaborate funeral.

Spend your time and money on obtaining quality authenticating documents.

In your new life, commit to a disguise for your new identity, and use your real first name.

Don't Google yourself and lead your hunters to your hideout.

And for the love of God, don't drive if you're supposed to be dead. Ditch the car.

But this is no how-to manual. I'm not a technologist or woman on the make. What I sought to know wasn't death but freedom—from debt, from myself.

In reporting this book, I found freedom in the strangest of places. Leaving Jonathan Roth behind in jail that day right before Christmas, I realized that if you don't learn to appreciate the tedium of life, you could easily end up groping for a quick fix. It seems antithetical to embrace that which plagues you. And there are exceptions. Battered wives need not invest in their violent husbands. But turning away from debts, personal and financial, has even graver consequences. One shortcut provokes the next, and before you know it, you're considering desperate measures. I often think of John Darwin's image of being perched atop the double black diamond ski run in Jackson Hole, Wyoming. Once you've turned away from the commonplace in favor of glory, there's no way out but down.

Witnessing people's reactions to my project also became a litmus test that revealed to me more about their backgrounds than they likely intended. When I tell the backstory of how my fascination with the topic originated from debt, people who carry a burden themselves understand immediately: I owe a tremendous amount of money, and I considered faking my death to escape it. People who come from more affluent backgrounds, who don't know the terror of a figure owed growing with interest despite monthly payments, assume I am writing a book about faked death to make a profit to pay my lenders. So innocent, those moneybags.

Yes, this quest began in retaliation for my student loan debt. But my relationship with the money I owed shifted when I listened back to interviews and denounced the entitlement that permeated several people's arguments: you fleeced those investors, you acquired all those homes you couldn't afford— shouldn't you pay it back? And it was so easy to recognize in others because I, too, possessed that same entitlement. I, too, thought I could live beyond my means and fly under the radar undetected. And though I think it's bullshit that universities gouge the middle class, I am grateful for the education that money gave me and how it led me—obliquely, bizarrely— to this topic. I will pay the bare minimum monthly payment for the rest of my life and call it the idiot tax. I will smile as I write those checks. Because here I am, this is what I get to do. And on the occasions when the monthly payment has exceeded the balance in my checking account, the customer service agent from Sallie Mae usually understands. Payment. Every debt has to be repaid. Repaying one's debts, according to Plato, at least, is the true definition of justice. Nothing is ever free. There is no such thing as getting away with it. When I looked, I saw ugliness, broken families, loneliness. Some people I spoke to clung to me as one of the few left who would listen to them. They had lost so much. Is transformation without annihilation possible? Freedom comes at a high cost. These lessons are not glamorous, like what I was hoping to find. But, God, are they true.

The Google search prompted by my feeling of despondence at my pauper fate was almost five years ago. Five years, though hardly a lifetime, has some heft. While I worked on this project and got on planes and trains to meet strangers who graciously took me in and shared their stories, life happened alongside. I lost one friend to cancer and another to suicide. I watched my knee swell to the size of a softball with Lyme disease. I cheated on the man I thought I was going to marry. I got away from myself. That sprawling empty openness where anything could happen was at my feet once more. But this time it was because I was in free fall. I didn't have to fake my death to torpedo my life.

I moved out of the rent-controlled apartment in Chelsea. I went to weddings and baby showers. I sent care packages to friends who lost parents and friends who miscarried. I finished graduate school and, mercifully, received a teaching fellowship to underwrite it. I edited the memoirs of nineteen-year-old Columbia University students. I did a stint as a substitute gym teacher. I fell in love and broke my own heart. (It is my contention that we always break our own hearts.) I saw the sun rise over water towers. I read and drank coffee in the same red armchair in a new corner of a different room. This is all there is, and I learned that it was all okay. That I would be okay. That people shoulder far worse than measly student loan debt. This isn't a story about death, or even about reinvention. This is a story about growing up, a little later in the game than I'm proud to admit.

These days, when I Google "fake your own death" (on the same dying laptop, during another interminable New York City winter), the results are pretty much the same. The wikiHow website still espouses "11 Steps (with pictures!)"; listicles enumerate "ridiculous" cases of people who tried and failed in exquisite fashion; new white-collar criminals continue to attempt schemes that result in outcomes so far afield from the release they imagined. There are details of getaway plans that might have worked with a little more finesse. There are components of each exit that probably did succeed. I know that the delicious moment of freedom they inevitably (if briefly) felt doesn't fit in a two-hundred-word newswire. I know now that beyond the headlines, there are families who bear scars.

But if life is a collection of choices that you experience in moments, then that moment of freedom—the ecstatic catharsis—also counts. When your weight is caught in the construction net, when you paddle the canoe away, when you piece together the clues, when you place your obituary in the paper, when the fixer's phone lights up with a Grim Reaper text, when you pass your backpack containing your death certificate through an X-ray machine, then, for just a moment, you are free.

Today my death certificate sits in my filing cabinet enclosed in the plastic sheath Snooky took me to buy at the mall after our seafood dinner. It is curling under the weight of tax returns, freelancing pay stubs, and news clippings of people who faked their deaths. I rarely dip into that filing cabinet unless I need to fish out a piece of evidence that my income, my self, exists. I'll thumb through the disorganized folders in search of some esoteric and half-ripped W-9 and catch a glint of light reflecting off the clear casing with a long manila dossier inside. I'll pull it out, undo the clasps, and run my fingers over the gold foil seal and red ribbons authenticating my death. This macabre souvenir, this possibility of an exit, returns me to a day when I could have died but didn't. I turn back to searching for the paper. I turn back to my boring old life, and smile.

ACKNOWLEDGMENTS

My agent, Dan Kirschen, for plucking me out of the gutter, hosing me down, and entertaining endless jokes about how we might one day employ the knowledge I acquired along the way.

All the heroes at Simon & Schuster, especially Jonathan Karp and Nick Greene, who took a chance on an obscure person with an unusual obsession. Massive thanks to Karyn Marcus and Megan Hogan for their genius editorial insights and vision for this book. Philip Bashe, I'm naming my firstborn for you, and you will ensure I spell the name correctly!

Readers who slogged through early drafts! Especially Valerie Seiling-Jacobs and Raina Lipsitz, who were my doulas in the birthing tub since conception. Kassi Underwood, Zoe Banks, Nicky Roe, Namwali Serpell, Craig Taylor, and Mike Thomsen.

Employers who gave me paychecks throughout! Heidi

Julavits and Patricia Minaya. Sally Mara Sturman, the most generous landlady and friend this lady could ask for.

The residencies that fed me in exotic locales as I wrote: Sangam House, the Ucross Foundation, the MacDowell Colony, Omi Ledig House, the Edward Albee Foundation, ArtFarm Nebraska, the Saltonstall Foundation for the Arts, the Norman Mailer Center. Thanks to the Columbia University School of the Arts for showing me what's possible. Thanks to the reference librarians at Butler, and to librarians everywhere.

Patricia O'Toole, fairy godmother to us all.

Margo Jefferson for unending support. Guy Lawson for so generously sharing his wisdom.

Kira Witkin for her eagle eyes. Julie Alongi, who annually sets my soul at ease. Petra Lee Ghin for her peroxide ninja superpowers.

Friends! Elijah Amitin, Kate Craig, Cathryne Czubek, Brooke Dawson, Dave Der-Sarkisian, Frances Dodds, Phil Eil, Madeline Felix, Sally Franson, Caty Gordon, Cherlyn Medina, Nick Milo, Dax Proctor, Michael Seidenberg, Alexa Vega, Chris Vieyra, Anya Yurchyshyn. Dawn and Eric, I miss you every day, and the world does, too.

Matt van Wingen for a crappy Vietnamese dinner and asking a question intended to be rhetorical.

The people who participated in this book and shared their stories. I am honored, grateful, and humbled.

And to my family—Janette Greenwood, Merritt Greenwood, Susannah Greenwood, Michael Rubin, Sam Rubin—most of all. Thank you.

ABOUT THE AUTHOR

Elizabeth Greenwood grew up in Worcester, Massachusetts. Prior to teaching in Columbia's Undergraduate Creative Writing Program, she taught in the New York City public schools. This is her first book.